The Origins of the Gods

SUNY Series, the Margins of Literature
Mihai I. Spariosu

The Origins of the Gods

James S. Hans

◆

State University of New York Press

Published by
State University of New York Press, Albany

© 1991 State University of New York

For information, address State University of New York
Press, State University Plaza, Albany, N.Y., 12246

Production by E. Moore
Marketing by Fran Keneston

Library of Congress Cataloging-in-Publication Data

Hans, James S., 1950–
    The origins of the gods / James S. Hans.
        p. cm. — (SUNY series, margins of literature)
    ISBN 0–7914–0660–1 (alk. paper). — ISBN 0–7914–0661–X (pbk.:
alk. paper)
    1. Philosophical anthropology. 2. Religion—Controversial
literature. 3. Myth. 4. Plato. Republic. 5. Socrates.
6. Nietzsche, Friedrich Wilhelm, 1844–1900—Contributions in concept
of superman. 7. Superman. I. Title. II. Series.
BD450.H273   1991
128—dc20
                                            90-40941
                                                CIP

For Heather,

arc-en-ciel de la vie

Contents

Acknowledgments

Chapter One of this book was previously published in somewhat different form as 'Shame and Desire in the Myths of Origins,' in *Philosophy Today*, vol. 33:4 (Winter 1989), pp. 330–346, and I should like to thank the journal for permission to reprint it here.

Excerpts from *The Unbearable Lightness of Being* by Milan Kundera, copyright © 1984 by Harper & Row, Publishers, Inc., are reprinted here by permission of HarperCollins Publishers.

Introduction

In the Beginning There Was . . .

Humans have always been interested in questions of origins, and they have regularly supplied any number of explanations for the beginning of the world, for the birth of consciousness and for the moment when their own particular culture began. Our own tradition has repeatedly gone back to two sites for its myths of origins, the Judeo-Christian Bible and Plato, the first providing us with the necessary accounts of the beginning of the world and of the human species, the second giving us the rational slant that is said to distinguish Western civilization for the past 2500 years. There have been other inquiries into origins, from the one pursued by the discipline of physics to those constructed by writers in virtually every other field of study, but the Bible and Plato remain the seminal moments in our culture, and they continue to supply us with the necessary ingredients for those explanations of ourselves and our behavior that we need.

At the same time, we have grown increasingly suspicious of accounts of origins over the past hundred years, and with good reason. Such myths can vivify and organize a culture and hence have great value, but they can—and do— inevitably authorize certain modes of power and behavior and restrict others. They artificially ground a set of circumstances that might otherwise be called into question, putting it out of play in order to give access to a straightforward account of the way things are. Myths of origin thus settle things that perhaps should not be settled, provide a false sense of the world as a site of established guarantees and

1

promises kept that bears little relationship to the dynamics of either the natural or the social world. So we have learned to be wary of accounts based on origins and have trained ourselves to sniff out the hidden motivations underlying any such foundational myth. This has been an important development in the history of our culture, for it has provided us with an unusual opportunity that seems to be unprecedented: we are in a position to question seriously both the needs that generate myths of origins *and* the issue of whether or not humans *require* such myths or can conceivably do without them.

Of late the majority of writing on these problems has dealt with the desires that generate the myths in the first place and the powers that consequently reinforce the value of them in order to establish their own positions in the social structure. These studies—from Nietzsche to Heidegger to Derrida and Foucault—have given us great insight into the ways in which we have manipulated ourselves and others to achieve our own ends and to deceive ourselves about the ways in which we deal with the world. But no one since Nietzsche has considered at length the other half of the problem, the more important half: if we assume that we have arrived at a fairly sound understanding of the desire that constructs the founding myths in individual lives and in cultures in general, can we imagine a human species and a culture that are capable of living with that knowledge? Or are we doomed always to have only a moment when we see between the operative myths and then inevitably slip back into the comforts of one of the interpretive grids? Can we imagine an unauthorized version of human existence that will prevent us from repeating the same kinds of horrors that previous cultures have inflicted upon the planet and the species, or must we finally accede to certain givens in human nature and conclude that people simply cannot accept the circumstances of their lives and will invariably recreate the same kinds of illusions again and again in order to sustain their belief in themselves?

It is worth remembering that Nietzsche invented that construct he called the overman in order to imagine a different kind of human attitude. If Nietzsche did more than any other figure of the modern era to undercut the myths of origins upon which we have depended, he also did more than anyone else to imagine what would be necessary to live without these myths, and he concluded that the human as we presently see him is incapable of living in such a way. This problem is regularly bypassed in discussions of the overman because of all the other issues that are associated with the word. There are questions of elitism to be addressed, and then there are those who see a call for an overman to be a declaration of a new and greater world built upon humans who have managed to transcend their fallible lot. Those who embrace utopian possibilities, from the Nazis to those who believe humans are capable of perfection, see in the overman a species that would have eliminated the problems of being human, yet this is clearly not what Nietzsche intended by the term. On the contrary, for him the overman was an image of a kind of human that was first and finally able to live with those problems that *cannot* be eliminated. The overman leads to no utopia but rather forces us to address what it means to be human and to accept it.

The overman is *not* a mythical marker of our hidden desire to become godlike creatures who have eliminated suffering from our lives. He is himself mythical, to be sure, but he partakes of a different kind of myth, the one that Nietzsche endlessly proclaimed: the myth that knows itself to be both a falsehood, an illusion, and a truth at the same time. The overman is a marker of the possible. He is a question to humanity: are you capable of being wholly human? Can you at least *imagine* such a human as a desirable—perhaps an inevitable—part of the world? Can you conceive of yourself as making strides in such a direction? These are the potential truths that reside in the overman, but they may also be illusions, and the strength of the concept of the overman is that it demonstrates the great difficulty of becoming what we need to become. The task is not an easy one and may well be impossible, but it is also the only goal worth pursuing, which is precisely what Nietzsche did throughout his working life. He may have failed miserably in all sorts of ways, but he saw his life in terms of the question of the overman and never ceased to address his own behavior in terms of that measure.

The overman is an image of our distance from what we need to become if we are to learn to live on the planet where we reside. In imagining him Nietzsche is simply calling us to the greatest of human tasks: the attempt to be wholly human for the first time, to realize that we are not authorized by God to be what we are and do not have laws passed down from another world to guide us in this one, but rather must make our own laws on the basis of our knowledge of what it means to live here and now. Between the death of God and the advent of the overman we are forced to put aside our illusions of grandeur and see ourselves for what we are in all of our tragic circumstances. We might have killed God off in order to usurp His place, but in the shadow of the moment when we denied Him we immediately recognized that that was not possible simply because He occupied no particular space at all and could not therefore cede His location to us. We *imagined* His place in order to authorize ourselves, then imagined that we could become both self-authorizing *and* perfectible, and were quickly confronted with the fact that we might in some senses have to be self-authorizing but could never achieve perfection. God died and left us only the hope that we could become ourselves. The overman is only an image of that prospect, one we have still not seriously addressed.

Given the question of the overman to which Nietzsche's thinking eventually led him, it is not an accident that he so reviled the two great cornerstones of the West, Christianity and Platonic thought, for he saw them as the foundational myths that took us away from our human potential rather than leading us toward it. He contended with them as he did because he saw in them the tragedy of endless human illusions, and it was the desire for those illusions against which he so strenuously fought. In time Nietzsche has become something of a mythical figure, reviled and idolized in turn by those who see written in him their own desires and who consequently wish to trade on whatever capital his name has left. Nietzsche himself, unfortunately, created the confusion that is associated with his name by the repeated declarations of elitism that lead readers to assume that his thought itself is necessarily predicated on an elite cadre of people taking charge of the world when in fact, I would argue, he maintains just the opposite. Nietzsche is the last philosopher seriously to declare that human beings are (perhaps) capable of becoming wholly human, and as such he is the most democratic and egalitarian of philosophers. He may be reviled by the masses and fetishized by those who seek to capture his power and make use of it as elitist priests of high truths, but Nietzsche's work declares again and again that humans are capable of imagining a world in which they are themselves, and there is no more egalitarian or democratic sentiment than that.

The best way to see how forcefully Nietzsche's philosophy undercuts an elitist and hierarchical view—however much Nietzsche regularly declared himself to be an elitist who believed in hierarchy—is to contrast his view of the overman and the potential that resides within that figure to his archenemy Plato and his way of construing the future of the species. And there is no better place to locate the difference between Nietzsche and Plato than that moment in the *Republic* when Socrates is busily dispensing with the poets and their lies. In imagining the ideal human community, Socrates and his interlocutor quickly construct the foundation of their future society in the following exchange:

> . . . the first thing will be to establish a censorship of the writers of fiction, and let the censors receive any tale of fiction which is good, and reject the bad; and we will persuade mothers and nurses to tell their children the authorized ones only. Let them fashion the mind with such tales, even more fondly than they mold the body with their hands; but most of those which are now in use must be discarded. . . .
>
> But which stories do you mean, he said; and what fault do you find with them?

A fault which is fundamental and most serious, I said; the fault of saying what is false, and doing so for no good purpose.

But when is this fault committed?

Whenever an erroneous representation is made of the nature of gods and heroes—as when a painter paints a picture not having the shadow of a likeness to his subject.

Yes, he said, that sort of thing is certainly very blamable; but what are the stories which you mean?

First of all, I said, there was that greatest of all falsehoods on great subjects, which the misguided poet told about Ouranos—I mean what Hesiod says that Ouranos did, and how Kronos retaliated on him. The doings of Kronos, and the sufferings which in turn his son inflicted upon him, even if they were true, ought certainly not to be lightly told to young and thoughtless persons; if possible, they had better be buried in silence. But if there is an absolute necessity for their mention, a chosen few might hear them in a mystery; and they should sacrifice not a common [Eleusinian] pig, but some huge and unprocurable victim, so that the number of the hearers may be very few indeed.[1]

This often-discussed passage bears continued commentary simply because it is so double-edged in nature, asserting on the one hand that the poets tell lies about the gods, suggesting on the other that even if they tell the truth about them what they say ought not to be heard by anyone. Hesiod may well have been misguided in what he said about Kronos and Ouranos, but his lack of judgment comes in thinking that stories of such savagery ought to be brought forth for poetic treatment. Socrates doesn't really spend enough time discussing Hesiod's lies for us to be convinced that he really thinks the falsehood of the poet's utterances is what is at issue, and the notion that such stories should not be told to children also seems to be less important than it might appear. These seem to be ruses designed to take the interlocutor—*and* the reader—off the track, for one cannot mistake the fact that Socrates is declaring that these stories simply should not be told, regardless of their veracity. Hesiod may well be right in his account, but that doesn't give him sufficient reason to tell these awful tales about the titanic struggles at the beginning of the world.

Socrates tells us that "there was that greatest of all falsehoods on great subjects, which the misguided poet told about Ouranos," but he fails to establish how he knows that what was said was indeed false. It may be the "greatest of all falsehoods," then, but we find no evidence to support that claim, and this reflects the excessively strong rhetoric that Socrates is using to cover up something. Likewise, Socrates suggests that Hesiod's poem was "lightly told to young and thoughtless persons," and there is no reason to assume this to be the case either. Hesiod may have known quite well what he was doing and may have done it with the most serious of intents, fully aware of the consequences that might come about as a result of the stories he told. But from Socrates' perspective, he was misguided and should not have told the story under any circumstances. If he didn't tell it without thought, then he didn't properly consider the nature of his audience, which would inevitably have someone young and/or thoughtless in it. That Hesiod might have a different idea of the nature and purpose of poetry, and the nature of its effects upon audiences, never occurs to Socrates simply because he assumes from the beginning that such a story can have only a negative effect upon an individual.

Indeed, Socrates demonstrates his falsity by undercutting his worries about young and thoughtless people, by arguing that even wise individuals should steer clear of such tales. We are told that "if possible, [the stories] had better be buried in silence," and this is hardly the kind of thing one does unless their virulence is considerably greater than Socrates is overtly suggesting. If they are to be buried in silence, then *no one* should hear them, including Socrates, who is wise enough to be able to deal with the violence and Oedipal bloodshed involved in them.[2] At the same time, Socrates concedes that there may be some "absolute necessity for their mention," but even then only "a chosen few might hear them in a mystery; and they should sacrifice not a common . . . pig, but some huge and unprocurable victim, so that the number of hearers may be very few indeed." The immediate upshot of these words is that Socrates realizes that the stories have a virulent subject matter that is potentially destructive to the republic, but he never states precisely what the risks are.

One could assume that the risks are not stated because they are obvious, but the passage suggests rather that they aren't named because Socrates is *afraid* to mention them, as though the very articulation of them might bring about disaster. Indeed, Socrates seems to have been deliberately vague in his account of what Ouranos and Kronos did, in part, perhaps, because he is concerned about what thoughtless youths might hear, but more likely because he is superstitious and therefore frightened by the possibility that simply uttering the heinous and bloody words would be enough to evoke an equivalent kind of violence in his own life and community. Thus, if anyone at all is to hear such stories, they should do so only in the context of a sacred mystery that will contain the potential violence within them, and even then they should make certain to sacrifice "some huge and unprocurable victim" to cleanse themselves of the taint that comes from simply hearing Hesiod's poem. Coming as they do from the master of reason, these words have a shocking effect, for there can be little doubt that Socrates himself is unwilling to contemplate the bloody fights between titans without the shroud of sacred mystery: to hear such things is to allow them once again to come into being, and once that happens their contagion could spread almost anywhere. Socrates seems to be quietly quaking here, and he quickly moves away from the subject of this originary violence and goes on to other topics, as though they are all of equal importance, when in fact the central issue—and the final justification for censorship of the poets—is to be found in this passage where we are told essentially that the singers of songs must be banished *because they tell the truth*.

In fairness to Socrates, one could argue that violence is

always a threat to the somewhat fragile threads of the social structure, and so one ought to do everything one can to put it out of play. The most vivid classical reminder of this is to be found in *Oedipus Rex* when the chorus begins to see that Oedipus and Iocasta have little regard for the gods. They assert with their own kind of threat and violence "why should I join these sacred public dances / if such acts [Oedipus's] are honored."[3] Their willingness to abide by the established laws wavers easily enough, even when one considers the nature of the crimes of which Oedipus is accused and when one remembers how shocking it would have been to hear someone in Iocasta's position state with vehemence that all lives are governed by fate rather than by the gods. The Thebans are ready to go the final step toward anarchy, and it is precisely that kind of violent movement that Socrates is trying to put out of play by banishing the poets. He understands the fragility of social order and the violence that lies just beneath its surface, and, having no real solution for it, he prefers to deal with it only in the presence of the purifying sacred rituals.

This central scene of *Oedipus* reveals the psychology underlying Socrates' acts of censorship, for we discover a tripartite reaction to Oedipus's putative acts. First we find the terrible fear of violence and chaos that the people feel, as seen when they assert

> fate
> be here let what I say be pure
> let all my acts be pure
> laws forged in the huge clear fields of heaven
> rove the sky
> shaping my words limiting what I do
> Olympos made those laws not men who live and die
> nothing lulls those laws to sleep
> they cannot die
> and the infinite god in them never ages. . . . (62)

The nature of this prayer reveals the psychological need at its own heart; it simply asserts that if the people are good, the gods will treat them well. They only need to keep the "laws forged in the huge clear fields of heaven" and nothing will happen to them. They are as frightened by the violation of the laws as Socrates was by the acts of Kronos and Ouranos, and they invoke the superstitions of the prayer here to protect themselves from whatever force might be unleashed as a result.

At the same time, they too demand in effect a mystery with a huge victim, in this case Oedipus. They prepare for his violent end well before it comes; indeed, they *demand* that it come about:

> arrogance insatiable pride
> breed the tyrant
> feed him on thing after thing blindly
> at the wrong time uselessly
> and he grows reaches so high
> nothing can stop his fall
> his feet thrashing the air standing on nothing
> and nowhere to stand he plunges down
> o god shatter the tyrant
> but let men compete let self-perfection grow
> let men sharpen their skills
> soldiers citizens building the good city
> Apollo
> protect me always
> always the god I will honor. . . (62)

If the chorus believes that "nothing can stop [the tyrant's] fall," that is because they *want* to believe it; if they think that "his feet thrashing the air standing on nothing / and nowhere to stand he plunges down," that is because this is the fate they determine he shall have. They first declare it to be inevitable, then call on god to bring it about—"o god shatter the tyrant"—then ask for social stability and civility—"let men compete let self-perfection grow," "soldiers citizens building the good city"—and then they come back to their own piety, the blood still dripping from their hands: "Apollo / protect me always / always the god I will honor." Never has a chorus more fully expressed the complex motivations underlying social violence in such a brief interlude, and never has a chorus more fully demonstrated how contradictory and irrational these motivations are. If Socrates is afraid of Hesiod's bloody story, he has good reason to be fearful, for he remains unaware of what calls these violent furies into play and disperses them.

Knowing the fragility of the human psyche and the social order that depends upon it, understanding full well the irrationality out of which human life comes and in the midst of which it spends so much of its time, and recognizing the degree to which nothing that humans can imagine is capable of controlling these irrational impulses, Socrates is willing both to participate in his own violent acts *and* to dispense with a democratic system to preserve order. He cannot *reasonably* deal with the dirty truths of human nature, so he sacrifices these truths on the sacred altar along with the pig that symbolizes their destruction and the cleansing of the priests who have tainted themselves with knowledge of that which the gods and humans are capable. Socrates will then very quickly go back to his lies about the lies poets tell and will thereby do everything he can to forget the abyss into which he has momentarily peered.

In effect we have two founding acts here, the acts upon which the Platonic world view are predicated. Socrates sacrifices his own knowledge, willingly pokes out his own eyes, so that he will not have to confront that for which he has no answer; and he seeks to bury this knowledge so deeply that neither he nor society will have to worry about its emergence in the future. This is one of the first major public acts of repression, and on it we have built our vision of humanity. More to the point in this context, Socrates has willingly and deliberately turned away from what he knows because what he knows frightens *him*—it is not just that he worries about how young and thoughtless people will deal with such knowledge but also that he is concerned about how *he* can deal with it. He concludes that he cannot do so and thus chooses to pull back from what he knows to be the case. Unlike the poets, he will deliberately lie to the people to protect them from what they too always already know. This is the only solution he has to the problem that Ouranos and

Kronos reflect in their violent battles for priority, for foundational status and authority.

In our own day, Socrates' willing abandonment of the truth in favor of social stability is all too easily rebuked as the misguided judgment of one who was in other respects wise enough to understand the greatest of human questions. But when we look at his reasons for running away from the truth, and particularly when we place them in the context of the chorus's fears and demands in *Oedipus*, we need to hold back a bit on a quick and easy denunciation. Socrates surely didn't bury the truth without careful thought, and only a glib response would fail to consider his reasons more seriously than they have been dealt with by most people throughout this century of great human violence. If, as I am arguing, there is a choice to be made between Nietzsche's vision of the overman who is capable of accepting what it means to be wholly human and Socrates' vision that humans are incapable of such acceptance, the choice is not an easy one. It is, on the contrary, a devilishly difficult one, as both Nietzsche and Socrates knew, and it will not do to reduce their dispute to minor issues and facile responses that would make both thinkers blush and would perhaps go some distance toward confirming the wisdom of Socrates. Without suggesting for a moment that totalitarian regimes and repressive structures are in the least desirable, we must still seriously address the possibility that *Socrates was right*. I suggest this possibility with Socrates placed next to Nietzsche precisely to define the situation as clearly as possible, for to most people Nietzsche remains an object of scorn and revulsion, and the question of whether or not Socrates was right is perhaps most contingent on the answers that will be provided by those who are appalled by Nietzsche and his thought.

What if Socrates was right? What might that change in our conception of ourselves and our social systems? We must begin by assuming that, unlike Nietzsche, Socrates decides to bury the violent origins of human society as a result of his own fear and loathing, not simply because he doesn't think young people can deal with such knowledge. He is not willing to confront this knowledge himself, though presumably he would agree to do so if it were necessary. Implicitly, he would be one of the elect who would try to bear this knowledge in order to spare others from doing so. Again, we need to separate the threat to the polis inherent in such knowledge—if Ouranos and Kronos can do such things, then why can't I—from the emotional effects of their brutality. The two are naturally related, but our tendency is always to move to the imitative level at which we see the contagion of violence spreading because the leaders have broken the laws too. First, though, we must realize that there is something totally revolting about murders and castrations, or in the case of Oedipus, about parricide and incest; there is something shameful, something that turns the stomach, something that makes one want to renounce one's part in a species that would be capable of such things. If we are not sickened by these acts, then part of our humanity is already gone.

At the same time, revulsion over the vile acts of Ouranos and Kronos folds into a double awareness that such acts can actually be committed *and* that they have been committed by those who authorize the community. When we add to this knowledge the fact that our revulsion is based in part upon our *excitement* in the face of such violent proceedings, we can begin to understand why the Theban chorus was so frightened, so outraged, and so determined to do Oedipus in at the same time. The world of decorum, of social forms and propriety, is contingent on a containment of the scandalous, on keeping it from the eyes of the people, for the sacrifices humans make on a daily basis to preserve the social order can quickly be foregone for the blood sacrifices of individuals if the eruption of violence manifests itself in the midst of the order designed to put it out of play. One believes in the gods and social decorum in order to get something back—a stable system through which one can anticipate the future with some certainty—and when the prospect of stability is called into question, the irrational immediately rises to the surface and threatens to overwhelm everything.

The violation of a social contract that comes about when violent acts are not punished by some kind of reciprocal, yet contained violence logically leads to outrage. If the social system is predicated on a variety of shared sacrifices, one is willing to give of oneself only to the extent that others contribute their portion as well. But the problem inherent in the outrage is that it is not in the least logical in its manifestations. Again, the Theban chorus trembles with fear for its life at what it has heard and superstitiously invokes the gods in the hope that the violence will pass it over just as it violently makes up its collective mind that someone must pay for the outrageous violation of decorum, just as it puts a name to the crime—pride—and establishes the agenda through which the tyrant will suffer, just as it finally demands of the gods to whom it is pleading for safety that they bring the tyrant down. It is a law of the universe that the tyrant must fall, even if that law is invoked by the people and violently asserted by them. And it can be assumed in this case that if Oedipus hadn't taken on himself the burden of guilt—and outrageously demonstrated this by poking out his eyes—the Thebans would have taken it upon themselves to rise up and tear Oedipus to shreds, confident retrospectively that they had simply done the gods' bidding, that they had fulfilled the sacred laws of the universe by acting as they did.

The chorus at no time considers its actions in a rational way, and it is likely that it never consciously addresses the reciprocal nature of the violence in which it is participating. On the contrary, such a knowledge would be so horrifying to the people that they might turn away from it in order to avoid being overcome by self-loathing. So there is a certainty, an almost entirely predictable course of action, that allows them to proceed in conscious ignorance of what they are doing, the most fundamental kind of repression known to humans. If Socrates is right that such knowledge ought to be buried, the initial reasons are to be found here in this circuitry that allows these violent acts to occur without any reflection on the nature of what is occurring. No self-awareness is necessary in such acts; indeed, lack of self-awareness is a precondition for them. And we are not dealing with the issue of whether or not the herd is capable of accepting its humanity; the question is whether *anyone* can do so, and the problem is simply that perhaps humans are constituted in a way that prevents them from adequately dealing with these phenomena.

We know, of course, that Aristotle took a different view and held that immersion into such violent scenes via tragic drama allowed one to purge oneself of one's pity and fear, but even if we concede that Aristotle may have been right in thinking that tragedy provides a social outlet for these pressures, he has not really addressed the central issue, for his belief in tragic drama is only slightly different from Socrates' argument that, if necessary, a very few individuals should deal with the violent acts in a mystery and then perform a major sacrifice afterward to cleanse themselves. The only crucial difference is that Aristotle argues that *everyone* should participate in the mystery and so cleanse himself. The secularization of society leads to the desacralized version of the mystery that tragic drama is, and the regular need for the drama and its purgations for all takes over the symbolic immersion into bloody origins that the priests had previously assumed on behalf of the city. In this way we could say that Aristotle is being more open about the mysteries of human nature, but at the same time there is nothing to suggest that either Aristotle or the people in the audience of a tragic drama are actually aware of the knowledge that is being placed before them. Does the tragic drama provide understanding along with its purgative effects, or is it designed to affect people and yet keep them in ignorance of what has been done to them? If so, Aristotle is suggesting that the knowledge is buried too; he simply argues for a collective burial of it rather than the private one of the sacred mystery.

One can consider the viability of Socrates' decision to bury the knowledge of violence from another angle if one looks at one of the central scenes in Hesiod's brutal account of the beginnings of the social world. Perhaps the most horrifying act in the story is that moment when Kronos castrates Ouranos and throws his genitalia into the sea, out of which in turn springs Aphrodite. Our more Botticellian version of this story has Aphrodite riding in on a shell, and there is no sight at all of genitalia or the drops of blood that sprang from them, indication enough of the success of Socrates' rite of burial in the *Republic*. We are told that "Eros and fair Desire attended her birth and accompanied her as she went to join the family of gods. And this has been her allotted province from the beginning among men and immortal gods:

> the whisperings of girls; smiles; deceptions;
> sweet pleasure, intimacy, and tenderness."[4]

Beauty in general has been added to "Eros and fair Desire" as part of Aphrodite's province, but she was quickly stripped of her horrifying origins—origins, one might add, that Hesiod immediately follows up on after his account of Aphrodite's birth: "As for those children of great Heaven, their father who begot them railed at them and gave them the surname of Titans, saying that straining *tight* in wickedness they had done a serious thing, and that he had a *title* to revenge for it later" (9). There is always a question of who has *title* to revenge, who is warranted in undertaking such a reciprocal act, and Ouranos establishes his title to the act at this moment: he shall forever afterward be entitled to take revenge on his sons for this act and reserves that right for himself in perpetuity. And it is his perpetual *right* to revenge this act that guarantees both his own sense of self-justification and the eternal return of the same violence in the lives of ever different people.

The "sweet pleasure, intimacy, and tenderness" that Aphrodite conjures up, then, are as sweet as they are precisely because they had their origins in the bloody castration of Ouranos. Death is *not* the mother of beauty, as Wallace Stevens had it; rather, *revenge* is the mother of beauty, bloody, violent revenge. Out of it comes whatever sweet pleasures we are to find in this world; out of it, or at least in the context of it, comes whatever intimacy and tenderness we are to possess. If there are also whisperings, smiles and deceptions written into desire and beauty, that is precisely because we should prefer to imagine that they had a cleaner birth. We should not have needed the scourge of AIDS to tell us that desire was not a "free" activity, if by "free" we mean an act without consequences done on holiday from the brutality of the "real" world. But again, there is something in this knowledge, whether one speaks about the relationship between sex and violence or beauty and bloody castration, that humans seem instinctively to run away from, even if they are also attracted to it. They don't have to *decide* to turn their heads from this; they do it without thinking. And as with all such situations, the repression of the knowledge, deliberate or otherwise, only guarantees that sooner or later it will return with even more virulence. Given this fact, Socrates may well have been right to try to bury as best he could the horrible truths he had uncovered, but at the same time his decision in turn assures the culture that the horrors will return again and again without warning, without preparation for their appearance, and without a serious hope of being able to deal with them appropriately, for they have been hidden away rather than considered in their fullest implications.

Socrates may be right. Humans may have no choice but to turn away from their knowledge of what they are and from what they came. And if this is so, then it is in the interests of the polis for a censorship committee to exist that will purge the sacred texts of the bloody truths that might in a moment undermine the entire structure of society. But if Socrates *is* right, then we must also concede that we are doomed to face this knowledge in any case, for it can never be buried deeply enough to keep from coming back to the surface eventually. It *will* return. Willed ignorance is always only a temporary expedient, the equivalent of public assurances that everything is in order, that everyone has chosen to obey the laws of the community, that there is no reason to think that anything will come along to violate these fragile accords among people. We may agree to work under such tacit circumstances, and we may also be aware of the fact that the agreement will eventually be violated once again, but even that knowledge does not lead to the exploration of whatever alternatives there might be. We simply turn away in horror from what we are and hope not to live to regret it at some later date. This has been the choice of our culture from the beginning, and there is nothing in the current socius to suggest that we have changed our ways of addressing the world or ourselves.

Nietzsche's overman, though, proposes a radically different solution to the problem, for the overman is a symbol of our knowledge of bloody origins and vengeful tendencies. He is the constant reminder of what we are because he is the measure of what we might become if we were to begin to think of alternative ways of dealing with our irrational impulses. Instead of trying to separate the sweet desires from the violent ones in the hope that he can cultivate the one and eliminate the other, the overman declares the inextricability of the two and asserts the need to confront this knowledge rather than repress it. It may be that humans are incapable of achieving that which the overman suggests to us, but as a measure, as a mark of our awareness of what we need to do to be more fully human, the overman is always only a gauge of what we are presently capable of conceiving and doing, no more and no less. He is a reflection of what we know of ourselves and a constant reminder of our situation, and as such he is simply a device designed to discourage the repression that we so easily accede to every time we confront something within ourselves that we should prefer to deny.

If the overman is only a mark of human potential that works to avoid repression, though, we also need to ask once again where his danger resides, for if matters were that simple surely by now we should have all declared his value and established his place in our lives. If the overman comes to occupy that space once held by God, what changes, and what happens to the horrors of life? Assuming that God was something of a shield from those aspects of being human that we chose to avoid, the overman does not provide us with that luxury. On the contrary, he makes our vulnerability to the dangers of life most evident, revealing that they never go away, demonstrating that for the most part they emanate from our own natures. He forces us to accept that which we secretly loathe—human nature—prompts us to recognize within ourselves precisely those things we should choose to eliminate if we were given the chance, from our mortality and fallibility to our fleshly mode of existence with all of its excretions and hormonal fluctuations. The overman does not give us control over these things but rather simply keeps us from forgetting about them, and this is what makes his image so hard to live with.

We have yet fully to explore the degree to which our shame before that which we conceive to be abject drives us to attempt to be something other than we are, but one could easily imagine that shame as the real origin of human discourse. Nietzsche argued that the gods grew out of guilt and debt to one's ancestors, and Freud postulated that society began when the primal horde of sons killed their father and then tried to keep the same thing from happening to themselves, but humanity may well have begun when the first person felt shame at what he or she was. The overman constantly reminds us of the revulsion we feel toward the beings we are, but revulsion is a mark of shame, of disgust, and hence is really the second-stage reaction rather than the first one. As a reminder of our shame, the overman would relentlessly be that which came between us and our willed ignorance, that which refused to allow us the easy illusions about human perfectibility and the utopian future.

Can humans bear to live with their revulsion? Is this a task they are capable of mastering, or is it precisely the mark of their perpetual failure to be at home on the planet? Again, if Nietzsche employed the term "overman," it was to argue that no human had yet overcome his self-loathing and that therefore the difference between the last man and the overman was great indeed. In a certain sense Christ represents within Christianity a similar kind of symbolic moment, for he willingly agrees to take on the form of a human—when presumably no god would prefer our abject state over that of a god—and assumes the burdens of living with the state that human being is. In so doing, it could be argued, he provides for us an exemplum, a model human life that demonstrates that at least one human being was able to live with who he was. The problem, of course, is that Christ *wasn't* a human, or at least *just* a human, and he conjured up the possibility of a future, far more godlike existence for humans and thus helped them escape the very humanity he was designed to help them accept. He suggests the impossibility of accepting the human condition for what it is, whereas Nietzsche's overman only demonstrates that humans would have to become something more than they presently are to be able to do so. The overman suggests that humans can at least *potentially* grow to the point where they can become what they are; he provides the alternative mode to Socrates' willed repression and offers humans whatever hope there is for the future.

The stakes involved in any agon between Socrates and the overman are clear and yet difficult to establish with fitting emphasis simply because they are two means through which we deal with that about which we believe nothing should be spoken. It is easy enough to say that the overman posits our ability to live with the horrors of life and our shame at being human, whereas Socrates argues we are incapable of doing so and hence must forever bury this knowledge, but inasmuch as we have been doing things Socrates' way for all these millennia, it almost seems incredible to us that there should really be that much to say about human revulsion and shame. If we have to disclose and accept certain things about our natures, that seems straightforward enough to do, we think, and should provide no great discomfort to us. Yet it does, and perhaps it does so more today than ever before. We saw Socrates in the act of denying the truths of the poets and refusing to state outright what Hesiod had said simply because he couldn't bring himself to utter the horrors the gods had done; we saw the Theban chorus quickly pray to have the horrors pass them by because of their devotion to the gods; and we have our own equivalent practices that are designed to allow us to imagine a free and clean space we can occupy without worry. And yet we do this kind of work at a level of consciousness that often hides itself from us, deliberately so, and thus helps us to think that we are above cant and superstition when the very structures of our everyday lives depend on them.

At the same time, the free and open space we work to imagine through our superstitions is closed off precisely to the degree that we fail to acknowledge the demons that drive us to imagine it. Socrates is thus a repressive force in more ways than one, and he demonstrates how the various modes of repression are interlocking aspects of one another. If he imagines a repressive state that censors what can and cannot be said, thereby limiting the openness and freedom of the socius, he does so because his model of human behavior is based on the same repressive state that limits psychological openness and freedom by keeping hidden from us those things that repeatedly cramp our vision and keep us from seeing the world the way it is. We are first imprisoned by the psychological model and the superstitions through which it seeks to close off inquiry into all the domains of human being, and the consequence of this incarceration is a social system that performs the same acts on large bodies of people. This is all the more ironic in that Plato, perhaps best known for his metaphorical depiction of life as a cavelike existence of shadows, has himself done more to make it a world of shadows by arguing that we cannot bear the full light of day. Nietzsche, on the contrary, seeks to overcome the repression and allow an openness and freedom to life— in both the psychological *and* the social realms—that has simply not been possible within our tradition. The price for this freedom, though, is full disclosure, complete awareness of all that we should prefer to hide from.

There were, of course, several things that Nietzsche himself doubtless managed to hide from, and one of the most prominent of these is suggested by his loathing for the herd. On the one hand, he conceived of the overman as he who would be most fully human and imagined that the species could progress gradually as more and more individuals became what the overman suggests. On the other hand, he also knew full well that the "strong" always need to be protected from the "weak," and that means that there is no way that a few overmen will do. They would quite simply be killed off, or perhaps less dramatically, simply ignored. The herd was that means through which Nietzsche could hide from the knowledge that *one* overman is not enough; either the entire species is capable of making this move *or no one is.* There are no distinctions of rank or strength or courage that will allow one to imagine a world in which some are capable of becoming what the overman posits and not others. This, after all, is precisely Socrates' vision of things, the one which Nietzsche so resolutely opposes through the overman. Socrates conceives of a world of philosopher kings and high priests who both bear the knowledge and the full weight of what it means to be human *and keep it from everyone else at the same time.* Nietzsche's thought denies the value of this model and yet depends on it at the same time.

Now this contradiction might well be little more than a reflection of the difficulty of achieving what Nietzsche sought to establish, and it is also no doubt an indication of the psychological devices he employed to sustain himself in the face of a studied indifference to his work—if his great thoughts are ignored or reviled, well, that is simply because the vast majority of humans are too stupid and herdlike to appreciate what he is offering them. The herd is thus for him a means through which his own difficulties with society are repressed. Instead of acknowledging that the "herd" is basically indifferent to him and his ideas because it is so hard for humans to confront the kinds of things Nietzsche insists on putting before them, because they are *unwilling* to dig into those things that were of central concern to Nietzsche, he registers contempt for them in order to protect himself from the full knowledge of his own existence. If he is going to press on and maintain his ideas, he has to have a way of working around the silence he faces everywhere. Therefore, knowing full well at one level that that silence is precisely a reflection of the repression he is trying to overcome with his books, in his capacity as an individual human being he is prompted to repress this awareness in order to live with himself and his ideas. For us this ought to be little more than a reminder of the great difficulty of imagining the wholly human, but it should also demonstrate that—at least outside the contradictions inherent in the person of Nietzsche himself—the conception of the overman is inherently *anti-hierarchical, anti-repressive, and anti-elitist.* Either *all* humans are capable of becoming the overman, or *no* human is capable of doing so. Nietzsche's work rises and falls with that fact, and it was one of the few facts he himself could not accept.

We of the twentieth century who are so much more avowedly democratic in spirit must confront this problem that Nietzsche himself was forced to repress. For us the matter is put in the opposite fashion: if we are to be truly democratic in spirit, if we are truly going to imagine an anti-hierarchical, anti-repressive, anti-elitist world, we can do so and be honest with ourselves only if we face the full consequences of Nietzsche's overman, only, that is, if we face our full revulsion at being human, only human. *Our* contradiction is to pay all kinds of lip service to the notion that the democratic spirit is the purest reflection of human being while at the same time refusing to confront those brute fears and horrors that always undermine democratic tendencies in practice. We advocate democratic social systems while secretly supporting repressive psychological practices in our own lives and in the lives of others, believing that somehow there is no problem with this schizoid attitude.

In fact, however—at least in the long run—democratic social systems can only survive if they are based upon an openness about what it means to be human. We cannot get rid of the philosopher kings and keep the high priests of human horrors in order to hide from ourselves. If we are to have free and open societies, we must be free and open about what we are, which means that we must turn to a concept like the overman for a mark of what we must strive to become. If democracy was in some senses the greatest social idea humans were capable of imagining, and if it drove the spirit of the Enlightenment that generated the modern world, Nietzsche simply provided the consequent moment in our tradition by arguing that it was time for us to apply that same democratic spirit to our individual and psychological lives. And if democracy was a vigorous test of our ability to organize human populations into coherent, yet more or less free systems, the conception of the overman is the equivalent test of our ability to organize our individual lives in coherent and yet more or less free ways. Socrates *may* be right, but there is little to be gained from assuming so, and perhaps a great deal to be lost. Nietzsche may force us to confront a whole series of things about our natures that we should prefer to avoid, but the possibilities are far richer—and the prospects for humanity much brighter—if we begin to ask the kinds of questions he did in the full knowledge of the difficulties that face us.

Chapter One

In the Beginning There Was Beauty

In our tradition we have always assumed that the religious impulse was the origin of culture, that the fire Prometheus brought to humans was first and foremost spiritual. As our commitment to the religious world waned over the millennia, we have posited alternative descriptions of that Promethean fire, but we have always construed them as derivative of the religion with which we began. Thus, writers like Matthew Arnold argue that poetry will eventually come to take the place of religion in our culture, and his assumption that the aesthetic derives from the theological is consistent with the way we have thought about the world. If we imagine the great poems at the beginning of Western civilization as compendia of religious, historical, philosophical, and poetic truths, we have thought that the poetic, the historical, and the philosophical are designed to serve the religious rather than the other way around. As we have grown suspicious of origins over the past century, we have indeed called into question the centrality of the religious impulse, but we have not yet sufficiently asked ourselves what our tradition would be like if we imagined its origin as an aesthetic rather than a theological one. What if we were wrong in assuming that in the beginning there were gods, or a God? What if in the beginning there was only the aesthetic play of the world, and we chose somehow to derive gods from that play rather than something else? What would change in our conceptions of things if we were seriously to ask these questions?

Perhaps the most striking change we would encounter would be the dehumanization and depersonalization of the world. Both the theological and the aesthetic provide descriptions of what is, and both of them articulate a sense of pattern, but the theological always has human interest written into it from the beginning. After all, a god has specific dealings with humans that explain why life is the way it is. This is so even in the Greek tradition, where the gods are far less concerned with humans than in the Judeo-Christian line. Zeus does not devote his time to working out plans for humans or laying down laws for them; whatever attention he pays to them is subsidiary, only one among many interests. In this sense the Greek gods are considerably less personal and human than the Judeo-Christian God, however human they appear to be in their thoughts and actions. They aren't quite indifferent to the disposition of human affairs, but they restrict themselves to thinking of particular individuals and clans and dispense their favors accordingly. Quite clearly, the great majority of humans can look to these gods for very little, certainly not for an acknowledgment of their importance.

The Judeo-Christian God is far more personalized and takes an active interest in human affairs; indeed, this seems to be His primary purpose. He monitors the behavior of the people and acts in accordance with the world that they establish. We are told that He has an interest in every individual and is aware of all of them, though this is more true of the Christian than the Jewish God. In this tradition, humans are in turn *given* the world; it is theirs to do with as they please, and the rest of the living creatures are at their disposal. There is no getting around the fact that the other animals and plants are to serve humans just as humans are to serve their God. In this way, everything that exists becomes centralized around the needs and wants of humans, so their concerns are written into everything, and their conception of the world is in turn designed to personalize the place so thoroughly that domestication is the only real value.

If we begin with an aesthetic world, however, this kind of personalization and humanization of the world is no longer necessary. If the ecstatic states out of which the religious impulse comes are oriented toward establishing a totally humanized world full of meaning, the ecstatic states of the purely aesthetic play of things have no such orientation. They give humans over to what is, but they don't dispose of it in human ways. They reveal patterns and shape and provide some sense of the dynamics of the universe, but they do not offer a *narrative* to go along with the scene into which the human has been placed. In this sense, the aesthetic opens humans up to the nonhuman in the world, and to the nonhuman in themselves; it situates them within the impersonal flows that determine the course of all living matter without judging those flows in terms of their equity or purpose, for they can be said to have no purpose within the aesthetic. The flows flow, and we are part of their flow, but there is nothing to be said beyond that. They do not flow *for* us, they don't lead *to* us; we are simply part of them, like it or not.

Now it is the human perception of these flows within ecstatic states—that mode of being we have characterized as the sublime—that generates the feelings that lead to the religious configuration of the world, for the powerful feelings of the aesthetic—both the joy and the rather fearful, overwhelming awe—can quickly split into the human need for a different kind of pattern, one that centralizes these powerful forces in anthropomorphic terms. If human need has drawn out of the aesthetic the consequent religious mode of interpretation, however, this doesn't legitimize the religious at all, but rather undercuts it. For the aesthetic mode is so entirely indifferent to the disposition of human lives and fates that there is no conceivable way to engender a system of meaning from it that would so personalize the world as to make every individual a valuable constituent of it. This is a fraudulent move driven by the force of a desire for protection from the cold indifference of the world; it can never follow from the original aesthetic context. It could be argued that the human world really begins *only* when the aesthetic has become the theological, but I would insist that, on the contrary, the human is always already present in the aesthetic mode out of which the theological comes, for we can assume that other creatures do not experience what we characterize as beauty in the way that we do. They do not seem to experience wonder, even if they are capable of delighting in the world, and wonder therefore would be the mark of the human, wonder and awe. From these two conjoined impulses we have derived our religions and our systems of laws, at least in the initial stages of our cultures, and we have gone on to assume that the aesthetic is really subordinate rather than primary.

Once we begin to see that the theological is an anthropomorphic projection of the desire for protection, for meaning, onto the aesthetic impulse out of which the human developed, we have to revise our ways of thinking about our status, and about the status of our disciplines of knowledge. Indeed, to begin with the aesthetic is simply to state what has been insisted upon since Nietzsche: that our knowledge is essentially ungrounded, that the play of things is so constituted as to be fundamentally indifferent to the human desire for certitude. But I want to insist again that we need to conceive of the aesthetic as that out of which the theological grows rather than as that with which we are left once we have lost faith in our religious modes of valuation. Arnold clearly thought he was praising poetry when he said that it would take the place of religion, but I would argue that he was in fact unintentionally *ruining* poetry by characterizing it as the supplement of the religious, first because this placed religious burdens on the aesthetic that it could never bear, second because it forced poetry into a mode of meaning that is alien to it. The aesthetic does provide humans with a sense of value, out of which in turn the particular values of our individual lives are constituted, but it does not offer guidelines for living or prescriptions and systems of value that are universally—or even seemingly universally—applicable.[1]

Perhaps the gravest problem we face as a species comes from the potential confusion that results from this moment of understanding when the aesthetic is seen to take precedence over the theological, even if such an origin is only an hypostatized one. For we are so used to attaching the aesthetic to the theological that once the religious impulse is stripped of its significance, the aesthetic itself too easily gets lost. We know, for example, that Arnold was wrong—poetry did not come to take the place of religion—and we might ask ourselves why it failed to do so. Part of the answer would seem to be that humans are so accustomed to finding everything of value connected to something that has a specific meaning to it that the aesthetic—which is fundamentally meaningless, at least as traditionally conceived—disappears when no meanings are to be found in it. It becomes the leftover that isn't even noticed. Put another way, we can say that the relentless course of the past hundred years has pushed us ever farther down the road toward conceding that the world is fundamentally an aesthetic domain, but the more definitively that realization emerges, the more the aesthetic slips into the background.

The sciences have been rigorously dehumanizing the world for some time now—at least in some senses—and have long devoted themselves to a conception of the world as a place that is indifferent to humans. The egalitarian push of democratic systems has increasingly led us to strip the false values from our way of looking at things in the social world and has thus in its own way demonstrated the general indifference of social systems to the individual as a particular interest. The consequences of our modes of production have increasingly forced us to recognize the hypothetical ecology of our planet, which in turn leads us to the conclusion that the earth is indifferent to our presence on it, and that indeed we can no longer afford to be indifferent to it. All of these shifts, I would argue, ought to lead us to the conclusion that the world is fundamentally an aesthetic entity, but instead they have led too often to the abandonment of the aesthetic altogether. The reason for this seems to be the human mania for personal meaning that drove the religious impulse to deny its aesthetic core in the first place.

The aesthetic has not been seen as the essential aspect of our world because it requires us to accept two interrelated theses, and we have so far only been willing to accede to one of them. We have grown to the point where we can concede that the world is *not* something over which we have dominion, in part because our own detritus has forced us to admit this. But we have so far been unwilling to follow through on this fact and recognize that as a consequence we must accept the world's indifference to our presence within it. It could even be said that we have failed to address the problems inherent in our way of life because we still tacitly assume that the earth—like the God who swore after the last major flood that He would never destroy everything again—*does* take our interests and our presence into account. We simply can't seem to get past the notion that it is totally indifferent to us, and until we arrive at that point, we cannot discern the ways in which the aesthetic is that which is left once we strip from the world the meanings we have imposed upon it out of the force of our desire.

If we begin with the aesthetic rather than the theological, we find pattern, flows, a rhythm to things, and we can do so precisely to the extent that we are willing to give ourselves up to those flows and experience our movement within them. The cost is that we must concede that the world has absolutely no personal interest in us and no particular interest in humanity either. This thought has been so staggering to us that we have literally been stuck at the edge of a kind of nihilism for a century, almost incapable of moving on to something else. Such knowledge, Camus will tell us, makes the world absurd, though it can be affirmed in its absurdity. Such truths, Sartre tells us, leave us as the fundamental makers of ourselves and confer upon us the heroic task of creating the world in our own image. These kinds of responses to the aesthetic world have clearly lost the aesthetic impulse from the outset, for their obsession remains with meaning and not with pattern. If the world is absurd, it is so only because it fails to subscribe to our narrow conceptions of significance and purpose. If we are the fundamental makers, then presumably we have really only taken over God's role and have at last truly arrived at the kind of dominion over things that we first arrogated to ourselves in Genesis. Camus and Sartre may be doing what they can to imagine a hearty response to the world's indifference, but they cannot escape from the abyss of nihilism simply because of their insistence on the same old kind of meaning that their work demonstrates the absence of. In refusing to give up the old metaphors of meaning and creation and making, they have left themselves stuck within a theological pattern that dooms their work to failure simply because, like Arnold's, it measures effects in terms of a supplementary reading of the theological impulse. And while it may have been understandable enough for the existentialists to be so caught, given the historical circumstances of their writings, the disconcerting fact is that all these decades later we are still lamenting the absence of the theological rather than praising the re-emergence of the aesthetic.

One of the refreshing aspects of the aesthetic view of the world that is so difficult to grasp is that in many respects it ought to be a relief to humans to see that the world is indifferent to them. Instead of being affronted by this fact, we ought to recognize it as something that frees us from the terrible obligations that came with being central, with being the particular reason for the world's existence. Other obligations follow in turn, but they are of a different sort, and if they require more self-discipline on our part, they demand less in the way of human capacity than the personal obligations that come from being the center of the universe. As the justification for the universe, we could never begin to live with our burdens; as one participant in it among others, we have only to learn how to work within its flows. Within the theological model we developed, virtually everything had a meaning attached to it—and hence a series of larger purposes and obligations—and this tended to make life more of a burden than it had to be. Within the aesthetic model, we can begin to distinguish those things that are meaningful parts of the flows through which our lives articulate themselves from those more or less gratuitous things that simply occur as a result of being who and where we are at any given moment in time. There is no need to reduce everything to a grid of possibilities and requirements. Some things just are and require no further justification.

The chief virtue of the aesthetic mode, however, at least when it comes to the consequences of its impersonality, is that for the most part we actually *prefer* its indifference, though we have accustomed ourselves to thinking otherwise. It is *pleasing* that the world is an impersonal, essentially indifferent place, however much we may have doubts about its lack of interest in us, and we simply have to reacquaint ourselves with this fact by reminding ourselves why we are always drawn to the aesthetic in the first place. Beauty draws us out of ourselves, provides us with the pleasure of being at home in the midst of whatever is aesthetically perceived. One can characterize this pleasure in negative terms, as someone like T. S. Eliot tended to do, explaining how the desire to escape from personality and emotion is that which prompts one to seek out aesthetic situations in the first place; or one can argue that the aesthetic is an essentially positive phenomenon that has its power over us because it gives us back the rhythms that are a part of our own being that are all too easily forgotten and lost in the social world. Regardless of the way one characterizes the experience, the same fact lies at the root: the world's indifference to our plight, to our everyday concerns and worries, to our crises and our shame, is that which makes possible the joy we experience through aesthetic perception. The indifference of the world, after all, is that which allows us temporarily to become indifferent about ourselves, and that is the precondition for an awareness that involves one in the larger flows of which one is a part.

The indifference at the center of the aesthetic cannot provide those things that religion offered to us, a meaning and a structure that made sense of our woes and justified our cause in every circumstance, but it is possible that it can erode our interest in such structures even as it provides the pleasure that displays the world to us as it is. More importantly, the question at this point is simply whether or not it makes better sense to see the religious as that which emerges from the aesthetic or vice versa, and given the powerful feelings at the center of religion—given its connection to the ecstatic—there can be little doubt that religion is simply an aesthetic discipline that has grafted the need for meaning and purpose onto the perception of beauty in the world. Because we failed to note that the aesthetic does provide structure, pattern and rhythm—which have truths of their own, even if they do not offer consoling fictions—we assumed once we declared God to be dead that beauty too had died, or at least those elements we valued, and we have since built our conception of the world on an aesthetic view all too similar to Eliot's: in the absence of religious consolations, beauty has become an essentially negative mode of being, a nugatory state that provides at best a momentary kind of relief from the anxieties we experience as a result of being alive. And Eliot's return to religion also suggests the total vapidity of this conception. We may not all feel the need to embrace a theological vision in the face of a failed aesthetic, but we have more or less come to create a world in which there is little to differentiate the aesthetic modes of those who merely seek oblivion from those whose interest in beauty is based upon the knowledge with which it provides them. Here is where the real nihilism lies, not in the assertion of the priority of the aesthetic. Here we find the abandonment of interest in the world upon which all aesthetic experience is based, a self-absorption so intense that the indifference of the world is incapable of drawing one out of one's own states of being.

Nihilism, then, is a product of self-pity, not of the indifference of the world to the human need for meaning and purpose; it comes about, as Wallace Stevens suggested more than forty years ago in "Esthétique du Mal," because our pain, the ordinary pain the comes from living, makes us indifferent to the sky, to the external world that provides some of the woe of life but also its pleasures and consolations.[2] Nihilism is the childlike assertion that these consolations won't do, that we require more in order to grant our assent to the world. It is therefore not overcome by a retreat to the sacred structures that our culture abandoned some time ago, for that is little more than a different way of refusing to accept the world on its own terms. We have to learn how to embrace the nonhuman without becoming inhuman; we have to see how we can become *more* human *only* by embracing the *non*human and its indifference toward us. And if we can do that, we will also recognize that the aesthetic mode of existence is the primary mode, that way of construing the world through which we originally worked, and that mode to which we shall have to return if we are going to find ways of dealing with the structures we ourselves have built.

Another way of phrasing the problem we face in the late twentieth century is to say that we are by now fully aware that the social powers that exert themselves in the world succeed to the extent that they attach themselves to the aesthetic. To be sure, this was always true, as suggested above: religion could not have had the power over people that it had if it did not derive its major force from the aesthetic. It loses its power over time as its aesthetic gestures are less and less convincing, less and less attached to the social world that emerges over the centuries. As secular powers gain more and more control over the socius, they seek more and more to usurp the force of the aesthetic, and they succeed to the extent that they do. Even repressive regimes in our time have to justify their behavior in aesthetic ways by providing convincing descriptions of social patterns that will justify their actions, though they are less under the sway of the aesthetic than democratic systems that depend more straightforwardly for their right to govern on the assent of large numbers of people. The most obvious example of the political usurpation of the aesthetic is found in the charismatic demagogue whose magic words convince the multitudes of the rightness of his plans for their future, but from the symbols through which political systems establish an emotive force that can approach the religious to the everyday arrangement of the socioeconomic apparatus through which people order their lives, social power depends upon the aesthetic for its sense of rightness.

The trend toward a greater and greater dependence on the aesthetic within the political comes about at a time when the political is also taking over the religious sense of mission previously dispensed by God, and because we are more aware of the ways political systems establish patterns of meaning and value, we have lost sight of their fundamental dependence on aesthetic forces that don't inherently belong to them. The most obvious cases where these forces manifest themselves have to do with the zealotry of crowds, whether they be those Islamic fundamentalists in Iran who chant for the death of the Great Satan or those in countries like the United States who have given their lives over to a cause. Ironically, in failing to acknowledge the effects of the aesthetic, the liberal parties in the West have done more to undermine their own position than any conservative group could do, though this has yet to be fully realized. The liberals were the ones who committed themselves thoroughly to the poststructuralist rhetoric that declared all positions ideological. They did so in order to argue for the need to have their own special interests addressed, but they failed to see how that in turn gave the more fundamentalist groups an equally valid claim to attention, one that was heightened because they could claim that only their eternal verities could save the society from relativism or total nihilism. In a totally ideological world, the will to power is all, and the liberals were willing to argue this point as long as they felt their own power to be in the ascendent. Now that there are some serious points of backlash, in local areas and in far away regions like Iran as well, they may have to confront the implications of their own arguments a bit more squarely than they have up to now.

The political left in the West has been able to ideologize everything by declaring the aesthetic to be a bourgeois ruse, but this ignores the fact that beauty can be found in all human life and all social strata. In assuming that the aesthetic is only a disguised ideology, such critics thereby deny that beauty has anything other than political effects in people's lives. It is true that certain *ways of conceiving* of the function of beauty in human life specifically reflect the socioeconomic context through which they are articulated, just as it is true that all conceptions of human existence, be they political or aesthetic or religious, bear the stamp of their time. But to deny the aesthetic altogether, to declare it nothing more than another kind of ideology, is to lose sight of that upon which all societies depend. And given this, it is not enough simply to be for the right cause, however admirable and just it may be. If the goal is the legitimate one of seeking to overcome some form of oppression or discrimination, it may in itself be admirable. But such goals cannot seriously be conceived over the long term through a scheme in which the will to power is all. If humans do nothing more during their lives than seek to exert power over others for their own benefit, then it is impossible to imagine a society in which discrimination comes to an end. One can do no more than hope for a world in which the dispossessed can take control and become the new masters.

The argument for the ideologization of the world comes about so easily because the aesthetic attaches itself to all disciplines without really being readily identifiable in itself. Because it lacks the structures upon which the West has based itself—because, that is, it is *irrational* and thereby defies reason, however sensible its own forms are in their own way—it appears not to exist at all and slips through the nets that would capture it. And because we have developed societies that make different kinds of appeals to the world, the questions we ask ourselves also turn away from the aesthetic. This is not simply because our self-absorption keeps us from recognizing a mode of life that is indifferent to us, though that is a good part of the problem. It is also because the very legitimate questions upon which all societies are based cannot be answered in a straightforward way for everyone on the basis of the aesthetic. The beautiful simply cannot provide the kinds of truths and structures upon which all social discourse depends, though all meaningful discourse derives from the aesthetic. And there is no reason why humans shouldn't demand meanings and a sense of purpose to their lives. The existentialists may have gone the wrong road when they began affirming an absurd universe and declared that we should create ourselves out of nothing, but they were right to be addressing these questions, however quaint they may seem in a world that is driven by the endless play of linguistic signs. Social systems must provide structure, meaning, and value, and their goal should be nothing else. The question is how they go about doing so, and dispensing with the aesthetic will inevitably fail to create the kind of community that those who argue so assiduously for an ideological world hope to bring about.

The problem of how to develop a social system out of the aesthetic should in theory be simple enough once one concedes the value in doing so, but the obstacles are not simply those that come from the seeming ineluctability of the forms of beauty. They also have to do with the questions that Socrates sought to bury, and we can perhaps best get a glimpse of these problems by looking at one of the most famous stories of Nathaniel Hawthorne, "My Kinsman, Major Molineux." Robin, the young man whose coming of age the story recounts, is the typical innocent who must learn about his potential for good and evil, though he himself believes he has simply come to the town to make his way in the world with the help of his kinsman Major Molineux. As a stranger in town, his resources are sorely tested from the beginning, largely because he was eager and foolish enough to arrive at a late hour without having any directions to his kinsman's house. The most striking thing about Robin's reactions, though, is how violent they are, how quickly he turns to thoughts of revenge the moment something goes wrong. The expressions of violence begin innocuously enough, in humorous fashion—"The man is old, or verily, I might be tempted to turn back and smite him on the nose"[3]—but the wish to strike out is very real, and it comes from the embarrassment Robin feels in the face of the town's reaction to him: "Ah, Robin, Robin! even the barber's boys laugh at you for choosing such a guide!" Robin feels negated by the ridicule to which he is exposed and therefore tries to redress his wounds by imagining revenge.

Of course it is not very long before the level of Robin's violence escalates in the face of further indignities. He goes from embarrassment to greater abjection, having to face the kind of situation from which he was protected in the past by his insular home life: "Hunger also pleaded loudly with him, and Robin began to balance the propriety of demanding, violently, and with lifted cudgel, the necessary guidance from the first solitary passenger whom he should meet" (36). Only his need for guidance and his desire for food keep him from threatening people with his cudgel, yet he fails to see that the guidance he requires cannot be had at the mere intrusion of a blunt instrument, that it is precisely his desire to make use of that instrument that must be guided. Nevertheless, his instincts get the better of him, and it is not long before he deliberately provokes someone: "The man was proceeding with the speed of earnest business, but Robin planted himself full before him, holding the oak cudgel with both hands across his body as a bar to further passage"(39).

These real and symbolic assertions of Robin's approaching manhood are designed to allow him to find his way in the world, but he doesn't realize that he is being forced to address his own internal desires through his confrontation with others, particularly through his contact with the man with the variegated countenance, who obviously symbolizes the adult state that Robin aspires to yet shrinks from:

> Robin gazed with dismay and astonishment on the unprecedented physiognomy of the speaker. The forehead with its double prominence, the broad hooked nose, the shaggy eyebrows, and fiery eyes were those which he had noticed at the inn, but the man's complexion had undergone a singular, or, more properly, a twofold change. One side of the face blazed an intense red, while the other was black as midnight, the division line being in the broad bridge of the nose; and a mouth which seemed to extend from ear to ear was black or red, in contrast to the color of the cheek. The effect was as if two individual devils, a fiend of fire and a fiend of darkness, had united themselves to form this infernal visage. The stranger grinned in Robin's face, muffled his particolored features, and was out of sight in a moment. (39)

Robin's own demons make their very graphic appearance to him through this man's visage, but like the man with the painted face, this grin shocks him with its horror and is "out of sight in a moment," for this is hardly what Robin wants to see. *He* is a good person and doesn't contain a fiend of fire and a fiend of darkness; *he* does not possess an infernal visage any more than he can discern infernal regions within himself, even if they are there. He may react with anger and the desire for violence at the slightest provocation, but to him that has nothing at all to do with the fiends represented in this figure.

When Robin is finally forced into a situation where his own behavior can no longer be ignored, when he has no other choice but to see at least momentarily that his guide was right, that a human may "have several voices . . . as well as two complexions" (44), he still cannot bring himself to admit what his own eyes and ears have shown him. Instead of seeing himself for what he is, he practices the sublime art of denial and repression. As his kinsman approaches in the midst of the feverish crowd that has tarred and feathered him, "The contagion was spreading among the multitude, when all at once it seized upon Robin, and he sent forth a shout of laughter that echoed through the street—every man shook his sides, every man emptied his lungs, but Robin's shout was the loudest there" (47). Caught up in the fever of the crowd, whose desire for the humiliation of the father figure is as strong for its own reasons as Robin's is, Robin unintentionally outlaughs those whose desires created the scene of Molineux's—and Robin's—humiliation. And when he recovers from his feverish outburst, his first response is to ask for the way to the ferry; he clearly wants to go back to where he was before he achieved self-knowledge and seeks to cover up his shame by saying that he is weary of town life (48). He has participated in Socrates' sacred mysteries, has been forever changed by them, but he remains uncertain whether or not, like Socrates, he wants to bury this knowledge forever or try to keep it in the forefront of his awareness.

Although Hawthorne ends the story before we find out whether Robin decides to remain in town, and hence accept his maturity with grace and insight rather than repression, the tone of the story would suggest that we are to expect

Robin to assume his fully adult position in the world. And although Hawthorne himself is clearly aware of the dangerous fuels he is playing with in this story, he too, like the mob who tars and feathers Molineux, chooses to point out the carnival atmosphere that surrounds these mysteries and mixes their violence with celebration: "The cloud spirits peeped from their silvery islands, as the congregated mirth went roaring up the sky! The Man in the Moon heard the far bellow. 'Oho,' quoth he, 'the old earth is frolicsome tonight!'" (48). The raging fires of the people may manifest themselves in colorful garb and mirthful laughter, but the joy of the crowd is mixed with the more potent forces of the cudgel Robin has so yearned to employ, and the mixture of emotions involved is as complex and variegated as the man's countenance: "On they went, like fiends that throng in mockery around some dead potentate, mighty no more, but majestic still in his agony. On they went, in counterfeited pomp, in senseless uproar, in frenzied merriment, trampling all on an old man's heart. On swept the tumult, and left a silent street behind." The "frenzied merriment," the ecstatic joy that sweeps the crowd out of its everyday state into the impersonal mass of the mob that can drive itself to deeds that none would accomplish in his or her ordinary disposition, is based on the triumph over an externally perceived evil that fully justifies both the merriment and the complete humiliation of the man who had previously symbolized the necessary order of the town.

The story itself, set just before the onset of the Revolutionary War, suggests that the United States, like Robin, is about to undergo its own maturation processes, is ready to assume the role of an adult in the world, but, as with Robin, it remains to be seen whether that role has even now been taken up, for it would depend on an acknowledgment of the variety of faces and voices inherent in every culture, an awareness of the fact that human motivations—and particularly that strong mixture of violence and merriment that dominates the story—are not always what them seem. Again, it is precisely to keep away from this kind of knowledge that Socrates prefers to bury the awareness of abjection and shame, for he believes that no social state can withstand this knowledge, that the knowledge itself breeds the contagion of the mob that continually undermines the socius. It is the fever that devours the state and can therefore never be acknowledged. Hawthorne takes a more sanguine view, one that suggests both the inevitability of our awareness of these phenomena and our ability to assume them with grace and dignity, even if the people in the story didn't do so. After all, the comic stance of the story mingles with the very real threat posed by the individual and collective demons within it to mitigate the forces of condemnation that would guarantee a repetition of this mode of abjection in the future.

Hawthorne is in this sense strangely tolerant of his characters at the same time that he distinguishes his view from Socrates', for their behavior is justified by their desire for freedom, the wish to govern themselves. If they are to become adults who manage their own social affairs, then they must put off the yoke of British rule, but they must also put on the knowledge of their own fully human potential for good and evil. The trade-off is assumed to be both inevitable and natural: one achieves freedom to dispose of one's life at the cost of the awareness of the potential violence and evil that are constant threats to one's freedom and the freedom of others. Hawthorne thus doesn't doubt here that the average human is capable of moving through this change of state and coming out of it with the wisdom that Robin and Socrates would prefer to bury.

What remains unclear in all this is why a commitment to the aesthetic, that which allows, if you will, a comic stance toward these infernal regions of human nature, inevitably forces one to face the variegated countenance of the aesthetic state. Why is the aesthetic predicated on an awareness of the joy and the shame that Robin experiences in the same moment as his laugh rises higher than any other in the crowd? In a way, this is a nonsensical question, for the only answer would be that the aesthetic is a composite state that embraces joy and wonder as much as violence, the abject, and shame. But the issue here is one of *awareness*. Socrates, after all, invoked the rites of the mystery to try to bury knowledge of the other side of the aesthetic, but even a mystery has written into it certain kinds of knowledge about its activities, just as most sacrificial rituals have built into them the symbolic knowledge of the blood sport of life, the sacrificing of a life in order to protect one's own, the symbolic exchange of one kind of violence for another. All sacrifice in this sense is a demonic assertion of power over the forces of death that surround one, a godlike demonstration of one's ability to trick the universe through a substitute murder, and one of the primary uses of the aesthetic takes place within this context of ritual, whether it be Socrates' desire to sacrifice a huge and unprocurable victim, Robin's desire to negate his kinsman in order to assume his own position in the world, or the rite of Holy Communion in the Christian Church. Some of these rites are sanctified, some are considered the devil's work, but seen from a distance they are all composed of the same kind of mysterious knowledge and ignorance. A mystery doesn't fully bury the infernal regions at all; it merely inscribes onto them a symbolic reminder of origin and intent.

Why, though, must there be some kind of awareness of these phenomena in spite of the very real desire for complete ignorance of them, and how does this contribute to the way the aesthetic is shaped by the political systems through which it chiefly manifests itself in our world today? If, like Robin, we should prefer to avert our eyes from Molineux's humiliation once we have had a chance to reflect upon what the contagion of the crowd had brought us to, why do we also seem to need such feverish states in order to sustain ourselves? One of the main problems with our current discourse is that it cannot answer these questions, cannot even approach them, perhaps out of a willed ignorance of them. We are still driven by images of utopian futures in which we shall no longer have to worry about the surges of the infernal regions that disrupt the smooth surfaces of people's lives, but such beliefs are no more than attempts to abjure the knowledge we possess, reflections of our desire to return with Robin to our presocial state in the forest.

Even more, we are still looking for *victims*, for those symbolic figures who will keep our full knowledge of the aesthetic contained. Victims serve the dual aesthetic role of obliterating and perpetuating the shame that prompts us to deny what we are. In externalizing what we disapprove of within ourselves and projecting it upon others, we seem to avoid the need to deal with it, but the very process of victimization leads to the awareness that we have indeed *victimized* someone, that is, unfairly treated another in order to avoid the full costs of accepting who we are. That shame is buried in turn, only to rise again at some future date to victimize someone else. If we have our mysteries to keep from seeing straight on that which we know to be within ourselves, they are mysterious only to the extent that this awareness—and its very real threat to our sense of self—is always hovering at the *edge* of the rite. If we victimize someone, that is because we feel victimized ourselves. A sacrifice is always a doubling of motivation, a symbolic and literal means of sustenance that commemorates a moment of recognition: we see ourselves for what we are. We love the brutality of the rite and are shamed by it at the same time. We applaud ourselves for our blood lust even as we are negated by the act that was supposed to uplift us. And because the emotions always oscillate from one side to the other, we can never get away from that which the rite is supposed to allow us to escape. The purpose of all sacrificial rites, then, becomes the need to perpetuate sacrificial rites.

Hawthorne's story and his greater tolerance of the vagaries of his characters suggest that we have learned something since Socrates' day, that we have found an alternative to the mysterious rites that Socrates preferred that better deals with the full richness of the aesthetic. We have increasingly learned that the concentrated effects of the mystery are different in quality from the play of difference through which the aesthetic can articulate itself in a more open social system. The problem is that it seems all too easy to say that an open social system allows for a play of difference that doesn't necessarily manifest itself in the violence of sacrificial rites. In some senses this seems to be true, at least in an intuitive way, as Freud's invention of the hydraulic machine of repression would suggest. It makes sense to think that knowledge of ourselves cannot really be buried, that it comes back with greater force the more we seek to keep it down. Likewise, therefore, it makes sense to assume that the pressures that grow out of the ordinary interaction of human beings are more likely to disperse themselves in benign ways if they are not repressed by an authoritarian regime. The return of the repressed is one of the clichés of our time, and it is hard to argue with its logic.

Socrates, we could say, produced the first public act of repression, contradictory though that is, and yet his very public declaration of the need for repression demonstrated its own impossibility. If Socrates really meant what he said, if he believed that one could indeed bury the knowledge of the violent truths of Ouranos and Kronos, then he should have done so without talking about it. He should have said that Hesiod lied and left it at that, *even if he believed otherwise*. To leave open the possibility that Hesiod told the truth, and to imagine remedies for this knowledge via the sacrificial mystery, is to be caught within the very contradiction that he seeks to escape: the declaration of repression that doesn't satisfactorily repress because it is declared. It may be that Socrates was simply conceding the obvious, that such things can never be wholly repressed for very long. It may be that he unknowingly demonstrated his ignorance of these matters by talking publicly about the need to bury this knowledge when it was quite clearly open for view in his discussion. And it may be that he simply had to preserve his reputation as wise man by acknowledging at least the possibility that the poet told the truth and then considering the consequences if he did. Regardless of the potential motivation, though, Socrates confers much greater power on the repressed by the degree to which he wants to repress it. He is not content simply to bury it. Instead, it must be buried in a mystery, and the mystery must be built around a huge and unprocurable victim, making it the greatest mystery of all. An ordinary sacrifice simply won't do; as with Christ, it has to be the sacrifice to end all sacrifices, for what is being sacrificed is the knowledge of the human desire to sacrifice, to supplement, demonically to take control of the forces of life and death in order to perpetuate one's life.

And yet, unlike Christ and his sacrifice, Socrates declares beforehand his knowledge of the purpose of the sacrifice—it is not an act done in *remembrance* of Ouranos and Kronos but one done *in forgetfulness;* it is not an act designed to put an end to sacrifice but rather to satiate that desire symbolically and under more or less controlled circumstances. Christ's sacrifice is presumably designed to bring to a close the endless chain of sacrifices upon which human communities have been based, and if it suffers from the same contradiction as Socrates'—that it depends on that which it seeks to dispense with—at least it does so with a kind of innocence. Socrates declares the purpose of his sacrifice to be the need to sacrifice our knowledge of why we need to sacrifice. It ends up commemorating the violent acts of Ouranos and Kronos through the mystery that pretends to put them out of play.

If the desires that generate the sacrificial tendencies within humans have both individual and social analogues, as Hawthorne suggests in "My Kinsman, Major Molineux," then it may well be easy enough to contain these forces of violence by dispersing them, by freeing humans from the need to provide endless victims to satiate their desire for blood. Here again, though, we run into the problem of the world's indifference, for it is precisely the world's lack of concern for our individual welfare that generates at least a part of the need for sacrificial violence. A good bit of the blood lust on the planet has its origin in the individual's perception of inequity, his belief that he has been unfairly dealt with. Democratic systems can come up with laws that are designed to address the social acts that create inequity, and that is their true strength, but they are incapable of dealing with the inequities that come about merely as part of the innocence of living. If one's neighbor steals from one, there is within the system a means of addressing the problem that ought at least in part to attend to the individual's desire to be paid back for his suffering.

But if one gets heart disease because of a genetic predisposition for the disorder, there is no system of recompense to address the feeling of being unfairly treated by the world. Even if we assume that an open society with a system of laws designed to protect the citizens from an unfair alteration in the play of differences goes a long way toward dispersing the pressures that might in less benign contexts lead to violence of one kind or another, we are still left with the very real indifference of the world itself to our individual affairs. This indifference creates its own kind of unfairness, at least as perceived by each individual, who is in the unique position of assessing the play of differences from his own singular position within them. And this indifference is that which our open systems have yet to deal with, the leftover of Socrates' problem that must be addressed.[4] This problem comes about because religion no longer provides sufficient assurances about the fair play of the world, and yet it is hard to imagine any society that could sufficiently deal with the manifold wrongs that individuals perceive to have been inflicted upon them without reason. Can political systems that are increasingly designed to offer constituents virtually anything in order to garner their support be depended upon to meet this need too? How could a political system—open *or* closed—ever hope to develop ways of asserting control over the random events of life?

It would seem more likely that our political systems would have to begin to discern a bit more carefully those wrongs that are indeed correctable, those that are worthy of addressing, from those about which nothing can be done. In the midst of societies that are designed to offer a great many temporal delights, we would have to be able to imagine systems that could simultaneously counsel a kind of stoicism about the ways in which fates are measured out, for nothing short of that kind of position can possibly address the problems we will need to face in the twenty-first century. In some respects the "difficulty" of an indifferent universe is more acute in the United States than elsewhere simply because the socioeconomic apparatus has been promising more than it can deliver for so long that it doesn't seem to know how to do anything else, even as the economic system itself is relatively less capable of meeting the needs that ought first to be addressed. If European communities are more amenable to a stoical viewpoint about the unfortunate twists of fate that come about at random, and if they have been more skeptical about religious consolations for some time, the problem of rectitude in the face of the world's indifference exists there as well.

Nevertheless, as was the case with the larger question of whether or not Socrates was right to argue that knowledge of the vicious acts of the gods ought to be buried, one would have to imagine that even if our societies were capable of articulating the proper stoicism in the face of the accidents of life, there would still be a problem with the pressures and violence that come from the individual's sense of being wronged. If the aesthetic can demonstrate that in the larger sense these "wrongs" are just part of the play of fields through which the world as a whole articulates itself, and if a stoical attitude toward one's own misfortunes allows one to accept that larger vision of things, the very senselessness of this view—as construed from the more traditional, so-called rational attitude—is likely to make it harder to accept than it might have been a century or more ago. There may have always been something of a triangular relationship between the aesthetic, the general indifference of the world to human suffering, and the violence that has plagued humans since they emerged as a species, but we have lost sight of it for so long that we have great difficulty recovering a less self-centered perspective on the events of life. The idea that one's pain is often nothing personal at all is hard for us to make any kind of sense out of because we have increasingly focused on the ego, on the self and its relation to the world, and our habituation to the fetishization of the self leads to the present impasse between our knowledge of the world and our desire for what it should be. Put most bluntly, it seems incredible to us that a person whom we may deem to be evil could have a better life than we do simply by chance.

There is something so corrosive in that notion that we have devoted millennia to putting it out of play. Regardless of whether we imagine our sorrows as tests of character, or whether we envision still another world to redress the imbalances of this one (as *we* perceive them), the West has regularly been prompted to find solutions to the problems of dissimilar fates, and while our era may be enlightened in many respects, it has not yet found ways of getting around this problem.

Indeed, we have yet to begin to understand why humans are so constituted as to be bedeviled by the corrosive influences of a perceived lack of fairness in the disposition of fates. We are aware of the degree to which the hierarchies of social systems in themselves tend to generate mimetic desires that feed the individual's sense of what is appropriate recompense for his or her virtues and the unfairnesses that have come irrespective of them, and we have a number of psychological conceptions that presume to address the psychic sense of loss and gain, desire and despair, that drives human beings, but even after Freud we remain more or less ignorant of the force our internal sense of fairness plays in the disposition of our lives and the way we think of ourselves. It could be supposed that much of the vengeance that seeks to overcome the lack of fair play an individual might perceive could come from a brutally pragmatic sense of temporality, from the irretrievable sense that we have, after all, only one life to live. Given that, it is all too easy to see the perceived unfairnesses as usurpations of our life. There are doubtless ample opportunities in every life for one to be overwhelmed by the fact that this or that simply should not have happened, that it ruined what might otherwise have been a good life, and that inasmuch as there is no alternative life to count on, the rage within builds and seeks an outlet. It is not *fair* that one's only life should be so polluted by this or that, not fair at all, and one is therefore unwilling to confer one's approval on a universe that metes out fates in such a way. As with the deaths of loved ones, most of us find ways of dealing with these moments when the world is destroyed for us by something that happened—

or failed to happen—but even so, the forces within us that circulate around such contexts are among the most pernicious, if also the most understandable, affective situations we are ever likely to face.

If we think back to Socrates yet again, we can see in his unwillingness to discuss in any detail at all the doings of Kronos and Ouranos—in his hurried proposition that if these things cannot be buried, a very few individuals should take upon themselves the burdens of these evils and then seek to purge themselves afterward—a fearfulness that surprises us in a man so wise. For his wisdom is not to be doubted in spite of his superstitiousness. On the contrary, his wisdom manifests itself here in conjunction with his superstitiousness. He simply does not want to risk saying anything more than he has to, for what he says could lead to an unpleasant dispensation from the gods. They might make him pay for his sacrilege, so he skirts the problem as delicately as he possibly can. As we watch the man who devoted his entire life to the rational exposition of the world, we can't help but be taken by his terribly human reaction to his confrontation with the defilement of the violent gods.

At the same time, we need to wonder why reason itself is not capable of dealing with this violence, and that is yet another way of addressing the problems humans feel in the face of the potential arbitrariness of their fates. The problem is not that people feel the world should be a fair place so much as they want to believe this to be the case at the same time that they suspect it is not so. It is their fear of its arbitrariness that prompts them to imagine alternative fates, ways around the potential disaster that could usurp their lives at any moment. And even Socrates is not about to disturb the fates any more than he has to. He may well be committed to a rational consideration of the world, but he knows when to pull up short and leave the rest to the sacred priests. If he wants to bury this knowledge finally it is because he himself does not want to risk the pollution that is involved in it. After all, Socrates could assume that the gods would know that he wasn't being sacrilegious in mentioning the evil acts of Ouranos and Kronos; surely the gods are capable of distinguishing intent, we would think. But Socrates doesn't assume this: the gods are irrational, and there is no accounting for what might offend them. Given this, when one begins to approach sacred ground, one ought to walk as quickly and quietly around it as possible. Hard though it may be to believe that Socrates is quickly trying to bury the subject of Kronos and Ouranos lest he be struck by a lightning bolt from Zeus, that certainly seems to be what he is doing.

And Socrates is a man who can bear his fate far better than the average human. He willingly takes on challenges that most of us would shrink from, confident that he is strong enough to deal with them. At the most crucial moment in the articulation of his Republic, though, he tells us that humans need superstitions—irrational and thoroughly implausible acts designed to convince one that one has the power to ward off any evil powers that might seek to destroy one's life—if they are going to live together in groups. They simply cannot coexist without repression, sacred mysteries and the rites of oblivion. In our own day writers like Daniel Bell have made arguments that don't stray too far from this position, though they would hardly put it that way.[5] But anyone who seriously argues for the need to maintain a sacred space that is purged of the contamination of the secular world—whether that person be an Iranian mullah or Daniel Bell—is essentially asserting that humans are incapable of living with the randomness—the so-called absurdity—of life. When one rewrites the world in terms of the aesthetic out of which it came, one inevitably comes up against this constraint, yet no aesthetic theory has ever found a viable solution to it. Plato thought the problem could be buried, Aristotle thought it could be purged through a full immersion into it via the ritual of tragic drama, and Kant assumed that it would lead to a rational assertion of power over the natural world that had the effrontery to suggest the irrelevance of our individual plans for its much larger schemes. None of these notions really establishes a proper relation to the problem, though it is no doubt true that repression of one's knowledge of the problem works for a while, and no doubt equally true that purgation through drama works as long as one participates in it regularly enough. Kant's solution, the assertion of the powers of reason over the lesser forces of the natural world, is something that Socrates realized as a foolish hope millennia before Kant proposed it, so it doesn't even merit serious discussion.

What has happened in our own day is that first the religious attitude was stripped of its value, and that left us with the political and the aesthetic attitudes. Next the political has assiduously sought to deny the existence of the aesthetic altogether—it is only politics by another means—in order to put out of play the very fates that determine the lives and actions of us all. The political vision—*any* political vision—can only succeed to the extent that it can put out of play the fact that, however much it may promise to deal with the inequities of life, and however well it in fact manages to do so, it cannot deal with the irreducible chanciness of life. It cannot overcome the play of chance that the play of difference is. It can rearrange some of the differences within the socius, but it cannot directly affect the way the differences play out. More pertinently, it cannot put out of play the totally understandable human fear that *nothing* can overcome the fundamental arbitrariness of the universe. And inasmuch as it cannot deal with these most basic concerns, it dispenses with them, declares them null and void, when it denies that there is such a thing as the aesthetic. I would go so far as to argue that the greatest flaw in all our current political systems is precisely this unwillingness to address the most basic of human situations, our relation to the nonpolitical world of nature. We may have environmental movements and protection agencies and scientists investigating ozone depletion and parties that color themselves green, but we have yet to develop a political party or system that is based on the aesthetic nature of existence, and only such a conception will make possible a means through which a better relation to the planet can come about.

Likewise, only such a conception will allow us to conceive of the relationship between human social systems and the larger flows of which they are but parts. It is not sufficient to begin with the social world and then try to address the ways in which it has a deleterious impact on the organisms around it, for that view fails to understand in a comprehensive fashion the position of humans in the midst of those other organisms. More importantly, without a politics that emerges out of the aesthetic we cannot begin to imagine a social system that is capable of addressing the dual heritage we have as a result of our aesthetic relationship to the world: that we both assiduously seek out the ecstatic indifference of the play of difference and at the same time live in mortal fear of it, that the very best moments of our lives are those in which we participate most fully in the natural flows of life, and the very worst moments—and the worst aspects of human being—derive from our inability to live in the world with a full knowledge of our vulnerability within it. Social inequities need to be addressed, as always; relationships between the various political systems need to be addressed, as always; the relationships between individuals in groups need to be addressed, as always; but all of these situations and our responses to them must finally be predicated on a sociopolitical understanding of the much larger forces that drive both us and the planet.

It is easy enough to declare the need to develop a politics that derives from rather than denies the aesthetic; it is another thing to imagine what such a creature would look like; it is again still another thing to wonder if such a system is even possible. If I have partially established that which an aesthetic politics would have to confront, I have yet to suggest what kind of possibilities are inherent in this idea. The most important point, perhaps, is that an aesthetic politics would have to be a politics for the entire planet, not simply for one group of people in a particular location, and certainly not just for human beings by themselves. It would have to address the politics of plants and animals as well, something we are already beginning to do in any number of ways that only lack a sufficiently coherent framework for bringing them together to have a significant impact on the way we begin to think of ourselves in relation to the earth.

The chief difficulty we face in building a system out of a larger conception of our own activities comes from our obsession with language and its limitations, specifically the question of whether or not it is possible to construe the nonhuman through language without writing humanity all over it. In a way, it is true that all language anthropomorphizes the nonhuman. Even the term "nonhuman" marks that which is other in terms of our own standard, and words like "nature" and "earth" are just as much connected to human conceptions of activities that transcend our thinking as "nonhuman" is. So we are not capable of looking at the world outside of our own interest in it, but that is less of an impediment than one might think given the current level of discourse on the nature of the illusions of language. We certainly note those things that are of value to us, and in naming them therefore develop ways of manipulating the world that have a human edge to them, but the patterns that we are able to draw out of the world through the interested namings we habitually employ attend to very real phenomena and hence allow us to achieve a greater and greater understanding of the way the flows of the world move.

One can use an example with much current interest, the question of what to do about the countless species of plants that are disappearing so rapidly as the tropical forests are plundered. Our scientists argue that the loss of these species is not merely a natural tragedy—that, after all, is also a human conception, for nature doesn't know tragedy—but also a human one, for any number of presently unknown plants might provide future benefits in the way of drugs and medications. Now this is surely an attitude with a human interest in mind, for the point is to save the species so that humans can benefit from a future understanding of their chemical properties. Indeed, this is a more interested perspective than a good many others that humans are also capable of taking, and yet the final result would be to provide for a world in which the diversity of flows is perpetuated as best as humans know how. If we have on the one hand created more and more rarefied species of plants and hence narrowed the gene pool in an effort to make more economically viable food products; and if we have in any number of other ways tried to reduce the diversity of the planet; still we are capable of realizing that it is in the planet's and our own interest to maintain as much diversity as possible.

From a less interested perspective—or actually in some senses a counter-interested perspective—we could use the example of the elephant, which we are presently told may well end up being extinct in a very short period of time if the ivory trade is allowed to continue. In economic—that is, human—terms, there is no particular reason why the preservation of elephants ought to take precedence over the abilities of some to make a fortune on the goods to be sold as a result of their slaughter. True, there are those who would argue that it is almost impossible to imagine the planet without its great elephants—I count myself among them—but countless species have already died out, and if there is a moral argument that distinguishes those species that died out from "natural" causes as opposed to those that died out as a result of human thoughtlessness, to a large degree humans are themselves no more than a natural cause, even if a potentially self-correcting one, so the sentimentality underlying the argument doesn't really work as long as the human species continues killing off countless other species from small fish to obscure plants every day. At the natural level, one species ought not to have a greater "right" to exist than another.

An argument on behalf of the preservation of the elephants is thus an *aesthetic* position: the world will be a more pleasing place for humans if elephants remain a visible part of it. Again, this is an interested viewpoint, but its interests are not parochial and economic. They are based on an assessment of the flows of life around us and our sense of how those flows ought to be allowed to continue, irrespective of our pragmatic needs and wants. An aesthetic understanding of the patterns of the world is as much a humanly interested perspective as any other viewpoint, yet its interest is not venal and purely self-serving. It is simply a perspective that argues that the greatest possible diversity of flows in the world provides humans with the most pleasing of environments in which to live. From there one can imagine the intrusion of other, more localized interests, such as the preservation of species in order to keep the gene bank rich and to provide future health benefits out of presently unknown compounds, but those are indeed arguments that begin to approach the self-interest that has been most destructive to the planet. The only thing that differentiates them from the common plunder we see around us every day is their awareness that we have a better chance of surviving as a species— and living more or less enjoyable lives—if we allow other species to thrive as well.

If the local point is that our various symbolic systems do indeed configure the world in anthropomorphized terms, these systems do *not* keep us from getting a sense of the flows of the world. We can discern the aesthetic nature of the world, even if the aesthetic is itself a human mode of perception, even if it is not "natural" or even a vision shared by other species. The aesthetic mode of construing the planet is simply that mode which most nearly allows us to see the world as it is with ourselves placed within its forces and flows. In this sense it is the most "natural" of human perspectives, even as it remains a human perspective. Other species may or may not have some sense of the beauty of the world—they certainly seem to be aware of some of its potential terrors—but even if they don't, the interested viewpoint of the aesthetic is all humans need in order to imagine a viable place for themselves within the vast scheme of the world as they are capable of perceiving it.

An aesthetic politics, however, would not proceed to give "rights" to the various animals and plants, for it would call into question the notion of rights to begin with. Rights can only be dispensed on the basis of shared *obligations,* something that is lost sight of in our present political climate, and there is no sense in imagining our relationship to the other species on the planet in terms of rights and obligations. Lacking self-awareness—at least as far as we know—other species can hardly be said to have obligations, to us or to anything else. Lacking self-awareness, they could hardly be said to have rights, which accrue to individuals in relation to their place within a social system. Lacking a social system, they ought not to be forcefully placed within ours, even if we perceive it to be for their own good. Even if we were to say that we were placing their "rights" in our trust, as we do with young children who are not yet capable of acting on the basis of their rights and responsibilities, we would be politicizing the species' relationship to the planet, which is precisely the problem they face at present. So we need to imagine an alternative relationship with them that is not based on the politics of rights but rather on some more neutral conception of their role within the flows of life.

If the politics of rights is not appropriate for the other species on the planet, neither is the sentimentality and bathos that is so often manifested toward the regular tribulations of various animals. We should certainly avoid inflicting any more pain on other species than is necessary for our own survival, but this does not mean that we should treat them as humans, with the same emotions and responses that we have. Some animals may well be capable of expressing grief, for example, yet this should not prompt us to assume their grief is the same as ours would be in similar circumstances. We waste large sums of money extricating a couple of whales from the frozen sea they are trapped in and at the same time ignore countless other cases where animal distress could be lessened simply by benign neglect or a little thought, and we ought to concentrate on those areas rather than on the humanizing attempts to name a few creatures and take them into our homes with us as pets, even if only for a week or so via television.

Outside of rights and sentimentality, the other species on the planet exist as we do, within vast flows of which they have all too little awareness but in which they manage more or less adequately to persist and even to thrive in certain circumstances. These flows are as indifferent to individual animals and particular species as they are to individual humans, and it is therefore appropriate for us to begin our own political aesthetics from that perspective, even as we must also inevitably confront the relationship between the particular differences of the world and the general indifference of the world to them. Politics is a system whereby the particular differences *are* noted, if not always addressed, and we must consequently begin by discerning the various differences that constitute the life of the planet in order to do what we can to allow them to persist. This does not mean that we attempt to hide our place within the food chain, for obviously humans need to consume living tissue in order to survive as much as any other species does, and we cannot imagine a viable politics outside of this awareness. But it does mean that we need to think through more carefully our role within that food chain in order to understand our relation to the other species who persist in similar ways.

The best example of the need to reconsider our place within the food chain is to be found in an examination of the human population as it disseminates itself over the planet. We have had grim forecasts about overpopulation at least since Malthus, most recently in the 1970s when the Club of Rome put out its pessimistic analysis of the relationship between the humans that were already alive and the available foodstuffs. And in turn we find that somehow we manage to subsist in any case, even as the billions turn into more billions. At present we are in the reactionary stage where we are told that population is not a problem at all, that the "doomsayers" have ignored the vast empty spaces of the planet that are still capable of sustaining human communities. There is no end in sight, we are told, to the number of humans the planet can maintain. Whatever starvation presently exists, we are further told, is the result of political battles and poor human planning, not the initial signs of the devastation humans will face as they grow in number and fight for increasingly scarce food products. And both of these statements may be true. At the very least, the viewpoint is as contestable as the "doomsaying" one.

What is in question, however, is not how many humans the planet can feed, but rather how many humans can exist on the planet before its flows have become overwhelmed by their presence within them. And again, this is as much an aesthetic matter as it is a practical one, for it is not simply a question of how to feed the mouths that exist; it is also an issue to do with whether or not we want to imagine a planet in which all the available space is filled with humans and *only* humans. Though the species would die long before this came about, one would have to imagine such a relationship to be an intolerable one, even if we were able somehow to feed all the people who existed. Life has the value it has for humans to the extent that it takes place within the diversity of nature, to the extent that we are regularly exposed to the differences of the nonhuman as well as the human. Even if a great many of us experience the nonhuman chiefly through cockroaches and the occasional tree, the *idea* of the natural world beyond our human communities is always available to us, and that would disappear if we were to "maximize" our presence on the planet.

Even aside from this argument, we have enough experience with the value of diversity at this point to know that the more one species dominates the flows of its fields, the less diversity there is, a situation that eventually works against the dominant species. Sooner or later the decline in diversity leads to the deaths of greater and greater numbers of the species. This is an inevitable result of the way the flows of fields are regulated. And if this works its way through rabbit populations in Idaho and lemmings in any number of places, there is no reason to think that it doesn't apply to humans as well, *regardless* of the technology we can imagine ourselves bringing to bear on food production in the future. Our capabilities are not such that we are able to discern just how many people can viably exist on the planet given the amount of food we can produce. We have no way of knowing the critical mass. We do know that within certain overpopulated communities—like those that exist in China—the political system itself recognizes its inability to deal with the geometric growth of the species and has therefore imposed stringent controls on the population, and we have to assume that at some point the same policies will have to apply to the entire species if we fail to do something about the problem now.

It may well take hundreds of years before the sheer magnitude of humans on the planet has so overwhelmed its resources that the earth can no longer sustain them. As with pollution problems and the like, these processes take a long time to build and are hard to stop once they have their own momentum. We could assume, I think, regardless of how many years it might take for our vast numbers to ruin the planet for human habitation, that there are at present already too many humans on the planet, and the goal ought not to be to slow down the growth—though that is obviously where we must begin—but rather to *reduce* the overall numbers of humans. The fact is that in terms of the aesthetics of the planet, the mere production of foodstuffs is not the only problem when it comes to numbers, for the magnitude of the numbers can also be reinforced by other factors, most obviously by the ability of any number of humans to lay waste to far more of the living matter on the planet than is necessary for their individual survival. Our scientific knowledge and technology may have led to higher crop yields and the like—though the question of the effects of these currently higher crop yields on *future* yields is an open issue— but they have also led to the greater plundering of other kinds of resources on the planet. When one thinks of how much of the energy resources and the minerals and the like are consumed by relatively small proportions of the species—one could use a single country like the United States as an example or the larger collocation of the West as a whole—one cannot ignore the fact that we are increasingly capable of destroying more of the planet per capita than ever before, and as development proceeds within the lesser-developed countries, our ability to destroy per capita can only increase, thereby *decreasing* the number of humans the planet will be able to sustain over the long term.

I want to stress that there are three interconnected aspects to the aesthetic politics that considers something like the relationship of the human population to the rest of the flows on the planet. There is the *purely* aesthetic angle—how we imagine the earth being overwhelmed by humans; how it simply *looks* to us when it seems little more than a giant ant colony or a metastasized cancer tumor overrun by people. There is also the aesthetic argument based on our perception of the flows of fields and their relationship to our general sustenance. And there is the immediate ability to sustain the lives that presently exist. In some ways these three aspects of the problem are separable: we can readily enough imagine being able to feed all the people on the planet right now at the same time that we can see that perhaps in ten years the sheer numbers might overwhelm the food supply. Or we can imagine the sheer beauty of the diversity of flows as being unrelated to the problem of one species sustaining itself at the expense of too many of the others. From an aesthetic politics, however, all three of these angles of vision must be considered together, for only then will we have the proper triangulation to assess our position responsibly. The essential beauty of the flows—irrespective for the moment of the very real brutality that they also involve—is an indication of the degree to which the other two angles are viable.

And the beauty is not simply a matter of "taste" or a subjective judgment based upon socioeconomic status, race or gender; it is a perception of the patterns that exist outside of our means of interpreting them. It *is* true that culture, race, and class play a part in whether or not one evaluates the world in this way, and that is worth emphasizing too. The human who struggles merely to keep food on the table is not likely to sit at home after a long day and consider the beauty of the flows of the planet. That conception requires leisure time and a culture that is interested in abstract speculation. And it is a peculiarly Western way of speaking about these things that would characterize them in terms of aesthetics and flows of fields and the like. But other cultures are as much based upon the laws of beauty as our own, whether they be construed in terms of yin and yang, the appropriateness of one's place in the karma of things, or some other cultural formation. And inasmuch as all cultures are based on the laws of beauty as they express themselves through the history/language that has passed them on from generation to generation, we can assume that the patterns themselves, however differently construed by this or that culture, are reflections of flows that exist extrinsic of our perception of them and hence the only place through which to begin articulating the politics upon which one's society should be based.

To return briefly once more to the question of rights, we can see if we begin with an aesthetic view that rights are based upon a particularly narrow, if also important, conception of human communities. Animals have no rights, nor within the natural world do humans. We have no *right* to live. We may be alive, and we may live in a society that grants us the right to do this or that *while* we are alive. But no one has a right to live. And if we were to begin thinking of animals and plants in terms of the "rights" they ought to have, we would end up so politicizing them that they would become negotiable instruments. It is in our aesthetic and pragmatic interests to let the flows of diversity play themselves out as richly as possible, and that means allowing other species to exist on their own terms as much as possible rather than simply on our own; but to start conferring rights upon them, however noble the intent, is to end up defeating the point at issue, for they will then come to have their existence defined solely in *our* terms. The aesthetic must begin with the general *indifference* to our interest, and we must then seek to construe our interests as best we can in terms of the indifference of the flows of the entire planet.

To express the need for an aesthetic politics from a more human angle, I should explore the value of it from a partisan perspective, one that might, for example, be devoted to establishing the rights and opportunities of one particular group of individuals. We have come to think of movements devoted to the promotion of racial or sexual equality as entities that focus singlemindedly on one group of issues, though of late some branches of the women's movement have also established links to environmental problems. In general the intent of these groups is simply to assert power within the community in order to ensure that the group gets more rights and opportunities than it would if no one were its advocate. Such advocacy has been all too necessary for certain segments of society simply because there has indeed been gross discrimination that continues to this day. For the most part, these groups are purely political in nature: their goal is to right the play of differences so that it does not unfairly work against large segments of the population that are easily identifiable simply because of their color or sex. As such these movements have done much good, though there is much still to be done.

The question here is whether an aesthetic politics can broaden the conception of such movements and thereby further legitimize their activities without at the same time usurping fallaciously a power that does not belong to them. It would not do, for instance, to argue that all human beings have a *natural* right to freedom and equality, for there is nothing in nature that would suggest that, even if there seems to be a desire within many humans for such a right. Likewise, it would be inappropriate to argue that the environmental movement and the women's movement are the same, for they are clearly not. The one is concerned with the political rights of a segment of the human population, the other confronts the human relation to the planet, and no one race or sex has priority over or a superior sense of this relationship. It would perhaps be politically viable to assert a connection between the two and defend women's rights as a reflection of environmental needs, but it would be disingenuous to do so, for the planet has no rights, and women's rights do not derive from anything within the environment. Indeed, it could be argued that the women's movement is often problematic precisely to the extent that it orients itself to a world *after* the natural world has been declared a fiction. For the most part it is simply not interested in our relationship to the environment; its concern is to address inequities within a social system that has long since abandoned any concept of the natural world. It is precisely this problem that an aesthetic politics would address, without at the same time creating a movement predicated on a problematic assertion of the forces of the planet or something like that in order to defend the rights that can be better established in other ways.

From an aesthetic point of view, rights are important, but they come *after* the recognition that the key problem within all human systems is the desire to freeze the play of differences. This is a situation—call it a reflection of the Freudian death instinct or whatever—that manifests itself in all human domains, most prominently in the relation to the planet and in the tendency to create hierarchical social constructs that are deliberately designed—even if they all eventually fail to support that design—to bring to an end the play of difference. The limitations of Socrates' polis, after all, can be expressed in any number of ways, but they all come back to the fact that the hierarchies he seeks to put in place, regardless of motivation, attempt to put out of play certain human attitudes and groups that will not forever willingly agree to be out of play. The attempt to create a mystery around the truths of Kronos and Ouranos is a means whereby the play of difference is frozen, for it is the play of difference that can lead to the undifferentiation of social violence that Socrates fears most, and he believes this problem can only be faced by declaring it dead or nonexistent, by freezing it out of the secular symbolic system. This move in turn depends on priests to attend the mystery, who then take on hierarchically superior roles within the polis that reflect their wisdom and their importance. And the same moves will be made on behalf of philosopher kings later on, reproducing in a purely social domain what Socrates began with when he sought to write the human connection to the nonhuman out of his social equation. All attempts to deny certain aspects of human being—whether they be the violent forces within us all or the tendency to distrust the other—end up presuming to rewrite the differences of the world in order to localize one's own difference at the top of a hierarchy that will then presumably be complete. And any movement that fails to take this problem into account from the beginning is inevitably bound to fail in the long run in what it seeks to establish, unless its goal is the purely political one of rewriting the differences in one's own favor, which can always theoretically be accomplished, at least for a period of time.

The issue, then, is not whether women can achieve the equality they deserve within the social system that declares them to be equal members, for that can be accomplished by the current political apparatus. It is whether a movement on behalf of such equality can build itself on a politics that has a legitimately broader base and justification for itself, and that could only come about to the extent that it addressed the play of difference at all levels of the socius. And the question is not whether one pays lip service to other displaced sectors—blacks or the environment or whatever—for that is easily enough done. It is whether one's arguments and tools reflect this broader base at every level. The fundamental proposition of an aesthetic politics is that the play of difference ought not to be arbitrarily frozen by a group in whose interests it is to do so, that the play of difference at whatever level ought to be as free as possible. This is not a *right*, for within the aesthetic mode it applies to the world as a whole and not simply to the sociopolitical system. It is a *principle* upon which one's actions are based as much as possible, and it is crucial to emphasize *as much as possible*, for to live within a human community is to seek to alter the play of difference on behalf of one's species and oneself. We attempt to eliminate certain bugs from our living environment; we try to establish more effective ways of growing crops; we work at addressing questions of land and water rights in terms of the resources available and the healthy disposition of them. So we contribute to the play of differences by giving shape to them, as does anything within their sway, though our ability to shape them is much greater than anything other than climatic and geological shifts. To argue on behalf of the play of difference is *not* to assert our passivity in the face of what used to be called the forces of nature, but it does establish a relation to those forces that is not as aggressive as the presumed dominion over the species that we once arrogated to ourselves.

A metaphorical example of the assertion of the play of

difference from a human perspective can be found in the way the United States Forest Service has developed a series of approaches to the disposition of the National Parks. For many years it had adopted a rigorous management style that dictated quite specifically what should be done with the land, and this meant that forest fires of natural or human origin were immediately put out. Then our scientific apparatus suggested to us that in the long run this was deleterious to the lands, so the Service changed its views and allowed natural fires to burn themselves out, in accord with the notion that the health of the park was contingent upon this burning that "naturally" weeded out dead wood and the like and thus contributed to the revivification of the overall system. This policy in turn came up against human desire in 1988 when Yellowstone Park was allowed to burn well past the point that anyone thought it would, and by the time the Forest Service decided to intervene in the fires, they were well nigh uncontrollable. We were told that the fires got so far out of hand precisely because all those years of aggressive management when no fire was allowed to burn left too many large stands of trees for the fires to overtake once they got started, but regardless of the reason, we now have in place a policy that seeks to compromise between the aggressive management of fires and the laissez faire approach that was in play until the fires of Yellowstone.

Our original desire to put out all the fires could be said to reflect the older viewpoint that sought to freeze the play of difference in whatever field as we asserted our authority over the activity within the field. The laissez faire approach was based on a commitment to the play of difference, at least in certain respects, and on a belief that it was truly possible for humans to remain outside of the play, to keep from interfering in the disposition of those nonhuman domains we sought to preserve. The latest approach, unhappy compromise though it might seem in terms of our desires for a "beautiful" park and our knowledge of how to dispose of "wilderness" land, is in fact a fair assessment of our present understanding of our relationship to the play of difference in such domains. We inevitably affect the play of difference within such parks, so there is no question of a laissez faire attitude, unless we choose to adopt a stance of deliberate ignorance. We must therefore do what we can to address the park on its own terms without unduly upsetting its ecology and yet without at the same time allowing the natural world to lay waste to it. If this means a return to a kind of "controlled burning" in order to let nature "take its course" and yet not devastate vast segments of the parks, then at least our disposition of the parks is based on a knowledge of the kinds of things that happen within such systems—and hence a willingness to let the play of forces go on—but it is also predicated on the obvious fact that we *use* the things of the natural world too, even if in this case the use is a purely aesthetic one, the desire to visit wilderness areas in which there remain vast stands of beautiful trees that put our own activities into perspective.

The play of difference is *never* the *pure* play of difference once a human community exists, and inasmuch as a human community does exist, and has existed for millennia, the only question is how to let the play of difference play itself out while we give shape to but do not seek to halt its processes. And this is an assertion upon which all movements for equality depend simply because it is the only orientation toward the problem of rights that will prevent a successful movement from seeking to freeze the play of difference on behalf of its own needs and interests once it has the power that was previously denied it. The only way out of the vicious circle of master/slave relationships is to build one's relationships instead on the play of difference and to argue one's political points on the basis of that rather than on a narrow conception of economic or social rights. At the same time, I want to stress yet again that this is *not* an argument from "natural" rights, nor is it an attempt to ground and justify such rights within the natural world in any way. From a nonhuman angle, there is no such thing as rights and hence no way of arriving at a conception of them from within the natural world. An aesthetic politics is not based upon the natural world simply because any aesthetic is by definition a human construct and thereby something supplemental to

whatever view of nature one might have. An aesthetic politics is based on an assessment of the play of difference and a
declaration of the value of that play, *including* the very real
effects we exert upon it in whatever domains we occupy.
And because the play of difference is truly groundless, there
is no way ever to assume that one has finally assessed the
play enough and can therefore build a shining city on a hill
on the basis of one's knowledge of it. One can only imagine a
mobile community that grows and changes in accord with
the play and its understanding of it.

If we were to adopt an aesthetic perspective that em-
braced the women's movement, we would thus not argue
that according to nature women deserve equality and more
rights than they have under the current sociopolitical regimes, nor would we assert that the play of difference provides a set of natural laws that demonstrates irretrievably
that women have been unfairly treated. Neither the play of
difference nor the natural world could demonstrate any such
thing. One would instead simply argue for the value of allowing the play of difference to play itself out as freely as
possible and demonstrate the ways it which its flows have
been arbitrarily restricted within the social domain—and
elsewhere—to prevent women (and other segments of the
population) from taking up their fitting place within its
flows.

The difference between this orientation and the present
one is that it takes into account the larger play of differences
outside of the domain of rights and privileges, but this
means that one has an expanded sense of how one's political
position relates to the disposition of other questions that
confront the human community, which in turn means that
one has to include within one's politics a different conception of the human. For it must be said that regardless of the
attempts to overcome the so-called man-centered vision of
the world that has developed out of the Renaissance, and
regardless of at least some feminist attempts to dissolve the
humanism that is the fullest expression of this man-centered
view, the fact is that the women's movement's conception of
the human is based upon the same humanistic view it pur-

ports to overturn. To be sure, it argues for the inclusion and positive valuation of the emotional and bodily domains that males have presumably denied, and it asserts the richness of being such an embodied creature in the world, presumably in contrast to that disembodied, hierarchical, and rational creature who ruled the planet for so long. But for the most part it has failed to address the reasons *why* this man-centered version of the world came about. It has yet adequately to take up the question of whether or not Socrates was right to want to bury the knowledge of Kronos and Ouranos, if you will, and until it assumes the burden of that issue in a very bodily way it will continue to work out of the definition of the human to which it presumably is opposed. For there can be no denying that the bodily creature that feminism seeks to affirm is also a creature that partakes of rich and horrifying mysteries that have been put out of play as much by the feminist movement as they were by Socrates. It is not enough to affirm the body and to delight in its pleasures; it is not enough to assert the virtues of the emotions and the irrational. One must also address the reasons why the body and the emotions were denied in the first place, and it was not the fear of women that led to their denial but rather a fear of the *human* that was projected onto women. And if we begin with the play of difference and assert its value in general and its specific value as a means of demonstrating the need to redress the artificial inequalities that have been established in our socius as a result of the human fear of the play of difference, then we must return first to the basic fear of the human that was put out of play when we asserted reason's power over the play of difference.

Chapter Two

In the Beginning There Was Shame

If human communities develop as a result of fears of what other humans are capable of doing, regardless if we use Freud's primal horde or the mark of Cain as our example, their symbolic expression of structure depends on the way in which they deal with these fears. Do they seek to hide from them, as Socrates would have it, and thereby develop a system based upon an initial repression of knowledge, or do they instead build the socius out of a full awareness of the fear of the human and hence affirm the play of difference of which this fear is a part? The West has consistently built its societies on a denial of that which is most fearful in humans, even as it has increasingly argued for open and democratic systems that allow the free play of ideas. It has regularly denied that there is any fundamental ignorance, willed or otherwise, about human nature. And like all societies, it depends on its myths for an articulation of those mysteries about which it would prefer to say nothing at all. When we look at the founding myth of the West, the story of Adam and Eve and their expulsion from the garden, we find there a knowledge of human nature that has yet to be fully exhausted, that has in some senses yet to be even properly addressed. We all know about the tree in the garden, and the fruit that was taken, and the tempting serpent and the weakness of Adam and Eve, but we don't really know exactly what is at stake in their fall, even if we believe that we are fallen creatures.

The crucial questions about this myth have always surrounded the tree of knowledge of good and evil in the center of the garden and God's reasons for expelling Adam and Eve from it as a result of their disobedience, and this account of the origin of humanity is so striking because of its difference from other myths. To be sure, some have a conception of the fall written into them, but if we seriously consider Nietzsche's arguments about the origin of the gods themselves, an origin out of fear and debt,[1] we see all the more strikingly how Adam and Eve present us with an unusual picture. When we observe Adam and Eve in flight from God, we can certainly assume that they fear Him mightily, that their disobedience is such that they feel both fear and shame. It is an open question which comes first, though, particularly when one considers their first act: "And the eyes of them both were opened, and they knew that they were naked; and they sewed fig leaves together, and made themselves aprons." The first thing Adam and Eve do is to sew some fig leaves together in order to cover themselves because of their knowledge of their nakedness. But this suggests nothing about fear in and of itself, even if we assume they dress themselves in anticipation of a future meeting with God. In the next verse, the fear emerges with clarity, but it is not readily observable in their first act: "And they heard the voice of the Lord God walking in the garden in the cool of the day: and Adam and his wife hid themselves from the presence of the Lord God amongst the trees of the garden." Once they hear God's voice, their fear is obvious, unquestionable, and they seek to hide from Him as quickly as possible. But they were first *ashamed* of their nakedness: they *knew* they were naked, and they tried to cover themselves so as not to be seen. Again, we can assume that it is the imagined vision of God from whom they wish to keep their private parts, but their awareness seems based on shame rather than on fear, even if the two are almost inextricable here, both being predicated on the awareness of a hierarchically superior individual.

The Bible tells us that the first fruit of knowledge Adam and Eve acquired was an awareness of themselves—particularly an awareness of themselves as sexual creatures—that shames them. And we know that humans do seem to feel shame to varying degrees about certain bodily features and functions, so the self-awareness and the shame about bodily functions make sense as markers of that which differentiates humans from other animals, and thus serve as a fitting account of the beginning of human society. But the fact that the shame of being human is the first thing that is felt and acknowledged once Adam and Eve put on the knowledge of good and evil remains an arresting fact, even when we consider the relation the West has established between sexual behavior and evil. Within our own culture these things are well understood, but as a myth of the origins of humanity, the story of Adam and Eve suggests that in the beginning there was shame, that *that* was the crucial marker of human existence, and one would then want to know why it is an inevitable fact that a self-aware human being would feel some kind of shame about his or her bodily nature. What is there about the body that so constitutes it as an object of shame once knowledge of self has been obtained? Why is it that other species seem not to feel shame as we do? And why does the Bible suggest that the knowledge of good and evil and shame are different sides of the same coin?

Adam and Eve eat of the fruit of the tree of the knowledge of good and evil and become aware of themselves, and as they do they feel shame because they recognize that they are bodily creatures. This in turn prompts them to make skirts to cover up their most prominent sexual and excretory orifices, and their true shame becomes fully known when they hear the voice of God in the garden, the voice that reminds them definitively of their change, of their difference. As we are presently constituted, all this makes sense enough precisely because we are the results of the myth and because humans in general seem to feel a degree of shame about these matters. When one combines the eating of the fruit—a physical act in itself with its own kind of shameful noises and gestures, to say nothing for the excretions that will come from it—with sexual intercourse, one gets shame. When one adds the smells of sex and excretions, one gets more shame, particularly, perhaps, because we can be both attracted to and repulsed by these smells, sometimes at the same time. When one considers the relative hairlessness of the human body, there may be still another reason for shame before it, for it seems so vulnerable and exposed. In these ways, it makes sense to see shame as manifesting itself in the disgust of the human body and all of its activities, and yet we know that the body's functions are "natural" and hence nothing to be ashamed of, much less to link to the evils of the world.

We could move to the next level and say that if there is nothing intrinsically shameful about the body and its functions, or even necessarily our knowledge of it, perhaps it is *desire* that is so shameful, that attraction for something outside of our own body that we feel so urgently when it comes to sexual matters. It is desire, after all, that attracts us to those things we feel considerable disgust about in other contexts; it is desire that, however self-aware we may be, prompts us to do things our own knowledge would make us think twice about. And inasmuch as we have construed our being in terms of a spiritual and a physical aspect, desire itself is shameful, for it relates to the physical aspects of life: we desire sexual activity or other kinds of bodily events before we desire anything else. But the divided self, the spiritual and physical demarcations, was employed to explain the shame rather than the other way around, and the fact is that it doesn't sufficiently explain it. It simply demonstrates that it exists, shows us that we are self-aware and declares the aware part our spiritual nature and that of which we are aware the physical part. And "desire" as a word that covers bodily forces over which we don't always have sufficient control is also a marker of an event rather than an explanation for it, for we need to know why we have problems controlling our desires just as we need to know why it is bad that we don't always have that control. Societies must be orderly places, and they therefore must be spared the arbitrary eruptions of sexual desire, so from that angle shame in the face of desire makes sense, but in and of itself it does not.

At still another level, we could think of shame as simply being what it is, the imagined (or real) gaze of another upon us, a gaze that in its fearful otherness would make us feel shameful and degraded—because it would denude us of our humanity and turn us into something less than we are— regardless of what features of our being it would attach to. In this scenario, the desire to cover up the private parts is not a reflection of the origin of shame per se—one could imagine Adam and Eve feeling shameful in another way—but rather an indication of shame in general. This may be partially true, for there is no doubt that the gaze of the other, that being who resides above them in nonbodily form, is that which they have really gained a knowledge of as they have come to see themselves in a new light. They see themselves *objectively,* purely as *animals,* as bodies without spirits, for the spirit, after all, cannot be seen. They see how the gaze of the other reduces them to their bodily activities and nothing else, and since they know themselves to be so much more, this makes them feel shame in the face of the bodily activities that could be said to go on only to allow the so-called higher functions to take place. Even if this is true, though, Genesis suggests the origin of shame in the awareness of the private parts, and if the gaze of the other is necessary for us to feel shame at our bodily natures, it is still within the body itself that shame is first located.

Shame is never first and foremost a metaphysical matter, as we know in observing the emergence of it in children. They begin with no knowledge of their sexual natures and a total indifference to the presumed offensiveness of their excretions. Indeed, they delight in excretions to an extent that is unimaginable to adults. They do not find the smell of them to be offensive and are quite capable of marveling at the strange things that come out of their body. They find none of this disgusting, and this leads us to declare that shame is not a matter of self-knowledge per se but rather a reflection of *socialization.* Inasmuch as the child feels no shame about its bodily functions early on, the theory goes, the only viable explanation for the fact that it emerges after a few years is to be found in the socius: we *make* the child feel shame by covering its body and by asserting that its excretions are offensive and not to be talked about in public. Our own shame is so readily apparent to the child that it cannot help but pick it up even if we try to make the body seem as natural and commonplace as it is.

It is possible that the socialization theory makes sense of the origin of shame, but I believe that Adam and Eve's story is more accurate: self-awareness is shame by another name, and it requires no socialization to come about. To be sure, as with all human knowledge, self-awareness comes *after* one is a social being: one is in language and makes use of it before one knows oneself as a separate creature, so one could argue that Adam and Eve's story is itself a reflection of the artificial play of signs that arbitrarily declares bodily matters to be shameful. There can be no definitive response to this argument beyond the one that asserts that all human beings in all cultures seem to feel a fair degree of shame about some parts of their bodily being. Even the most unself-consciously physical of societies tends to have some kind of covering over at least some of the private parts, and this would suggest that shame is an intrinsic aspect of being human rather than something culture *adds* to people in order to socialize them into useful citizens.

It would seem, rather, that shame is a function of the combination of two forces that are really the same: emerging self-awareness and development of the nervous system. If children do not find their excretions to be offensive in their first years, it may be that they do not simply because their nervous systems are not yet sufficiently developed to allow them the kinds of discrimination of tastes and smell that would make them find some things shameful. We know that young children will eat almost anything, even if its poisonous nature is obvious to an adult simply as a result of the offensiveness of the taste or the smell, and there is no reason to think that the so-called blissful indifference to excretory matters and smells is therefore a product of acculturation. It is rather a function of normal nervous system development: the child grows to the point where it can distinguish between "good" and "bad" smells, even if at times the smells are combined, even if at other times that which is "good" and "bad" is somewhat arbitrary and/or culturally defined.

And the child seems to have sufficient discernment to begin to make these distinctions between good and bad smells, tastes and the like at the same time that it begins seriously to be aware of itself as a distinct human being, an autonomous and self-aware creature. Shame, then, seems to appear about the same time that offensiveness of smell and self-awareness appear, and in this sense the story of Adam and Eve rings true. When one feels shame, the first thing one recognizes is that one is a *bodily* creature, one knows this by having some dim sense of being seen by an other, and one feels shame.

At still another level, we could argue that the shame Adam and Eve feel after they have eaten the fruit of the tree of the knowledge of good and evil comes from a kind of built-in safety mechanism in human beings and other creatures as well. Their self-awareness is that which allows them to distinguish what is good and bad for them, what is life-promoting and what is life-threatening, and, so the theory would go, they could have no knowledge of these things without first recognizing themselves as bodily creatures in the midst of other creatures whose alien nature can contaminate and hence destroy them. The awareness of the other, that is to say, is an awareness of the fragility of life—the fear of God comes from the sense of mortality. This mechanism isn't perfect, for we are fully capable of eating things that poison us—taste isn't always a sufficient indicator of toxicity—but it does contribute to the overall well being of the species. Even if this were true, though, it would fail to account for the shame at the center of the story. To be repelled by a substance due to its smell or texture is one thing, but it is quite another to be shamed by one's ingestion of it. The term is in excess of what we would feel in the presence of something noxious.

It would seem that regardless of the hypothesis, there is no sufficient means for accounting for the shame Adam and Eve feel after they achieve self-awareness. We can say that humans tend to feel shame once self-awareness emerges, and we can see that the shame manifests itself particularly when an individual confronts his or her bodily nature, from eating and excreting to sexual matters, and we can know that the intensity of the feeling of shame is considerable. But we seem not to be able to make sense out of this phenomenon. It is not enough to say that we are revulsed by our connection to the mortal processes of the body and the planet, nor will it suffice to argue that we are disgusted by our connection to the other species of animals, as though that were beneath our dignity. Both of these are retrospective ways of explaining why we feel shame that concede its presence without making sense of it.

If we approach the subject from another angle, we can establish some of the characteristics of our sense of shame in the face of the bodily, and that will at least begin to account for this mysterious process, if not fully cover the terrain it occupies. Shame is related to and yet different from fear, for both are based on the human sense of vulnerability. If Adam and Eve first feel shame when they come to possess knowledge, that is indeed because they feel vulnerable, because they are capable of imagining how an other would perceive them, which is to say that they are capable of imagining an other. To be able to imagine an other is to be aware of the risks of living, for any other can harm one. And to see oneself as an other might would therefore make one crucially vulnerable to *any* other. Adam and Eve's second act, after all, is to hide from God, full of the knowledge that the Other will know that they know what they shouldn't, that He can harm them.

At the same time, fear and shame are separable events, for we more often feel fear without shame than shame without fear. If vulnerability is at the heart of both, the emotions that accompany the two states are different. Fear may make one want to fight back against that which one has concern about, or it might make one wish to capitulate to it, but it does not as a rule lead to shame, unless one is forced to capitulate to what one perceives to be a lesser force. Shame and fear both depend on a sense of hierarchy, but their relation to it differs, shame leading to a sense of abjection, fear simply to an awareness of relative differences in power. Shame is a function of a psychological sense of rejection, whereas fear is based on a purely pragmatic assessment of one's ability to sustain one's being in a particular set of circumstances. So fear can lead to shame, but shame always depends on fear—it is a part of shame in a way that shame is not of fear.

Self-loathing or revulsion is at the center of shame, a rejection at some level of the circumstances that constitute the nature of one's being. One simply refuses to accept some element of the world of which one is a part, and this can only come about by the intrusion of another measure. In and of itself, there is nothing problematic about human being; it is what it is, and it ought to be sufficient as it is. But the self-awareness that is part of being human is also predicated on a dual perspective, on being who one is and being able to imagine who one is from an other's perspective. Self-awareness in this sense is really always first and foremost *other*-awareness that leads to a change in conception of the self. To be aware of the other is not simply to recognize potential threats, for any animal is capable of discerning that which might undermine its being. It is to have a dual perspective on who one is. As far as we know, other animals are not capable of imagining how others perceive their actions whereas humans quite clearly do this all the time. And while that split awareness may develop into conceptions of body and spirit or simply into multiple perspectives on the nature of existence, it always introduces the element of shame. Once we recognize the fact that others see us differently than we ourselves do, we feel shame when we imagine them watching us.

Social life is thus predicated on our feelings of abjection and on our awareness of the fact that others perceive our lives differently than we do, and the socius trains us to feel shame in contexts where we might not ordinarily experience it. But inasmuch as society *begins* with the first moment of shame—the human community asserts its presence the moment one recognizes the gaze of the other—shame is not something created by society in order to manipulate its constituents, even if it does make full use of it for its own purposes. And if it is a hierarchical state, it is not always dependent on the feelings of an inferior in relation to a superior.

We may well feel shamed most often by those we perceive to be our superiors, but we are also quite capable of feeling the same way in the face of demonstrable inferiors, though not necessarily so. One's child can make one as privy to the sense of shame as any superior could, for example, even if some people also assume that they can do anything in the presence of children. Such individuals might believe that a child, like a slave in earlier eras, is not sufficiently human to engender a sense of shame, having no real awareness of being human. Because they are ignorant of the conditions through which one lives one's life, one cannot imagine their gaze upon one. This is clearly one of the reasons why society has to protect children from adults, for once adults negate the child's humanity by declaring it to be incapable of being an other, they can more easily manipulate it for their own purposes, even if the child itself feels shame at what the adult makes it do.

In the beginning we were revulsed by our own natures, and we have been feeling shame ever since. And this shame comes not from a sense of guilt, from a sense that we owe a great burden to God or to the ancestors, as Nietzsche would have it, though that may account for later social developments. In the beginning we simply find the conditions of our existence to be unsatisfactory; this is another way of saying that we have self-awareness. Once the fruit of the apple has its effect upon us, we are both aware of ourselves and shamed by who we are. This is at once a personal and a purely human thing. Again, the gaze of the other focuses our attention on who we are as particular individuals, makes us aware of our own distinctive features. But that gaze also makes us feel shame about those elements of human being that have nothing to do with one individual. We may be shamed by some aspect of our bodies, for example—we don't like the shape of our ears, say—but we are always first shamed by the fact that we *are* bodies. So our shame is predicated on both particular and general conditions of human existence. Adam and Eve seem to feel shame merely at being human, for the gaze of their other is a God who casts a harsh light on humanity, but we who follow after them always feel shame in both particular and general contexts, even if the first moment of shame is always a general one. Children may begin by being simply amazed at the things that come out of their bodies; they can see the act of defecation as a reflection of the miraculous nature of their bodies, as they well should. But when they change their attitude toward defecation, when the smell of it turns offensive and the act itself becomes a private one to be hidden away, their shame is not particular at all. Once shame intrudes itself into their lives, however, children quickly begin to focus on the particular elements of their beings with which they are in disagreement.

The nature of the shame humans feel is always a matter of some controversy because one can never state precisely to what extent it is a learned or an innate effect. Most recently the issue came up in an essay by John Berger that attempted to set Milan Kundera straight about his misperceptions on the matter. Berger quickly undercuts Kundera in the most disdainful way, and then, having shamed him properly, he goes on to demonstrate his great superiority over him by showing how little he is bothered by excretory matters himself:

> In one of his books, Milan Kundera dismisses the idea of God because, according to him, no God would have designed a life in which shitting was necessary. The way Kundera asserts this makes one believe it's more than a joke. He is expressing a deep affront. And such an affront is typically elitist. It transforms a natural repugnance into a moral shock. Elites have a habit of doing this. Courage, for instance, is a quality that all admire. But only elites condemn cowardice as vile. The dispossessed know very well that under certain circumstances everyone is capable of being a coward.[2]

One can begin by noting the ways in which Berger manifests his contempt for Kundera's views, first by refusing to state in which book Kundera makes his assertion, second by refusing to use any of Kundera's own words, third by making the glib accusation that Kundera is being "typically" elitist, and fourth by quickly suggesting via example that Kundera would also be the kind of person who would revile cowards, even though Kundera's own work demonstrates repeatedly that this is not so. Obviously Kundera's views about the nature of shit upset Berger enough for him to prompt a rhetorically scurrilous attach on Kundera. Equally interesting is the way that Berger asserts his own moral superiority throughout the piece by claiming that he has no problems with shoveling shit and by demonstrating his close acquaintance with it. No elitist would ever consider shoveling shit, and we certainly have no evidence that Kundera was ever given to this activity, much less that he would profit from doing so if given the chance. Only a true egalitarian would both shovel shit and appreciate the value of doing so.

So Berger patiently shovels the shit of his friends to make a space for the new leavings and contemplates the varieties of excretion: the shit of cows and horses is "relatively agreeable" because they don't eat meat, whereas "Chicken shit is disagreeable and rasps the throat because of the quantity of ammonia," and "Pig and human excrement . . . smell the worst because men and pigs are carnivorous and their appetites are indiscriminate" (60). This worst of shits has a smell that "includes the sickeningly sweet one of decay. And on the far side of it there is death." Berger thus courageously addresses the full implications of shit, from the unpleasant smell to the confrontation with death that one smells in the decay. No reason to be affronted by any of this, and certainly no reason to dismiss the idea of God.

The fact is that we find ourselves in the presence of a man who understands these things much better that we civilized and elitist individuals who try to keep a safe distance from such matters. He is both comfortable in the presence of shit and fully capable of articulating a metaphysic on the basis of it, as he very quickly demonstrates: "While shoveling, images of Paradise come into my mind. Not the angels and heavenly trumpets, but the walled garden, the fountain of pure water, the fresh colors of flowers, the spotless white cloth spread on the grass, ambrosia. The dream of purity and freshness was born from the omnipresence of muck and dust. This polarity is surely one of the deepest in the human imagination, intimately connected with the idea of home as a shelter—shelter against many things, including dirt" (60). At this point Berger almost seems to be suggesting the kind of thing he accuses Kundera of, that we are so repulsed by our need to shit that we are driven to imagine paradises where such activities need not take place.

But no, he would be satisfied with a paradise here on earth, one with a walled garden, a fountain of pure water, nice flowers and the like. And this paradise is to be differentiated from the conventional one because its purity is of a different order: "In the world of modern hygiene, purity has become a purely metaphorical or moralistic term. It has lost all sensuous reality. By contrast, in poor homes in Turkey the first act of hospitality is the offer of lemon eau de cologne to apply to the visitor's hands, arms, neck, face. Which reminds me of a Turkish proverb about elitists: 'He thinks he is a sprig of parsley in the shit of the world'" (60). It would seem that Berger's elitism springs from his identification with the Turks and their proverbs about "civilized" people. We are in the presence of a rustic who knows full well that the poor Turks understand much more about what is and is not valuable in human life than any Czech possibly could, to say nothing for an American who might agree with Kundera that shit presents a metaphysical problem to humans. We have these difficulties because we have turned the word "purity" into a "purely moralistic term," because we are no longer content with clean hands or clean water or clean houses like the poor of the world. We have stripped the "sensuous reality" from purity, presumably because we have so little to do with shit and dirt and the general "muck" of life. The way to achieve moral superiority, then, is to deny that one is morally superior, to assert one's willingness to shovel shit and to identify with the poor who are grateful for a spot of lemon juice to cover up the unpleasant smells that come from dirty people. *That* will show those clean Czech emigrés.

Of course Berger's morally righteous position fails to take into account Kundera's views on the matter just as Berger manifests his own sense of shame in the presence of shit. After all, among other things he is most repulsed by pig and human shit because it doesn't smell as good as the excretions of more vegetarian species, and his revulsion for the human is therefore not to be cast off by the simple declaration of his willingness to shovel the stuff or to assert his happiness in the face of walled gardens and clean fountains. He finds shit to be unpleasant himself, even if he also feels virtuous in cleaning it up once a year, thereby reminding himself of his connections to the sickly sweet smells of decay that direct his attention to the endpoint for all living matter.

The Romantic assertion underlying Berger's piety, though, is indeed a simple one, even if it is restated twice for emphasis: "Evil begins not with decomposing matter but with the human capacity *to talk oneself into*" (61). Nature knows no evil; only morally superior human beings who declare the universe to be unfit know evil: "Nothing in the nature around us is evil. This needs to be repeated since one of the human ways of *talking oneself into* inhuman acts is to cite the supposed cruelty of nature." True enough, one supposes, and yet one wonders how this is relevant to an attack on Kundera's work. The argument seems to be that Kundera has taken purely natural phenomena and made out of them a moral disgust with the nature of human existence that in turn could potentially justify all kinds of human evil. By moving from "repugnant" to "evil," Kundera has committed the typical human act of allowing evil to emerge in the first place. If we just stuck with the fact that certain things about the world are "repugnant," there would be no real excuse to perpetrate any evil in the world. Or so it would seem. More obviously, we are being counselled here to remain close to nature and to resist transforming "good" and "bad" from pleasing and repugnant to virtuous and evil. Not bad advice as far as these things go, but certainly not the kind of advice that someone like Kundera would need, for this is simply a slightly updated, albeit rather too pious, rendition of Nietzsche's marvelous account of the generation of good and evil out of our sense of fear and indebtedness. And inasmuch as Kundera is about as Nietzschean a writer as one could imagine, one would have trouble believing he needs this advice.

The problem with Berger's objections to Kundera's work is that they fail to take into account the fact that humans do feel shame in the face of a pile of shit. The other animals don't, we assume, feel this shame, and that needs to be noted, but there is no way humans can avoid feelings of shame and still be human. Yet Berger seems to be arguing that he is beyond shame simply because he takes shit to be a normal part of his universe, in contrast to Kundera, who finds it to be a violation of an acceptable world. Berger's moral superiority is based on the denial of morality and the assertion of a *natural* morality based upon sensuous rather than spiritual purity. The problem is that this assertion of superiority is no different in kind from the one that Berger (erroneously) accuses Kundera of reflecting. Berger is simply putting the shit in someone else's (Kundera's) house while he declares his own abode to be clean. He accuses someone else of spreading false rumors about the nature of evil and at the same time denies his own evil tendencies. After all, he immerses himself into the simple life—he seems to *glory* in the fact that he gets to clean outhouses and thereby remain close to his origins—and maintains his purity of soul by keeping close to the rhythms and processes of nature. No evil civilization for this man; he was born to be a rustic who was capable of discerning the various nuances to be found in the shit of different species the way an "elitist" sorts out the subtleties in the varieties of wine. There is, it would seem, no need for shame if one gets close enough to the earth.

Kundera does indeed seem to take a different view of these matters than Berger, as we can see when we look at the passages in *The Unbearable Lightness of Being* to which Berger alludes. Kundera tells us that "Spontaneously, without any theological training, I, a child, grasped the incompatibility of God and shit and thus came to question the basic thesis of Christian anthropology, namely, that man was created in God's image. Either/or: either man was created in God's image—and God has intestines!—or God lacks intestines and man is not like Him."[3] There is nothing here that suggests Kundera is making a moral issue out of intestines; he is simply asserting that he believes the Christian conception of God is incompatible with the digestive processes as they exist in humans. Inasmuch as he believes this to be the case, he argues that there is a contradiction at the heart of Christianity, for it declares that humans were made in God's image at the same time that it makes it impossible to conceive of God as having intestines. In part this is Kundera's way of suggesting that our bodily nature in general doesn't go along with the conceptions of God that we have accustomed ourselves to—in this sense the idea of God having intestines is something of a limit case. We can imagine Him eating food, but we can't imagine Him digesting it. At another level, though, it is indeed the repugnance of the digestive processes and the shit that is the final product that doesn't fit into our conceptions of our own images or of God's, whose visage we are presumed to reflect in some way.

Far from making a moral issue out of shit, Kundera is arguing for a need to redress our conception of existence to accommodate who and what we are. In spite of the fact that the contradictory vision of humans at the heart of Christianity has been problematic for a long time, we remain saddled with this way of looking at ourselves that makes it difficult for us to accept the nature of our lives. And this is far from an elitist concern. Kundera recognizes that we feel shame about excretory processes, and he realizes that the Judeo-Christian tradition reinforces this sense of shame, not simply because it begins with Adam and Eve's shame but rather because it prompts us to imagine ourselves as possessing the kind of purity that Berger himself rightly takes issue with. Far from trying to remove his conception of the human from the bodily, Kundera is rather seeking to ground it in the bodily in order to emphasize the value of the *heaviness* of life as opposed to the non-sensuous paradisal vision that encourages disgust for our bodily processes.

To make the point even more clearly, Kundera writes that "Shit is a more onerous theological problem than is evil. Since God gave man freedom, we can, if need be, accept the idea that He is not responsible for man's crimes. The responsibility for shit, however, rests entirely with Him, the Creator of man" (246). Quite clearly shit and evil are unrelated in Kundera's moral vision. Indeed, evil is more easily dealt with simply because we can imagine a world in which we are responsible for the evil things we do whereas we can hardly be responsible for the fact that we defecate. As long as we are alive, we have no choice in the matter; we simply must digest and excrete our food. Now Berger might argue that there is nothing wrong with these digestive processes, however much they lead to the contemplation of shit, and however much the smell of our shit reminds us of our mortality, and Kundera would have no problem with that.

In theory, of course, Berger is right. There is no reason whatsoever why one ought to be offended and shamed by these most fundamental of bodily processes. Our opposition to them is obviously not rational in the least, but this is not a result of any kind of elitism, nor is it due to the rarefied social circumstances in which many in the West find themselves where the level of cleanliness is such that they can *almost* imagine a world without shit. Berger might insist that he feels no shame in the face of shit and demonstrate this fact with his lengthy discussion of what is involved in moving it from his outhouse to its grave, and he might supplement this demonstration with discussions of Turks and lemon eau du cologne, but the anecdote reveals how well Berger understands the shame involved in thinking of his shit. He too wants to be rid of the smell, and surely there is nothing intrinsic to the smell that ought to make it so repugnant to him, particularly if he has forgone meat and thereby generated a sweeter kind of excretion. If he weren't shamed by the final product, he would not feel the repugnance he admits to, even if the smell was less than endearing.

What is at stake in Kundera's work is not the question of whether shit is a moral phenomenon or not—he and Berger are in agreement that it should not be construed in that way—or the question of sensuous and non-sensuous purity, for again he agrees with Berger that we need to learn how to live within the bodily domain we inhabit. But Kundera admits what Berger refuses to concede, that humans feel shame in the face of their own shit, that they feel degraded by it and find it to be a repugnant subject matter as well as a disgusting physical presence. There is no rational reason why this should be so, and any number of good reasons for arguing that the species would be alot better off if it did not feel so strongly about one of its most regular products, but that does not change the fact that we begin with shame and spend most of our lives running from it, as Berger himself seems to be doing in a perverse way by reveling in the fact that he confronts his and other's shit on a yearly basis and provides it with a personal and proper burial. He may move it out of the way, both metaphorically and literally, but he will never get away from the shame to which it is connected in human life.

To get the full sense of what is at stake in Kundera's views of these fundamental questions, I need to quote a more lengthy passage in which he delineates clearly his basic position:

> The dispute between those who believe that the world was created by God and those who think it came into being of its own accord deals with phenomena that go beyond our reason and experience. Much more real is the line separating those who doubt being as it is granted to man (no matter how or by whom) from those who accept it without reservation.
>
> Behind all the European faiths, religious and political, we find the first chapter of Genesis, which tells us that the world was created properly, that human existence is good, and that we are therefore entitled to multiply. Let us call this basic faith a *categorical agreement with being.*
>
> The fact that until recently the word "shit" appeared in print as s——— has nothing to do with moral considerations. You can't claim that shit is immoral, after all! The objection to shit is a metaphysical one. The daily defecation session is daily proof of the unacceptability of Creation. Either/or: either shit is ac-

ceptable (in which case don't lock yourself in the bathroom!) or we are created in an unacceptable manner.

It follows, then, that the aesthetic ideal of the categorical agreement with being is a world in which shit is denied and everyone acts as though it did not exist. This aesthetic ideal is called *kitsch*.

"Kitsch" is a German word born in the middle of the sentimental nineteenth century, and from German it entered all Western languages. Repeated use, however, has obliterated its original metaphysical meaning: kitsch is the absolute denial of shit, in both the literal and the figurative senses of the word; kitsch excludes everything from its purview which is essentially unacceptable in human existence. (247,48)

One might begin by suggesting that if Berger accuses Kundera of an elitist kind of moral shock, perhaps Kundera would see him as a manifestation of retro-kitsch. Berger thinks he has escaped the kitsch of the world by the work he does every year in transplanting his shit, but the few whiffs that remind him of his own mortality seem to be more symbolic than real, and even if the act of moving the shit is a necessary one, it is quite clear from Berger's essay that he has been waiting some time to demonstrate his superiority to the reader by displaying his ability to confront that which we so readily reject. In this he demonstrates that moving the shit is far more of a symbolic and *moral* act that anything he might accuse us of; he proffers his moral superiority to us through the casual way he can deal with and talk about shit in its various permutations. His is a kitsch of the farm, of the peasant, and in that it is not necessarily preferable to any illusions more elitist types might hold to.

Kundera's remarks about shit and their relation to Genesis point in another direction. They state the simple fact that there is a profound difference to be found in human attitudes in the West, and it is based less on whether or not the individual believes in God than on whether or not the person accepts without reservation the nature of existence.

That divide in turn could lead to a belief in God or a lack thereof, but it could just as easily lead to a belief in science or to the greatest of skepticisms about the nature of human valuation. In the face of this duality, though, we must confront the fact that "Behind all the European faiths, religious and political, we find the first chapter of Genesis, which tells us that the world was created properly, that human existence is good, and that we are therefore entitled to multiply." Yet at the same time we have built a civilization on the notion that existence is *not* necessarily good, that there are certain things—shit and everything literal and symbolic it carries with it—with which we simply cannot agree. Life is good and acceptable to a point, but shit and death and the stinks of life are not to be approved of. And whereas some of us may be more or less open about the basic act of defecation—we may be more willing to leave the bathroom door open than most—our social system is based upon a disgust for the human that is predicated on a fundamental *rejection* of defecation and its consequences. We believe in God yet still find His creation to be unacceptable and live uncomfortably within that bind.

So, Kundera argues, we have based our society on a categorical agreement with being, and we have refused to agree categorically that being is good. And given our unwillingness to face the hopeless contradiction at the heart of our system, we create an "an aesthetic ideal of the categorical agreement with being . . . in which shit is denied and everyone [except John Berger] acts as though it did not exist." If we cannot face certain aspects of human being, we shall create an ideal in which it no longer exists; we shall invent what Kundera calls kitsch, that which "excludes everything from its purview which is essentially unacceptable in human existence." And then we pride ourselves on the fact that we have constructed a world that is *almost* acceptable to us as long as we remain comfortably within the confines of the kitsch that fends off the unpleasant. If kitsch is the absolute denial of shit in both literal and figurative respects, it allows us to put out of play our shame at being human and prompts us to imagine a world in which bodies no longer exist to embarrass us with their "imperfections" and fluids. Adam and Eve are born in beauty, they live briefly and then eat of the apple, feel shame and are sent out of the garden for their sin, and live the hard life we all now must face as well. But we quickly forget about their shame and content ourselves with the awareness that they ate of a tree they were forbidden to touch, and if that involves shame, it is a different kind than the one we most want to hide from, the bodily one.

Is Kundera right that we create kitsch in order to hide from ourselves and that which we find most loathsome about our lives? Is it true that we cloak our shame in the robes of an artificial beauty that keeps from our eyes those processes we have never been able to deal with? And are we in the West unique in this respect? If so, what is the harm in doing this? Are we better or worse off as individuals and as a culture? And finally, is beauty *always* inevitably based on kitsch, or is kitsch in some senses rather what I have suggested it is, a denial of the fundamentally aesthetic processes of the world to which we are drawn and from which we turn away when they force us to see ourselves most fully?

Kundera makes his point by suggesting that the question of kitsch doesn't simply appear in the religious world. On the contrary, *all* of our faiths are based on kitsch as far as he is concerned, and *The Unbearable Lightness of Being* is clearly more interested in the kitsch of the political world than in its religious manifestations. Our faiths are predicated on a kitsch that denies who we are and builds up a "folding screen" against shit and death so that we don't have to see them. As Nietzsche half believed, art is thus an Apollonian lie that we tell ourselves to keep from dying of the truth. But Nietzsche didn't always believe that art lied to keep us from dying of the truth, and Kundera is arguing the opposite in his novel. If European conceptions of beauty have been based on a denial of the human, it by no means follows that beauty *must* be based on a denial of it. After all, *The Unbearable Lightness of Being* is clearly an aesthetic medium devoted to the notion that humans are indeed capable of a categorical agreement with being that at least comes close to accepting the world on its terms.

If we do live in a world of kitsch, and if we have built our conceptions of beauty out of kitsch, we come back again to the shame that Adam and Eve first experience after they eat the fruit. There was shame, and there was the attempt to hide from it, to deny it. The fig leaves in that sense are the first manifestation of kitsch in the human world; they cover up that which humans would like to imagine away. First Adam and Eve hide their bodies, or parts of them, with fig leaves, and then they hide among the trees of the garden in order to escape from the gaze of God, two screens designed to keep the Other from seeing the shame that only appears once an awareness of the Other comes into being. The layers of kitsch are necessary in order to forget the shame with which we began, or so it would seem in the world we have created, and because of this we have truly built an aesthetic vision of denial, of categorical rejection of the realm of human being, because we have declared the world to be unacceptable as it is. The shame of shit is more than we can bear, and the gaze of the other who makes us aware of the shame of shit—even if the other is only imagined, as it often is—is that first fierce denial of our sense of self that emerges along with our original moments of self-awareness.

Kundera's either/or is nevertheless more a dramatic device than anything else, a way of demonstrating the contradiction at the heart of our social structure. If he states that "either shit is acceptable (in which case don't lock yourself in the bathroom!) or we are created in an unacceptable manner," he doesn't really mean to suggest that we have only those two choices. As with kitsch, which Kundera declares unavoidable in order to undercut those elitists like Berger who think they can cut through it, shame too is unavoidable, even if the *degree* to which we let shame affect the outcomes of our lives is not, and given that we are for the most part metaphorically constructed to want to lock ourselves in the bathroom when we feel the need to defecate. Other cultures might not so obviously hide themselves away when performing this act, but they do so in other ways. V.S. Naipaul, for example, in *An Area of Darkness*, talks at length about the tendency of Indians to defecate anywhere they please, and to do so in groups. His own sensibility, framed by the shame that wants to lock the bathroom door, keeps coming back to these improbable scenes of men and women simply defecating wherever they may be when the urge seems to hit. He sees, for example, a group of women who continue to talk as they squat and shit completely out in the open, and he simply cannot believe that this is happening. Where is their shame? Where is their sense of decency, which derives from the sense of shame? Where the decorum that Naipaul himself has come to expect? These people truly are barbarians. Yet from their perspective it would seem to be just the opposite: "Shankaracharya Hill, overlooking Dal Lake, is one of the beauty spots of Srinagar. It has to be climbed with care, for large areas of its lower slopes are used as latrines by Indian tourists. If you surprise a group of three women, companiably defecating, they will giggle: the shame is yours, for exposing yourself to such a scene."[4] Such a reversal of the vectors of shame inclines one to think that perhaps the act of defecation isn't necessarily shameful at all, that only we in the West have made it so.

Indeed, Naipaul begins to assume precisely this. India suggests that only Western or Westernized individuals have difficulty dealing with excrement, as numerous sequences in *An Area of Darkness* would seem to indicate:

> In Goa you might think of taking an early morning walk along the balustraded avenue that runs beside the Mandovi River. Six feet below, on the water's edge, and as far as you can see, there is a line, like a wavering tidewrack, of squatters. For the people of Goa, as for those of imperial Rome, defecating is a social activity; they squat close to one another; they chatter. When they are done they advance, trousers still down, backsides bare, into the water, to wash themselves. They climb back on to the avenue, jump

on their cycles or get into their cars, and go away. The
strand is littered with excrement; amid this excrement
fish is being haggled over as it is landed from the
boats; and every hundred yards or so there is a blue-
and-white enamelled notice in Portuguese threatening punishment for soiling the river. But no one no-
tices. (74)

Such visions disgust Naipaul and leave him incredulous, as
they would most of us, and they suggest radically different
conceptions of the abject that imply there is nothing intrinsically shameful about the act of defecation.

Then it occurs to Naipaul that the Indians do not *see*
themselves as defecating in this way. They are totally oblivious of shit and the seemingly public act they are undertaking:

These squatting figures—to the visitor, after a time,
as eternal and emblematic as Rodin's Thinker—are
never spoken of; they are never written about; they
are not mentioned in novels or stories; they do not
appear in feature films or documentaries. This might
be regarded as part of a permissible prettifying intention. But the truth is that *Indians do not see these squatters* and might even, with complete sincerity, deny
that they exist: a collective blindness arising out of the
Indian fear of pollution and the resulting conviction
that Indians are the cleanest people in the world.
They are required by their religion to take a bath
every day. This is central; and they have devised mi-
nute rules to protect themselves from every conceivable contamination. (74, 75)

The Indians are capable of throwing a wall around their shit
that makes their public acts of defecation invisible. Because
of their fervent belief in rites of purity and the need to avoid
pollution, they wish it away, deny it is there, whereas a
foreigner is confronted by the presence of human excrement
in all sorts of unusual places. Naipaul can only account for
this strange (to Westerners) practice of publicly voiding one's
wastes at the same time that one has the capacity totally to

deny the presence of shit or shitting by recognizing the manner in which the possibilities for pollution have "all been regulated and purified" by a peculiarly Indian "method of argument, an Indian way of seeing" that makes "squatters and wayside filth begin to disappear" (75).

We should keep in mind that it may be Naipaul's Western orientation that makes him *think* the Indians are actually blocking out their awareness of the seeming omnipresence of shit—perhaps they are fully aware of it and simply indifferent to its presence—but if his observations are correct, then we find graphically depicted among the Indians the same contradiction that is found in the West in our categorical agreement with the state of being that is denied every time we lock ourselves in the bathroom. There seems to be no way of getting out from under the contradiction, just as there is no way of escaping from kitsch, and for the same reason: human reality is predicated on a denial of shame and those acts that make one aware of it, and it is therefore constructed on a tissue of illusions that is designed to curtain off our awareness of these "lesser" aspects of our being so that we can act as though we are comfortable within the flow of life.

The either/or, then, is not a choice but a point of awareness, a question directed to the future of the species. Kundera isn't arguing that it is possible to eliminate the shame that humans feel—they would no longer be human if it could be cut away, for it was there from the beginning. Nor is Kundera maintaining that we therefore have to be condemned forever to finding the world unacceptable in human terms. These are the horns of the dilemma through which human societies constitute themselves, but there are other responses to them than the ones the West (or the East) has made use of. This does not mean that we all ought to start shoveling our own shit, as Berger does, for that is only a kind of symbolism that avoids the problem. But it does mean that as far as Kundera is concerned, the problem of shit and our shame in the face of it is central to our futures because of the political systems we devise to hide from ourselves and our excrement. Kitsch is everywhere, in communist and capitalist societies alike, and it threatens to kill us off, all because we are caught in a contradiction we do not wish to face, all because we *almost* prefer the unreality of the world of kitsch to having to face up to the shame that we began with and can never leave behind.

If we cannot escape from our shame and yet find it necessary to arrive at a categorical agreement with being that overcomes our disgust with being human, we clearly have to reimagine the structures that govern our lives. *That* is Kundera's main concern, for he is quick to point out that our political systems today are most adept at making use of our shame for their own ends. The communist system that Tomas and Tereza live within in the novel is indeed a kind of Big Brother, with an eternally vigilant gaze surveying the acts of the people, and the very thought that there is such a gaze makes it a reality. Adam and Eve, in this sense, really only had to *imagine* God as out walking in the garden in the cool of the day; He could have been their shame transformed into the ghost of a spirit that haunted them because their self-awareness was really other-awareness, and they were therefore prompted to imagine a huge and forbidding (and *invisible*) Other that could see them while they could not see Him. It is in this sense that God was created out of our shame rather than out of fear or out of a sense of obligation, and we didn't even have to think about creating Him. We became aware of ourselves as distinct creatures, we felt shame at what we imagined an other would see, and because we could not hide from that awareness ourselves, we imagined an Other who could see everything too and who therefore knew of our shame as much as we did. We invented God because we had no choice; He is the supplement to our shame, the measure of our self-awareness and our self-loathing.

Tomas and Tereza live in a world where the system has become God and has found ways to manipulate people through their shame. Inasmuch as women have traditionally been the focus of bodily shame, given the sexist orientations of Western societies, it is not an accident that most of Tereza's shame has to do with her body as an unfaithful rendering of who she thinks she is or would like to be. The rumblings of her stomach and the fever that intrude on her most important moments of love are a reflection of the bodily revulsion she feels toward herself. If these feelings tend to be more intense in women, that is because they have lived under the practiced gaze of men, even if that gaze is often inflicted upon them—as was true in Tereza's case—by their mothers, who have spent a lifetime suffering under the masculine eye and know how to project it upon others. Our societies are constituted to make the bodily fluids of women more shameful than male fluids, even if there is no intrinsic reason why menstrual blood ought to be any more or less offensive in the cosmological scheme of things than ejaculations of sperm. Thus, shame is much more obviously a bodily question in Tereza's life, whereas Tomas, however much he is dominated by the desire for sexual conquest, has an almost disembodied existence and locates his shame elsewhere, in the way that he treats Tereza, for example, or at the center of his contradictory desires for both heaviness and lightness.

In Tomas's world, shame is much more a function of the political structure, as he finds when he is prompted to recant his essay on Oedipus. The state puts him in the uncomfortable position of having to capitulate to its desires for "confession" in order to keep his prestigious position as a surgeon, and yet all it asks him to do is to write a simple letter in which he takes back what he said about the Oedipal desire to put off one's knowledge of the crimes that were committed by those who zealously willed communism into being in Czechoslovakia by metaphorically poking out their eyes. No one has to know that he has written such a retraction, Tomas is told; the letter simply must be put on file to "protect" the authorities in case anyone should protest about his presence at the hospital. Of course, Tomas's colleagues already know about the state's request, and he is surprised to see how eager most of them are to have him recant. Tomas sees in their eagerness their own shame and the desire to make their own denial of self more bearable through Tomas's act of recantation.

The eagerness to see Tomas deny himself through a letter

of retraction is in turn translated into Tomas's entire negation as a person once he refuses to sign. For Tomas it makes no sense to retract what he said about Oedipus and the people of the revolution, for to do so would be to deny who he was, would be indeed to poke out his own eyes in a very public way while at the same time opening them up all the wider, and even though he is enough like everyone else to be prompted to sign a retraction, he refuses. But this makes the shame of those who have indeed recanted their past and denied themselves all the greater, so much so that they can no longer bear to see Tomas. They must avert their eyes, act as though he no longer exists, in order to live with themselves. Kundera shows through this public shame—and the masterful way the government puts pressure on its citizens to deny a part of themselves—how shame has been put to use so well because those who resist the pressures of the government are faced with the almost unendurable situation wherein they have to live with the omnipresent gaze of the state that is always present in the others who can inform on them while at the same time they are continually denied by the averted eyes of their fellow citizens who shame and are shamed by their inability to recognize their existence. The omnipotent other constantly watches, while the others out of which the intimacy and pleasures of social life are built turn away from one in a refusal to acknowledge one's being. No wonder the likes of Tomas, those who actually resist the pressures publicly to put out their eyes, are so hard to find. And no wonder that Kundera is so concerned about shit and shame and the way they shape human life in modern societies.

Shit is a problem because it turns us against ourselves, and because consequently we are manipulated through the shame we feel at being human. In democratic societies the kitsch may be more in evidence as a force of manipulation than the heavy hand of the state, but Kundera's novel demonstrates the ways in which we allow ourselves to be captives of the kitsch we desire as well as the pressures the social system exerts as people express their power on our bodies. If the communist world has the kitsch of the grand march, democratic societies have the myth of the free and autonomous individual who asserts his independent spirit. Inasmuch as both myths focus on thoroughly unreal conceptions of human existence—total solidarity and total independence—they encourage us to think about ourselves outside of the normal constraints we face in everyday life. They prompt us to imagine a world devoid of those things about our humanity we don't like. The march of solidarity can take place only when we are willing to embrace ourselves and others and the lives we must perforce live as bodily creatures; the independent individual is in turn only possible if he is willing to accept totally who he or she may be. Yet the kitsch tells us that these human states are possible *without* reference to any of those disgustingly mortal aspects of life we so want to run away from. In this Berger is certainly right, that our kitsch in the West has tended to connect purity to nonphysical conceptions and then to project those conceptions as moral phenomena. We have created this kind of kitsch in order to avoid the more unpleasant features of life that made purity a virtue in the first place, those features that make clean water and air and the like truly life-enhancing elements.

Kitsch is designed to deny our connection to the body, to that animal world that our bodies connect us to. It would be wrong, I think, to argue that humans feel shame because they see little to distinguish their physical being from other animals and thus bear the collapsing weight of their presumed spirits every time they see themselves for what they truly are, but one of the residual effects is indeed our disgust with the animal connection we have to other primates in particular. When Adam and Eve ate the fruit, they did not feel shame because they recognized a connection between their bodily make-up and that of chimpanzees, but one of the consequences of their awareness of their embodied existence was indeed a kind of shame to be derived from their lack of difference from other animals. The West has worked for millennia to put space between the "human" and the "animal" world, even if that same distance has been seriously called into question at least since Darwin's time. It could be said that Adam and Eve first felt shame because they recognized they were bodily creatures, and their sense of abjection came from the disembodied voice of God, thereby demonstrating their great difference from Him; but there is nothing in Genesis to suggest that they made the bodily comparison first with animals and felt abject because of their lack of difference from them.

Likewise, children first learn shame not in the context of their likeness to animals but rather in terms of their difference from whoever they perceive to be the gauge of what is appropriate. In some situations this is a parent, in which case the child feels shame because its behavior is demonstrably different from the parent's, and the parent has perceived this. In other contexts the shame comes from a difference from those whom the child construes as its peers. But the idea of loathing the body and its animality is nowhere noticeable in the early years when shame first comes upon children. The body is not bad *in itself* for them; rather, the *products* of the body are bad, and not because other animals also have them but rather because they seem to be difficult to deal with in social situations. The gaze of otherness doesn't need psychologically to force the child into the category of animal to work; it only needs to push it into the category of hopelessly different other.

The shame that comes from our connection to the other animals is much more of a learned response, and much more of a metaphysical objection, than the original shame with which we all begin. All shame may be the product of a social awareness, but it isn't necessarily a trained response. By the time the individual comes to feel the kind of self-loathing that might derive from seeing oneself as *only* a body like all the other animals, one has already long since learned to distinguish the cultural categories of body and mind, body and soul, or whatever. A perceived difference of social caste is at that point intruded into the development of shame. What was once disgust over being human, all too human, becomes in turn a revulsion over being *less* than human, over being just another animal, no better than the monkeys. Once this step has been made, it becomes difficult—if not impossible—to distinguish between the original shame that simply came from a difference worked out between two pairs of eyes and the social abjection that comes from construing oneself as occupying a less than human status.

When we look at the kitsch that is produced by our society, it is thus no accident that its relationship to animals is curiously devoid of those things we don't like to face in ourselves. Our aesthetic is based on animals that have been anthropomorphized into creatures without smells or unpleasant fluids, creatures that have been sentimentalized into good or bad beings who represent metaphysical states we embrace or turn away from in disgust. Like God, we busily condemn the snake to a life on its belly because of its loathsome nature, and we freely dispense such absurd nominations to the other animals simply depending on whether we like them or not. The sanitized animal kingdom is in turn a reflection of our own sterilized world, and if we celebrate the great natural world around us, we end up doing so on our own terms. Once the smell of dung filters into our nostrils, we have had enough of nature and are more than ready to retreat to our more pleasant, imaginary conceptions of the beasts of the fields. We know full well that Western civilization has in effect been waging war on the natural world since its inception, and if the only thing that distinguishes it as a civilization is the greater degree to which it has been able to wage that war, it is also true that the war continues, both in the moralized images we have of the other living things on the planet, and in terms of those sentimental visions of ecological processes we think we are learning better to accept. We may be at the point where we shall begin to think about things like acid rain or chemical contamination of the ground water, but we haven't really arrived at the point where we embrace the ecological vision simply because it is too *natural* and hence unpleasant. It may be only a human conception of certain natural processes, but it is probably the nearest thing humans have to an understanding of what "nature" really is, and even at that it is far too unpleasant a view of things.

We take our ecological movements these days the way

we take our animals: in the quiet confines of an ordered structure, be that structure a zoo or a piece of legislation that is designed to address a problem that we know we are causing. Once the legislation is passed, or the zoo visit ended, our connection with the natural world returns to its kitschy state, perhaps with a bit of self-righteousness on our part for our interest in it. To take seriously the flows of fields that any ecological vision entails would require such radical disruptions in our conceptions of the human and of society that few of us are the least bit interested in moving in that direction. If we were to proceed further, we would indeed have to break down the artificially contrived border we have established between our own life and the life that other things on the planet also seek to maintain. And if we were to do that, we would have to confront our shame at being what we are in the knowledge that becoming aware of it doesn't make it go away, which is finally the real problem. We live in a world, after all, where the prevailing psychologies usually offer us the view that in confronting our problems, in facing that which bedevils us, we shall be able to make it go away. We tend to assume that we can overcome all problems simply by confronting them squarely, when in fact the most basic of human and social problems will not go away even if they are confronted. It may be unwise to repress our knowledge of phenomena within ourselves and elsewhere of which we don't approve, just as it may be useless finally to project them elsewhere or deflect them or even to sublimate them into useful social activity; but whatever we do with the most basic of human contexts like the one that produces our shame at what we are, we shall also have to deal with the fact that facing them will not make them go away.

When we consider how our shame is written into our relationship to the rest of the natural world and further contemplate the ways in which we use this relationship to run from knowledge that seems unbearable to us, we can find yet another useful commentary in *The Unbearable Lightness of Being*. First Kundera returns to Genesis to offer his own remarks about our rights over the animals: "The very beginning of Genesis tells us that God created man in order to give him dominion over fish and fowl and all creatures. Of course, Genesis was written by a man, not a horse. There is no certainty that God actually did grant dominion over other creatures. What seems more likely, in fact, is that man invented God to sanctify the dominion that he had usurped for himself over the cow and the horse. Yes, the right to kill a deer or a cow is the only thing all of mankind can agree upon, even during the bloodiest of wars" (286). Kundera does not argue here as I do that the origin of God is to be found in shame, but what he says certainly supports that view in a general way. He is taking issue with our standard relationship to the rest of the creatures on the planet, on the presumed dominion over the other species we were supposed to have. Near to Nietzsche's view here, Kundera asserts that God was invented to allow us to usurp dominion over the cow and the horse and to sanctify—that is, cover up our guilt over—the ways in which we have dealt with the animals around us. What we find here is yet another explanation for that later kind of shame we feel when we find ourselves to be too close to the other animals in nature: we have created a two-tiered system with ourselves at the top and the rest of the living world beneath us in order to see ourselves as non-bodily creatures. If we are made in God's image, we create a hierarchy in which we are the disembodied lord over the embodied species below us. If we first felt shame in the face of that anonymous and disembodied voice, we shall seek to occupy that space ourselves by declaring our definitive difference from the animals. So we create an unreal distance from them to cover up our shame, yet bring ourselves more perilously close to shame by doing so simply because we cannot keep the difference between living creatures as different as we like. We may be able to master the other animals in all sorts of ways, but our mastery never lets us achieve what we had hoped for in the first place, a disembodied status in the world devoid of the shame that so haunts us.

If we humans can tacitly agree on our difference from the other living creatures, Kundera suggests, we can thereby turn them collectively into the scapegoat for our shame, which derives first from our self-awareness and then from an awareness of the fact that we can maintain our lives only at the expense of other species. Without our self-awareness, other animals lack the shame that comes from stripping something of its life, but we live in constant danger of being crippled by this knowledge, and the only way we have found to deal with it has been collectively to sacrifice both literally and through the notion that we were specifically intended to have dominion over them. In this light it is not an accident that the God who gave us dominion over the other species also demanded regular sacrifices of those animals to satiate His own blood lust. The complex web of rationalizations in this mixture reflects incredible human ingenuity, for on the one hand, as images of God, we can see in our sacrifices to Him those acts that would make us more like Him—the hierarchical relationships parallel one another and thereby uphold our position over our own somewhat more tenuous domain; and on the other we can justify our killing of animals by arguing that God demands it. These two are then brought together by the fact that just as God metaphorically "eats" the fruits of the kill, so too do we; killing animals thereby becomes a godly act that is sanctified and fully supported by the supplement that is always set aside for that jealous God.

The parallels are even stronger when one considers what must be the most astonishing passage in the Bible, that moment when God explains why he feels the need to throw Adam and Eve out of the garden: "And the Lord God said, Behold, the man is become as one of us, to know good and evil: and now, lest he put forth his hand, and take also of the tree of life, and eat, and live for ever: Therefore the Lord God sent him forth from the garden of Eden, to till the ground from whence he was taken." An anthropological reading of these lines would suggest that God is more than just angry over man's disobedience; He is resentful of the fact that "man is become as one of us" with his newly acquired knowledge and fearful that, now that he knows good and evil, he will "take also of the tree of life, and eat, and live for ever." To keep this from happening, to overcome His fears of losing His hierarchical position, God therefore feels compelled to throw Adam and Eve out of the garden so they don't have the opportunity to achieve the same state that He has. And in order further to demonstrate the reasons for this change, God makes it clear that He wants to remind Adam of his origin by forcing him to "till the ground from whence he was taken."

Humans, in turn, once they have taken dominion over animals and have learned blood sacrifice, deliberately kill other species in an equivalent way: the sacrifice demonstrates their power over "lesser" beings and stresses their connection to a disembodied God, and it also symbolically destroys the life of animals via the sacrifice, asserts the power of life and death over animals in order to keep them from achieving the same status humans have as mortal creatures with the potential for eternal life. We thus mimic the God who so threatens us—and of whom we are at a certain level mightily resentful because of the mortal stink of our lives—in the hope that such imitation will grant us the status we lost when we were thrown out of the garden for experiencing the knowledge of shame and realizing our potential abilities to usurp the place of God. To say that we invented God to sanctify our murderous intentions toward the rest of the species on the planet is to argue that out of our shame also came an awareness of our lust for blood and our desire both to kill and to be relieved of the guilt associated with killing. And it is further to demonstrate the way in which we tried to put great distance between ourselves and the rest of the animals from the very beginning in order to avoid contemplating ourselves.

This point is made in another way in *The Unbearable Lightness of Being* when Kundera talks about the ways in which certain animals were treated in Czechoslovakia after the Russian invasion of 1968:

> The first years following the Russian invasion could not yet be characterized as a reign of terror. Because practically no one in the entire nation agreed with the occupation regime, the Russians had to ferret out the few exceptions and push them into power. But where could they look? All faith in Communism and love for Russia was dead. So they sought people who wished to get back at life for something, people with revenge on the brain. Then they had to focus, cultivate, and maintain those people's aggressiveness, give them a temporary substitute to practice on. The substitute they lit upon was animals.
>
> All at once the papers started coming out with cycles of features and organized letters-to-the-editor campaigns demanding, for example, the extermination of all pigeons within city limits. And the pigeons would be exterminated. But the major drive was directed against dogs. People were still disconsolate over the catastrophe of the occupation, but radio, television, and the press went on and on about dogs: how they soil our streets and parks, endanger our children's health, fulfill no useful function, yet must be fed. They whipped up such a psychotic fever that Tereza had been afraid that the crazed mob would do harm to Karenin. Only after a year did the accumulated malice (which had then been vented, for the sake of training, on animals) find its true goal: people. People started being removed from their jobs, arrested, put on trial. At last the animals could breathe freely. (289)

The sacrificial motif returns under a communist regime to feed and discipline the fears and resentments of the populace. Disconsolate over their loss of freedom, the people are looking for something to take their loss out on, and animals make the logical substitute. After all, as in Genesis, they are relatively powerless before the people as the people are before the government, so they make perfect victims. As Kundera asserts, the attacks on the animals depend on the human desire for revenge, the wish to lash out at something because of one's own powerlessness. In need of citizens to help govern, the regime deliberately "sought people who wished to get back at life for something." Only such resentment can feed the fires necessary for an equivalent arbitrary move on another living species in order to reciprocate the blow that has been inflicted upon the presumed injured party.

According to Kundera, the regime only used the animals to train the people to do the same things to their neighbors and simply employed them until the idea was properly developed and allowed to fester. Once the people knew that there was *someone* to blame for the fact that their lives were so bad, they could easily transfer their hatred from pigeons and dogs to people because their hatred was not for a particular species *but of life itself.* The human need for victims in the face of the arbitrariness and relative unpleasantness of life is inexhaustible, it would seem, and readily finds an outlet in the expression of violence toward another animal, be the victim a human or some other species. This is precisely why it is so necessary to face the shame at the center of human consciousness, for only that confrontation holds any hope of allowing us to escape from the endless symbolic shuffle of victims we search for every time we feel some resentment toward life and wish to get back at it.

If our God had not given us dominion over the animals, then, we would have had to invent such a dominion simply to preserve ourselves and to deal with the things about life in the face of which we feel helpless. There was at that point only one step left, the one taken by the modern era that Kundera symbolizes in Descartes (Kundera too needs his victims):

> Even though Genesis says that God gave man dominion over all animals, we can also construe it to mean that He merely entrusted them to man's care. Man was not the planet's master, merely its administrator, and therefore eventually responsible for his administration. Descartes took a decisive step forward: he

made man *"maître et propriétaire de la nature."* And surely there is a deep connection between that step and the fact that he was also the one who point-blank denied animals a soul. Man is master and proprietor, says Descartes, whereas the beast is merely an automaton, an animated machine, a *machina animata*. When an animal laments, it is not a lament; it is merely the rasp of a poorly functioning mechanism. When a wagon wheel grates, the wagon is not in pain; it simply needs oiling. Thus, we have no reason to grieve for a dog being carved up alive in the laboratory. (288)

When Descartes denies animals souls and turns them into machines, he completes the role we sought to establish for ourselves via the account of our dominion in the Bible. The link between ourselves and the animals is completely severed, and we no longer have to deal with the animal per se, for it should concern us no more than would any other *thing*. We can thus rest easy in our victimizing of animals without fear of reprisal or of a vivid and constant reminder of our bodily state. Modern consumer society, which does so much to hide from its constituents the fact that the meat they eat actually comes from those loveable animals they see grazing out in the fields (though they seldom even get to graze anymore unless they are milk cows) is the logical endpoint to Descartes' way of thinking. One is eating meat, but *not* the flesh of an animal.

The point here is not that humans should avoid the meat of animals, though that too is worth considering; it is rather the way in which we deal with both the animals in general and with the fact that we live through their wanton destruction. And both of these problems relate to our shame in the face of what we must do to keep alive. If the first shameful act was one of eating—albeit only a fruit—we still feel shame over eating the meat that we find so satisfying, as we doubtless also feel shame over the act of eating itself, not only because it leads to end products like shit, but also because the act of eating, even in the midst of the savory tastes and the magnificent smells, is somehow inherently degrading to us, yet another link to that kingdom of dirt and death we so want to avoid thinking about. Socrates may be right that we are better off hiding from our shame, but we have arrived at the point where we know too well that from which we are hiding, and this makes our situation somewhat different from the one Socrates faced, for he was among the very few who knew how savagely the human species could be driven to escape from knowledge of its savagery.

At the same time, we must also ask what the alternatives to our present attitudes toward animals and the shame of life are, for it is not enough simply to indict our present ways of conceiving of our lot in the world. Kundera clearly provides the necessary questions to an alternative consideration of the world through his emphasis on the value of the *heaviness* of being. If life is so hard, so difficult, so heavy for us, that need not be construed as something from which to flee; it could also be seen as that which gives life the value it has. The value in heaviness would be that it would overcome the feeling within us that leads us to think we have the right and the need to get back at life for its unfairness, its arbitrariness, its simple shamefulness. Instead of trying to overcome the heaviness we feel in life by destroying other life, metaphorically or literally, perhaps we can address that which we have perceived as shameful if we begin to see the burdens as the richness out of which valuable living comes and the shamefulness we feel as a result of being an embodied creature as that which establishes the context through which the beauty of the world is perceived by humans. If our shame and our sense of beauty are the twin armatures of our measure of life, we need to begin to see just how this is so.

One of the ways Kundera addresses the relationship between beauty and shame is through the question of love, and this is also his means for questioning the value that the other animals have for us. He asserts that Tereza's love for her dog Karenin is in many respects superior to any love she could feel for a human. Kundera arrives at this notion by arguing that "The longing for Paradise is man's longing not to be man" (296) and by suggesting that the animals are our connection to whatever dim conceptions of paradise we might have because they were never thrown out of Eden the way we were. This link is further established by a scene in which the author questions why Tereza would not be discommoded by Karenin's menstruation and concludes: "The answer seems simple to me: dogs were never expelled from Paradise. Karenin knew nothing about the duality of body and soul and had no concept of disgust. That is why Tereza felt so free and easy with him. (And that is why it is so dangerous to turn an animal into a *machina animata,* a cow into an automaton for the production of milk. By so doing, man cuts the thread binding him to Paradise and has nothing left to hold or comfort him on his flight through the emptiness of time.)" (297). Because animals feel no disgust over their being, have no sense of shame about life itself, they prompt us to imagine a world in which we too could put off our shame and disgust at our physical nature and simply rest content with what we are. This is our vision of paradise, and our only connection to that vision is indeed the animals we so mightily abuse because of our shame.

For Kundera, or at least for his character Tereza, the connection between animals and paradise leads to the "sacrilegious thought that . . . the love that tied [Tereza] to Karenin was better than the love between her and Tomas." We are told that "Her feeling was rather that, given the nature of the human couple, the love of man and woman is a priori inferior to that which can exist (at least in the best instances) in the love between man and dog, that oddity of human history probably unplanned by the Creator." The reason for this superiority, presumably, is that "It is a completely selfless love: Tereza did not want anything of Karenin; she did not ever ask him to love her back. Nor had she ever asked herself the questions that plague human couples: Does he love me? Does he love anyone more than me? Does he love me more than I love him?" (297). It would seem that Kundera wants us to take this argument seriously, and I confess that I have great difficulty with it even if it makes a certain amount of sense. Tereza might not want anything of Karenin, and so the love might in some respects be selfless, but one might also question whether or not such a totally selfless love is superior to the more fallible kind that Tereza has with Tomas, the kind that does indeed lead to concerns about relative value and equality. One might also argue that it really isn't selfless at all, that what Karenin gives to Tereza is precisely a situation in which she doesn't have to be concerned about how the other perceives her—she knows Karenin will always greet her with joy—and so in some respects her love for the dog is the most selfish kind of all, even if she also gives love to Karenin. The dog can clearly give Tereza something that Tomas cannot, unconditional love, unconditional acceptance, but one might ask about the value of an unconditional acceptance that comes from a creature who would not be capable of a conditional love in the first place.

Tereza's love for the dog does indeed have its place in her life, and it is an important one. It provides her with the unconditional acceptance she needs in the face of the uncertainties Tomas and the other aspects of her life present her with, and it also gives her that crucial connection to the animal world and the idea of paradise that Kundera thinks is important to humans. I would add that Karenin also has the value of presenting not so much a vision of paradise as a sense of human silliness to Tereza, something that might be linked to utopian dreams of a nonhuman world, but also something that has the more tangible benefit of focusing one's attention of the absurdity of the shame humans feel as a result of their bodies. It is clearly impossible, for example, for Tereza to confront her own menstrual periods with the same indifference that she has toward Karenin's, but the value of Karenin's example isn't necessarily that it shows what humans would like to feel about such basic bodily processes—that is indeed a paradisal vision that is beyond our capabilities. Karenin's value is rather that he reminds Tereza—even if she cannot hope to escape from the shame that attends her own periods—that they are, after all, only natural processes of the most ordinary kind and hardly something to lose face over.

Karenin in particular and animals in general thus point us not toward an unobtainable paradise so much as they remind us of our arrogant denial of who we are, force us to see how silly we become when, driven by shame, we seek to deny the body that we are. The end of *The Unbearable Lightness of Being* suggests that Kundera himself indeed wants to go farther than this, prefers to argue for the superiority of human/animal love over human/human love; this would at least account for what I would argue is a rather sentimental dawdling over the all-too-lengthy demise of Karenin. Tereza and Tomas would surely mourn her loss, for she was an intrinsic part of their lives and one of the fundamental links between them; they indeed might choose to get as mawkish about her death as they do, but Kundera rides their sentimentality too long to escape from it—he too seems to believe in their mawkish vision of animals and their relationship to humans, and this becomes in turn perhaps a mark of his own kind of special loathing for humans.

Regardless of the possible sentimentality that brings the novel to its close, we can see, I think, that Kundera is deliberately setting about on the heels of Nietzsche to revise our conceptions of our place on the planet and our relationships to the other species with which we share it. As he recounts the famous episode at the onset of Nietzsche's madness when he went up to a horse that had just been beaten by its master and hugged it, Kundera asserts that "Nietzsche was trying to apologize to the horse for Descartes" (290), and that is as moving an interpretation of the event as one can imagine, and certainly a plausible one. If Nietzsche sought to overturn the older ways of looking at things, it wasn't simply out of the delight that comes from anarchic destruction but rather out of his own instinctive sense of the wrongheadedness of the disembodied vision of humanity that the West had foisted upon its societies. And out of his distress over this flawed way of construing our world came both a sense of the incredible difficulties involved in seeking to provide

more accurate ways of viewing human behavior and a serious attempt to articulate such a revaluation. Although it is
not a part of the archive he left behind, his gesture to the
horse must surely be seen in the same light, as an attempt to
make amends for what humans had done to horses from the
moment they were first domesticated. Nietzsche felt shame
in the face of the inhumanity of the master, not at the weakness of the enslaved and mechanized horse, and this is as
much a reflection of his revaluation of values as is the overman, the thought of the eternal return, or any other concept
he came up with. And perhaps it is superior to those other
gestures because it was nonverbal; if it wasn't precisely on
the horse's terms, it wasn't an attempt to anthropomorphize
the horse either. Beyond that gesture, there would seem to
lie only sentimentality.

Animals and their relation to the human concept of the
idyll are important to Kundera's revisionist view of human
reality, but I would argue that to keep the animals connected
to the notion of the idyll is to keep them penned up in the
anthropomorphism that Kundera himself does such a masterful job of undermining. It is true that animals *can* be seen
as part of our dream of paradise, but one must ask how that
differs from traditional kitsch, from the views of reality we
construct to screen ourselves off from the shit and the death
of the world. One must make a distinction between the fact
that humans do indeed have within them the desire for this
unreal paradise (and may well see animals as their sole tangible connection to it) and the fact that even if we can no more
escape that desire than we can the shame that is part of it,
that is no reason why we should embrace or cultivate it, as
Kundera himself seems to do. It is a fact to be noted, but not
necessarily one that we ought to continue to pursue.

We might be better off if we concentrated instead on the
more important link we have with the animals, our finite and
embodied status in the world. That would prompt us to
make the connection to the environment around us in a way
that would indeed be preferable to the artificial and overly
sanitized one we presently have, but it would also force us to
go back to the origin of our shame and to ask about the

inevitable connection between shame and beauty. Again, if the aesthetic world has been overtaken by the "beauty" of a kitsch that denies everything that humans find unpalatable about the world, it doesn't follow that the aesthetic world itself is necessarily kitschy. On the contrary, our recognition of the animals would lead us to see things in another light, one that would allow the beauty of the world to present itself in the midst of our shame rather than as a cover over it. The idyll dreams of that time when we have no shame to hide from; the pragmatic connection to the animal world suggests that even if we cannot escape from the shame that is an intrinsic part of being human, we are capable as a result of our shame of experiencing the beauty of the world. If the animals have no shame, they also lack a sense of the beauty of the world, and while we may think we would be willing to forgo the beauty if we could get rid of the shame, we can no longer afford to chase that futile and destructive dream. Nor can we hope simply to accept life on its own terms, for we are incapable of doing this as well. Instead, we must work to understand the circumstances that define our lives well before reason intrudes itself into the mechanisms of life and well before we start providing reasons for being who and what we are. That is the point where our world begins, out of the couplet of shame and beauty through which our lives are always constituted.

Chapter Three

In the Beginning There Was Shame and Beauty

When we think about the first moment of shame that Adam and Eve feel in the garden as they furtively sew the fig-leaf skirts they hope will cover both their private parts and the self-awareness that brought them the curse of this shame, we might wonder if our relationship to the sense of abjection would be different in a tradition other than the Judeo-Christian one. In one sense I have argued that not much changes when one investigates other cultural responses to shame; the circumstances change, and they appear to provide different ways of living with one's humanity, but closer scrutiny usually suggests that there are simply different ways through which cultures seek to hide from the shame that constituted them in the first place. Naipaul is doubtless right that the Indians too feel shame in the face of shit; their circumstances are simply such that they hide from it in ways that seem to suggest indifference to it to us.

Our tradition also goes back through the polytheism of the early Greeks, though, and in some respects it is this polytheistic view of human existence that Socrates was trying to bury. From this angle, he was not simply seeking to destroy the knowledge of vicious and bloody acts on the part of gods, though he was certainly doing that; he was really attempting to cover over the polytheistic tradition of which those acts were a part in the belief that the emerging mono-theistic tradition would not find its origins in the acts of Ouranos and Kronos. Socrates was thus offering a "new beginning" with his Republic, one that shunned the true origins of humanity and argued instead for a rational root at the heart of the tree that Western civilization became. And if we see Socrates as assiduously working to bury polytheism, we might ask ourselves what differences those polytheistic structures provided as a response to the shame and the beauty humans found in the world.

Would many gods rather than one make any difference in the conception of human life? Did the far more "human" gods of early Greek culture provide a different vantage point through which to construe our own situation? In some respects, it would seem to make little difference whether there was one god or ten simply because of the power any god would wield over a human. If part of the abject nature of humans comes from the self-awareness that prompts them to predicate another pair of eyes upon them, then the polytheism of the early Greeks wasn't that much of a benefit, for we know that people waited for their gods to assume particular human forms and test their hospitality with a visit and a request for food and shelter. If one could at any moment expect a god in disguise to visit, the gaze remains in effect as a way of focusing one's attention on one's difference from the powerful other. True, the early gods did take up human form and didn't present themselves as disembodied voices, and this is an important difference, for they were sometimes easier to monitor, but as far as the gaze of the other is concerned, the polytheistic world was based upon it as much as the monotheism of the Judeo-Christian world was.

The early gods were indeed much more like humans, though, and this must have had some effect upon the shame that the people who imagined them felt. If the gods on Olympus are indeed the descendants of titans like Ouranos and Kronos, then they partake of the violence and the fears of these early gods as well, just as their humans do. These gods themselves are almost completely shameless, and they don't really expect humans to be much better, even if there are certain codes for them to follow, so one would think that the sense of abjection would be less under the polytheistic regime than it is in the present system of values. We might assume that even if shame were present—as I assume it to be, as a defining characteristic of the human—it did not dominate the socius the way it could during the height of Christian influence in the West. Beyond the laws of hospitality, the rules forbidding parricide and incest and the like, there wasn't as much of an emphasis on deliberate attempts to shame people. There was more of a stress on the major crimes that threatened society in general—and hence a much greater sense of scandal when such crimes occurred— but the so-called venial sin was probably less shameful than it was in the Christian world. Shame in this context would be present but not manipulated in an intentional and oppressive way, forcing itself to the center of consciousness only when an egregious mistake prompted the gaze of the entire community to focus on one. So the abject was present, but the more human status of the gods, and their consequent greater tolerance of the minor excesses of human life, tended to mitigate it far more than would the system to follow.

Another aspect of the polytheism that relates to the sense of the abject is the relative lack of interest the gods had in the average individual's life. If the exceptional humans were the ones who chiefly mattered to the gods—and only then if they were the favorites or the reverse of a particular god— the gaze would once again be less intense than under a God who had numbered the hairs on everyone's head. Again, the indifference of one in power is not always a bad thing, as we seem to think, for if the god has more or less forgotten about one, or is simply indifferent to the outcome of one's life, one is at least spared what would otherwise be constant scrutiny. True, one has forgone the comfort of knowing that a god is looking out for one, and this makes one's fate considerably more chancy, but one also does not have to spend as much time thinking about how the god or gods will look upon what one is doing at any particular time.

Telemachus, like Odysseus, is a great man, and so he is someone the gods pay attention to. But that also means that he must pay much more attention to them and in effect invite them into his daily life. He will have to learn how to see Athena in the humans who come his way, which means he will constantly have to keep his eyes out for that special gaze that marks the presence of the goddess. Likewise,

Odysseus has to attend more to what the gods might wish and how they might construe his behavior, for otherwise he might be punished. In a system where a god can look out for one but still not spare one the woes of Job because other gods are offended by the first god's interest in one, that interest can be a curse as well as a blessing.

Regardless, the fact was that the lives of the great individuals of early Greek society were assumed to be affected by the gods—Odysseus has both a powerful defender in Athena and a powerful attacker in Poseidon, and his heroic adventures were memorable as a result. But another way of looking at the situation is to say that when a society interpreted an individual like Odysseus, it came to look upon his victories and defeats, his triumphs and his struggles, as a reflection of the battles between gods for their own kinds of priority. When a setback occurs, it is blamed on Poseidon; when Odysseus overcomes an obstacle, it is due to the influence of Athena, who is always looking out for him. For the most part we can assume that this kind of interpretation didn't apply to the vast majority of people as much as it did to those legendary lives that were passed down in song. Odysseus, if you will, simply struggled more or less triumphantly through his life, if we can assume that he lived. Afterward, when the tale of his tribulations was told, the hermeneutic screen through which his acts were construed was articulated through the battles of the gods as they wrote themselves into his life. And in this sense even Odysseus was unaware of the gods' interest in the events of his existence.

If the gods were less interested in humans, the humans were less interested in the gods. There were certain situations in which they had to pay particular attention to them, but there was a much larger realm of activity, including acts of discretion *and* indiscretion, with which the gods were not concerned, and so the emphasis on them in the individual's life doubtless also was less focused. Indeed, it is this contrast with the early Greek sense of what is right and wrong, and with the degree to which such questions involve the gods and to which the gods themselves are interested in the humans, that suggests to us how much of the shame of being human is related to the society that makes use of it as a sociopolitical force. Certainly the people we see in the old Greek songs seem much less shamed by their bodies and their actions than we in the Judeo Christian tradition are, and it in the past we might have characterized them as more barbaric than we are, we did so precisely because shame was much less in evidence in their lives. The human lot was in this sense less circumscribed; more of the typical daily activities were simply actions that didn't merit severe judgment of one kind or another—they just happened without a great deal of attention. Good things happened and bad things happened, and people performed good and evil acts, but the moral watchfulness was simply not as intense as it was to become, and this suggests inevitably that the people who lived under such a regime were less shamed by being human.

If there are a great many writers in our culture who have nostalgically posited a time before humans fell into the split consciousness of body and soul that Kundera works through, they most often return to the early Greek world for their idyllic moment, and people as diverse as Schiller and Nietzsche and Heidegger have moved in that direction. Now Schiller and Nietzsche and Heidegger and all the others don't speak of the presumed wholeness of early Greek culture in terms of its relative lack of shame, but that is simply because they have misunderstood the precise relations that established the split in consciousness that they perceive to be the enemy of human happiness. They assume that the split itself is the cause for the discontinuities and psychological tribulations of life, and therefore they simply imagine a time before the gaze of the other was perceived to be directed at us and characterize such a period as the ideal. What they miss is that it is the relative lack of shame in the face of a less intense gaze that they really desire.

When writers imagine the early Greek world as that ideal context from which we have fallen, many of them are really pointing toward the kind of paradise to which Kundera repeatedly refers: they are wishing for an end to the human altogether; they desire the complete oblivion of the purely animal world, the total negation of self-consciousness. This kind of nostalgia is pernicious in its consequences because it so thoroughly undercuts the value of the life we have and because it makes self-awareness the devil that has ruined human existence. Other writers, though, do not imagine early Greek life—or any other kind of idyllic moment—as a prehuman world devoid of self-awareness. Rather, they argue for a self-awareness that has some kind of perspective, that is not so obsessed with itself and the gaze that *everything* must be filtered through that knowledge. And it is no doubt true that the early Greeks were less obsessed by the minutiae of their behavior than we are, just as there is little doubt that in some respects they were clearly better off in being much less interested in the everyday details of everyone's life. In this sense, the gaze was much less in evidence in their culture, the self-awareness much less crippling, the shame much less of a force in everyday life. It was still present, and its effects could be all the stronger when they did manifest themselves, but in being less preoccupied with their lives than we are, and in assuming shame simply to be a part of life that is no more worth agonizing over than the degree to which the meat is over- or undercooked, they had a perspective on that which humans have always found loathsome that we seem incapable of adopting. In this their gods followed along.

The early Greek gods, then, more human in their delights and sins, less consumed by an interest in the human world in general, more willing to imagine the world as a constant battle between various forces than any grandly unified structure, did seem to offer an orientation to life that was better capable of putting shame into perspective. They didn't eliminate it, for then the human itself would disappear, but they didn't turn it into the overriding force of the culture either, and this makes the people either barbaric or else sufficiently tolerant of human behavior to be less obsessed by that which can shame humans and less wary of an omnipresent gaze that would direct their attention to that which made them abject. There was at the same time a greater fragility to the social systems, a greater likelihood for them to dissolve into the anarchy of war, and also considerably less interest in the rights and privileges of individuals, and given these factors we need to keep our awareness of their relative lack of shame in perspective.

But we must also ask the chicken/egg question, for it is of paramount importance: did the Greek gods, as reflections of their own interests and assumptions, create a world that was less obsessed by the gaze and by the shame it introduces because they were more human and more indifferent to the human, or was there an essential relationship between the fact that there were many gods rather than one and the relative lack of emphasis on shame? Is a monotheistic system *inherently* more obsessed by the shameful in the human world, or is this simply a function of the culture through which the god makes his or her presence known? In some respects we can probably never know the answer to this question because the particular conditions through which the culture creates its gods have so much to do with their effects and importance. But it still seems plausible to argue that a polytheistic system is inherently more likely to generate a human community that has a sounder perspective on the abject simply because of the kinds of things that Socrates was trying to bury. If we consider the acts of Ouranos and Kronos, the first thing to remember is that they were bloody and that they violated familial bonds, something that is hard to avoid when everyone is family. These are the things that make their crimes such a horror to Socrates, as they well should. If there were lies told about gods, it would seem that they were declared lies because gods simply shouldn't take part in such inherently unstable acts of violence, for it gives the humans beneath them the wrong ideas about how communities ought to be structured. The constant struggles between literally titanic forces that we see worked out in the acts of Ouranos and Kronos suggest that life itself is an endless play of titanic forces that are often bloody, and that often violate the structures that societies establish to contain them.

Not only are these bad things for the community to see, but they are also even worse when it is the gods themselves who are performing the horrific acts.

More to the point in the context at hand, there is no final resolution of these kinds of conflict. Because the titans can only win by conquering the parent, and the parent could only win if he could successfully kill off all of his progeny, either the world would come to an end or the conflicts will continue. And when we move from the ranks of the titans down to those gods who are in the same league as Zeus, we have different kinds of conflicts between equally elemental forces, so even if there are some changes—crucially, that Zeus is the equivalent of a kind of mediator in major disputes between the gods—the battles between or among gods would seem to have no end. Kronos lives on as time, and the gods too live through time, even if they are immortal, and therefore there will always be other things for them to have disputes about, other questions of priority and turf, other interests to defend and jealousies to play out and foes to undermine. Even if we assume that Zeus adds the stabilizing force of mediation, we still cannot imagine that these gods will ever come to terms with one another. Their regime too is unstable, if not quite as intensely so as the titans' regime was. So the gods articulate a structure of meaning for the humans, but they do not convey to the humans a world in which the forces of life have a stable and predictable order. In this the Greek gods more accurately mimic the natural forces out of which they grew. There is simply little to do in the face of turbulent weather or earthquakes or volcanic eruptions, and that kind of natural instability is written into the gods' relations as well.

The unpleasant side of the instability of the structure the gods establish is that daily life is a more chancy affair. There is no telling on any given day just what might happen, and this reflects not only the instability of natural forces but also the greater instability of the socius as a whole. Given the greater chances for death on any given day, if you will, and given a world in which the gods themselves reflect that greater chance of mortality, there is nothing in the cosmol-

ogy that provides a buttress against the uncertainties of existence. And when one adds the indifference of these forces
into the equation, one has to imagine a world in which the
gods are of little use when it comes to protection and preservation. That is simply not their domain, except in the rare
case of the hero or the leader, who by definition demonstrates the presence of the gods in his life by being heroic or
by being a good leader. And because one knows that the
gods themselves are regularly in conflict—and that their
conflicts often have considerable effects in the human
world—one simply has to assume that there are no consolations to be offered for the riskiness of life either.

In exchange for a greater vulnerability in the face of the
instability of the forces of life, though, the Greeks got in
return a lesser quotient of shame. In part this was simply
because the gods were generally indifferent to humans, but
more importantly, that very indifference was a product of
their multiplicity and their own conflicts. In reflecting the
instability of life, they exhibit the instability of human beings
as well, and in so doing they suggest a different vision of the
human psyche. Shame, to the extent that it is predicated on
the gaze of an other who seems to see only one thing, is
based on the ability of the other to strip away one's other
characteristics and to reduce one's being to the single feature
upon which the gaze rests. The implication of such a gaze is
that one is *only* that which generates shame, that one's definition is indeed based first and foremost upon that shameful
aspect that one feels called upon to recognize. In a polytheistic world such a gaze is also possible, but the sense of the
human world is more flexible, more based upon a conception of the fluidities of life than it is on the need for a single
identity that is established through the gaze of the other. If
the gods fight with each other, fall in and out of love, are
violent and caring by turns, none of this is unexpected or
untoward in the least. The gods take their cues from Proteus
in this respect, fluidly responding to the situation they find

themselves in and needing no justification for doing so. This doesn't excuse their behavior to themselves or to the humans, who can still very easily be appalled at some of the things the gods do. But it does provide a vision of the gods that doesn't tie their nasty acts to a shameful persona ever after. The gods have specific characters, but they take on many shapes, and there is no reason to deny the power of the god—or his or her value in particular contexts that are relevant to humans—simply because one knows they can also do horrible things to each other and to humans as well.

The gods thus reflect a fluid sense of the psyche. It is always part of a character that is discernible, but different environments can bring different things out of it. Consistency is not prized or expected when one assumes that, for better and worse, humans are capable of erupting at what might seem to be the slightest provocation with either joy or violent anger. If there is a consistency that delineates character, it doesn't necessarily hold the character responsible for the acts that might be provoked by things beyond the control of the person, including the arbitrary eruption of other states that would deny the character. With only a loose sense of coherence, the polytheistic system is more generous toward the fallibilities written into human beings, and less inclined to interpret everything an individual does in terms of a unifying grid. And without that grid, or the demand that everything a person does measure up to a certain (arbitrarily defined) standard, the sense of shame is considerably diminished.

These humans still dress to cover themselves and their sense of shame, and they still perform sacrifices of various sorts that are designed to purge them of their shame even as they make them feel more shameful. They degrade themselves with some of their acts, are doubtless occasionally appalled by the things they (and their gods) do, but they do not view these things the way we do within the Judeo-Christian system of values. Their life is not idyllic in the least, for they don't have sufficient ignorance of existence to live without self-awareness and shame, and the fragility of their societies and the relatively primitive nature of their understanding of human motivation hardly qualify them as candidates for an ideal paradise. One ought not to make more out of such distant people than is pertinent or plausible. But their polytheism had a kind of robust, if tenuous, attitude toward humans that seems from our own vantage point to be rather refreshingly free of needless moralizing and frenzied attempts to shame people into doing things they might not otherwise be interested in doing.

Early Greek society was also unquestionably more bodily than the one of which we are currently a part, and this too has to do with some of the mitigation of shame, and doubtless as well some of the unpredictability of their characterization of their gods. Socrates may indeed cheat by irrationally hoping to bury the violence of the gods before he seeks to institute the regime of reason, but he thinks he can still succeed in imposing a centralized site above the body that will filter the bodily urges in such a way as to flatten out the surges of chemicals or hormones or whatever one chooses to use to describe the considerable fluctuations bodies go through on a regular basis. Socrates is not pleased by the potential *risk* involved in letting bodies be bodies. He is not content to let the gods go on their way and provide bad examples for humans even if their characters are indeed unpredictable and horrifying as a result. Instead, he wants to replace Zeus with reason, the central processor that cannot only mediate disputes—which Zeus already did well enough in the realm of the gods—but can also impose order on unruly actions, asserting priority over all the other impulses that emanate from the body. Zeus for the most part could not really override the major gods; he had to address all their special provinces and seek to placate them in order to address their grievances. He could not dictate to Poseidon what he ought to do any more than he could insist that Athena do what Zeus thought she should. His accommodations were thus not outside impositions but rather attempts to work through solutions that would satisfy autonomous regions with their own integrity. Socrates' reason does not want to grant to the body and its impulses that kind of autonomy or that kind of integrity. So again we find that in an important respect Socrates really does begin the Western obsession with an externally-imposed order to be placed upon the bodily regime that most of us would more or less willingly shape our lives around if we were given the freedom to do so.

I need to emphasize that while the body has its own truths written into the impulses that seek to move it in this or that direction, it is no more of a supreme arbiter of human value than reason is. Socrates may have made a fatal move when he attempted to overturn the body's basic governance of life in favor of reason, but he was certainly correct in assuming that the bodily regime is no panacea, as our own societies should have rediscovered as recently as the sixties and seventies. My point is not that the body's "wisdom" is superior to the "mind's," for that is only another kind of nostalgia; it is rather that the body never sought to impose hierarchical systems upon human life, and one part of its loose collectivity never attempted to usurp the force of the other regions for its own benefit, at least until the mind and its assertion of reason began to insist that humans were indeed totalizable in this way. The polytheism of the Greeks prompts us to return to a more bodily conception of the world than the one we presently maintain, and it does so at present in the midst of a society that declares itself to be all too bodily through its obsessions with beauty and fitness and aging while at the same time once again forcing the body to submit to a *disembodied* idea of how we as individuals should look and how our bodies should reflect the kind of self-image we think we deserve or hope to have.

We are as revulsed by our bodies as we ever were, and as shamed by their processes, but our public rhetoric—and particularly the language of commercials and other kitsch (and even academic discourse these days, yet another kind of kitsch)—repeatedly suggests to us that *only* the bodily is important, and *only* it can provide a fitting image for our sense of self. The obsession with fitness and beauty, with liposuction and plastic surgery and vitamin pills and weight regimes, demonstrates how great our sense of abjection is in the face of these bodies that of themselves seem repulsive to us and become all the more so as they age and the skin sags and the wrinkles develop and the joints work less well. In this sense we may have become a more irrational society in the past few decades, but we have hardly escaped from the imposition of totalitarian rule that Socrates sought to impose on both the body and the socius as a whole.

The trade-off that Western civilization made when it moved away from the polytheism of the body toward the monotheism of the mind has been clear to us for quite some time: we traded the uncertainty and fludity of polyvalent looks for the gaze of the Other, the *invisible* Other with the omnipresent stare, and the potential security to be found in that unifying focus. In Socrates' time, this may well have been the right move to make. There can be no doubt that Socrates knew full well the feverish pulsations that drove the polytheism he undercut with his dialogues, and we can assume he therefore believed that the only conceivable way to construct a viable polis was to establish once and for all the regime of reason and to hope that the violent impulses that were buried at the founding moment of the Republic would not return to overwhelm the minister he put in their place.

For us at the end of the twentieth century, though, the matter is entirely different inasmuch as we have learned too well in this century alone how futile it is to hope that reason can master the fluidity of the body, the emotions, the mind, or any other human domain. And as the repressed returned in Freud's theory of the return of the repressed, we have been forced to recognize that we cannot go along with Socrates' choice, first because it was based upon the erroneous judgment that human irrationality could indeed be buried— and *should* be buried—and second because his polis is based upon the ignorance of the citizens, and the false beliefs that the philosopher kings and priests must articulate in order to keep from their constituents what they all already privately know in any case: that they attempted to bury certain human phenomena and failed to get rid of them in spite of all their efforts. We at this point in our civilization can no longer afford to arrogate such power to a few, even if we were to determine that it was for the best. And given this situation, we have no choice but to return to that initial trade-off and to ask yet again which side of the equation has the more accurate vision of existence and which is more likely to provide us with a pattern through which we can make more viable social choices.

The sociopolitical ramifications of the metaphorical choice between a polytheistic and a monotheistic system are closely related to the virtues and limitations of the two viewpoints. To return for a moment to the now clichéd notion of a society in which the equivalent of "Big Brother" monitors the moves of every citizen through the reports of neighbors, loved ones and other means, we can see within such a system the fullest manifestation of a monotheistic system written into the sociopolitical domain. The gaze of the government reaches into every corner of one's life, putting one at odds both with oneself and with others, engendering suspicion of those around one and focusing intently on the kinds of shame that would keep the citizens in their place. Public opprobrium becomes the *least* significant thing likely to happen to one who has violated the tenets that are established by such a regime, and the pressures for silence and conformity are thus enormous. As one can see in a place like China where the huge numbers of the system create less of a private space in any case, leaders in such societies often seem to believe that the only way they can preserve order with so many people is through the repressive gaze and the humiliations and potential execution that can follow upon it. Whatever the excuse, those societies that are committed to the exploitation of the people through the visible and yet all-too-invisible gaze of the other invariably ground their system on shame.

We have certainly had enough experience with repressive regimes of various sorts in this century to realize how closely they are patterned on the monotheistic model, even if the most repressive systems are often found in polytheistic societies. At the same time, the madness of a Hitler takes part in the same exploitation of shame through the gaze that is both public and private and depends on the idea of a central gaze for its development and frenetic energy. Without the establishment of *two* others—the one who will always be watching everyone in order to find the other who ought to be eliminated in order to purify the society—fascistic systems cannot work for even a short time, though it is precisely the duality of others that creates the instability in the mechanism that drives them, for it invariably becomes more and more difficult to distinguish between the two kinds of other. The gaze is predicated on the purification of humans that will engender the security that is presumed to inaugurate the ideal regime, but all purification rites are based on the artificial establishment of an other who must be sacrificed, which in turn makes unclean those who have had complicity in the sacrifice, which in turn engenders the need for further sacrifice. This is the kind of vicious circle with which we have become all too familiar, and if it is true today that most Western societies are no longer based on the gaze of the omnipotent other even though they grew out of the monotheism that sought to disperse the gaze into every corner of life, this results from their awareness of the consequences of such systems, an awareness bought with payments to their own sacrificial past.

The polytheism that comes from the multiplicity of locations of authority can also be highly problematic depending on the circumstances of its articulation, but in theory at least it works best to overcome a system based on the pollution of the horrific gaze that focuses on the shame that each individual feels. The effect of having *many* "gazes" rather than one, many areas of power rather than an omnipotent and nearly invisible one (because omnipresent), is to disperse attention to many areas rather than concentrate it into one, and this applies both to the regions of authority and to the constituents whose social lives are mediated through the authorities. As is the case with the so-called "checks and balances" of the United States government, the distribution of power among the various regions of the system—like the establishment of separate but equal legislative, executive and judicial branches of government—prevents any one from asserting the kind of authority that would reintroduce the focusing effects of the gaze.

Democratic systems in general could be said to be polytheistic in this sense, as their images of government are derived from the kinds of mediation between autonomous branches that we found evident in the relations between the early Greek gods. However much democratic systems may seem to be based upon the rock of specific grounding certitudes (the certitudes and their ground differ from system to system), they are in fact based on the fluidity of the play of forces within the socius itself. This is in some respects true of any society, for even fascistic ones are susceptible to the violence that can be sparked by repressed or overzealous people, but it is not a principle of governance in such systems, whereas in democratic societies it is. The grounding principles, like the symbolic heritage upon which they are invariably based, only *seem* to ground the system in order to give the various branches of government the necessary symbolic authority to do their work without being constantly concerned about their legitimacy. In fact, however, there is no ground to their action beyond the historical circumstances that legitimate them as regions of power in the first place. They can assume the symbolic trappings of larger forces, as with the robes of the judiciary or the sacred precincts of the houses of legislation and the titles that come with the position and the title and aura of the chief figure of government, and they can create thereby an aura that suggests a more-than-human origin—"In God We Trust"—but the workings of the systems clearly show that the pressures of history, tradition and immediate context provide the flows through which the forces of government administer the socius.

Given this, we are once again back to the fact that even our democratic forms of government have at least tacitly been based upon the larger authority of the monotheistic system out of which they have grown. At the end of the century, that higher authority is for the most part only a nominal attachment to the system, and in any case it was always there only to provide legitimacy in times of crisis, just as Oedipus turns to Tieresias for help when things go bad in Thebes. But we have indeed built our systems on sacred grounds that are in effect denied by the very processes of the governments we have found most workable. Monotheism and democracy simply don't go together, and it is not just the clash of symbolic systems that is at stake here, for one can easily enough imagine a sociopolitical system that is based on the multiplicity of realms of power and a religious system based on a central force; it is rather that the vision of *order* underlying a democratic system is contrary to the notion upon which a monotheistic religious order is based. We have been able to maintain these two incompatible systems together for two reasons: first, and particularly in the United States, we have insisted on the separation of church and state, a principle that is more or less operative in the other Western democracies as well by now; and second—the belief upon which the first is predicated—we have insisted on the separation of body and spirit or soul, the move that allows us to assume that political systems administer human lives in the secular world while religious systems do so in the sacred world. The secular world is tied to the regime of *nature*, however that word might be defined at any given moment, and thus the flow of its power must take into account the fallibility of humans, the bodily impulses and hormonal surges, the conflicts between sites every time there is more than one of them, and so forth. Thus, we have discovered that the greatest political wisdom does indeed lie in democratic systems with many sites of power that disperse interests in order to prevent the focusing of shame that drives more repressive regimes. This system is based on the bodily domain of human life and responds in its own way to the natural flows and patterns that invariably determine the outcomes of all the forces on the planet in different ways.

Democratic systems are in fact derived from a knowledge of certain "natural laws" that are inferred from "natural laws" of bodily existence, about what creatures with the bodies we have do and desire and expect. Because a good part of the knowledge of bodies has to do with the *instability* of the forces they comprise and are capable of releasing, we have also tried to connect them to nonsecular laws in order to assure a higher order to which to appeal in times of instability. But as Oedipus shows, at a certain level we all know that when the appeal to the higher authority comes, it comes at a time of crisis, and it invariably has nothing to do with the higher authority but rather concerns the human urge to project our own diabolical needs onto an other who can take responsibility for them. In the best of times, in other words, the authority of the other is not needed, for the flows of forces upon which the system is based work fine; in the worst of times, the authority of the other is needed only to keep from ourselves the knowledge that we are about to commit horrible crimes that we cannot admit to ourselves as being *our* crimes. When the need for sacrifice arises, there must not simply be a victim; there must also be an *authority* to establish who the victim is and who declares the rite of sacrifice to be holy. This last resort always comes precisely when all else has failed, when the system is about to tumble irretrievably into chaos. The only question is whether we are more or less likely to arrive at that kind of crisis in democratic systems with or without a nominal association with an other, monotheistic regime of power.

Put another way, the issue is quite straightforward: we all know that monotheism is simply *unnatural*. It defies the flows of the natural world and overrides the sense of order that we derive from our understanding of the patterns through which "nature" asserts itself. Most religious systems have been unnatural in this sense, though some—like the polytheism of the early Greeks—attempt to articulate themselves on the basis of an understanding of the natural world as it is perceived by the makers of the system. Their virtue has always resided in their decided unnaturalness, and we have understood that at an individual level without realizing fully the parallels at the political level. If the Judeo-Christian religion is unnatural, that is precisely because it seeks to provide a vision of things through which humans can *escape* from their ties to the natural world. We know that well enough, and the appeals to eternal life, the purity of a life without the decay and shit of embodied existence, have a certain amount of plausibility in the face of the corruptions all around us, even if we also believe that the origin of the vision lies in human need rather than in an other.

What we fail to see as clearly is that the very idea of a centralized power, omnipotent or otherwise, is entirely antithetical to the flows of the world and the multiplicity of forces within it. In some respects this is simply saying that monotheism is a deliberate attempt to escape from the forces of the natural world, but it is usually not recognized as an escape at this level, and this is most curious precisely because we have arrived at a secular sense of power that depends on those "checks and balances" at the same time that we have so far refused to follow through in a similar way in the religious domain. One could argue that the trinitarian scheme of Christianity is an attempt to embrace a kind of multiplicity, but it would seem rather to be a concession to human nature that doesn't really deny the centrality of the gaze with which the Bible begins in the Old Testament. One could attempt to distinguish between what has come of Christ's teachings—which for the most part until recently has been an entirely hierarchical, centralized state—and what He Himself said, but that would not change the fact that the monotheism that has been practiced in the West is based upon a monolithic power that succeeds by commanding an omnipresent and invisible view of the shame of our being in order to achieve our submission.

The separation between church and state—while the state remains tacitly grounded in the law of an other that must in some senses be associated with the church—thus provides for the dual motivations of humans: it gives them a secular power that more or less presumes to take them seriously as individuals and that bases its governance on the flows of the fields of which they are a part; and it also allows both the citizens and the government to appeal to the other power in times of need. This in its own way is the legacy of Socrates' assessment of human communities in *The Republic*, for it too assumes that some things ought to be buried or at least not discussed in public, and that when the results of the incomplete and inevitably ineffective burial come to the surface, one must then call in the priests to offer more sacred rites, search for some huge and unprocurable victim, and hope that these devices will overcome the unnatural—really the all *too* natural—intrusion of violent disorder into the socius.

We are thus back to the same crux we have confronted before, the question of whether or not humans can imagine communities that work without resorting to the repression or projection of the religious, whether they can implement their knowledge of the polyvalent forces that govern their lives throughout the human domain or whether they are incapable of doing without the unnatural imposition of the other with the invisible gaze. If the world is always a question posed to humanity, as Heidegger liked to phrase it, then this would seem to be the question it has been asking us since Adam and Eve ate the fruit in the garden. The only thing that has changed over the millennia is that we have come to see better what is embodied in the question and how thoroughly our response to the world to this point has deliberately violated its order and denied the question it has asked us.

It must also be said that the multivalency of a polytheistic system does indeed have its own potential problems. Most obviously, as we see within the checks and balances of the United States government, a kind of gridlock or inertia can overtake the various branches when they are seriously at odds with each other. When the community itself is divided over what course it ought to follow, as it most decidedly seems to be at present, the tendency is for the various branches not simply to check the others but rather to bring them to a halt. The result is not that nothing happens, for something is always happening; it is rather that the system is incapable of dealing with what is happening and allows it to occur on its own without any shaping from the modes of governance that are supposed to be directing it as much as possible. At times such breakdowns can indeed occur because the populace itself is divided and uncertain of its desires, and at others it could also be a function of the way the system itself developed. Bureaucracies, for example, have a habit of intruding so many layers of procedure between the purposes they are meant to serve and the people for whom they are supposed to be working that the system breaks down.

In *An Area of Darkness,* Naipaul provides an all too common account of what happens when the bureaucracy is designed to frustrate the desires of those it is supposed to serve. He wants to bring alcohol into India, but in order to do so he must go through so many levels of procedure that hardly anyone ends up with the alcohol he sought to obtain. There is always another form to be filled out, always therefore another office to go to with another line and another person who is not quite sure what form it is that one needs. In this case it would seem that the system is deliberately schizoid: it does not want to deny outright the right of visitors to take alcohol into the country, but it does want to discourage it for all that, so it creates a system that so frustrates the individual in his attempts to get the alcohol that only the most persistent and patient are capable of following through successfully.[1] These kinds of procedure are fine as long as their schizoid intent is shared by the people as well, or as long as the people find a way of dealing with the system, but if they do not, and if the procedures are designed deliberately to frustrate the will of a large number of people, one is once again in the midst of those flows that come into being when one's will is regularly frustrated for no particular visible reason. When something goes repeatedly wrong and no agent for the difficulty can be found, then potential violence looms as a very real prospect. The multiplicity of regions of authority can in this way lead not only to inertia but also to precisely the thing that political structures are designed to avoid: violence that threatens to undermine the fabric of society.

If a multivalent system of power can also conceivably lead to violence and chaos, it might seem as though it would therefore have nothing more to offer as a mode of governance than the centralized authority it sought to supplant, for if the goal of all social systems is to avoid the violence that can so easily overwhelm them, and the multivalent one is recognized to be incapable of preventing such violence in all cases—and particularly without the diligence and care of its constituents—then one could ask what the value would be in abandoning the kind of schizoid system we presently have where the multivalent secular system is backed up by a monolithic sacred domain. The answer could only be that we know for certain that violence is always a potential problem for human communities and that the older, centralized system could not avoid it precisely because of the centralized nature of its power. We *do not* know for certain that violence could be avoided if we made our political apparatus more consonant with our knowledge of the flows of the world and our place within them, but the risks to our future in the present regime are such that it would be worth our while to try a different way of construing the socius. If we can assume that any system that is based upon a schizoid dichotomy between secular polyvalency and sacred centrality reveals a human community deeply at odds with itself, then we can also assume that the forces underlying the divisions within the community will inevitably result in some kind of violence. And if this is so, then we have an obligation to try the alternative vision that eliminates the authority of the invisible gaze and redistributes its forces throughout the community.

The problem that comes about when we imagine the value of attempting to create a political system with an entirely multivalent flow of authority is that it founders on the chicken/egg problem we have encountered in other contexts before. Such a political system would only work if its members were willing to abjure the denial of the shame that centralizes their vision of themselves within the sacred domain. The citizens would have to be *complete* citizens in that they would have to be willing to take responsibility for what it means to be human, to be an embodied creature; they would have to imagine a system in which there was no resort to a higher authority beyond the ones that were established out of the members of the system itself. They would have to confront collectively and individually that mystery which Socrates sought to bury. In the current political climate this is problematic precisely because the shame is already buried from view by both the conservative and liberal traditions. One would expect this to be so in a system wherein there was a tacit reference to the sacred authority beyond politics. Even in European societies where the governments appear to be more secular, one still finds the violent truths of Socrates to be buried away, and as long as this is true, the political system depends on the sacred for its authority, regardless of whether or not it acknowledges that dependence.

Both the conservative and liberal traditions have indeed abandoned any attempt to confront the shame that founds the socius in the first place, but they have different strategies they employ to deny its foundational importance to their views. If the conservatives share Socrates' assumption that the abject is that which humans are incapable of addressing, they therefore assume that its part in existence should simply not be spoken of. The flawed human world depends upon a strong authority to keep the knowledge—and the violence that might attend it—from coming to the surface, and the conventions one employs in order to escape from these truths become the medium through which any civilizing impulses can take place. In most cases, again like Socrates, the conservative attitude toward shame attaches itself to a vision of the sacred that is capable of redeeming the abject condition of life and allowing humans to overcome that which is so central to their being. The parallel authority of the other order provides relief from the guilt that attends the fallibility that constantly undermines human plans and works against the social order. And when necessary, the combined authorities of the political and sacred domains authorize the expedient of victimage; when a localized mystery seems to be the only thing that could restore order, the two interlocking networks provide both the rite and the victim, consecrate the sacrifice, and move the socius forward without too much thought about the mystery itself, lest that create greater problems and allow the violent impulses to get out of hand.

The conservative response to shame is thus based on what our culture has called original sin, and its strength is that it at least concedes we are inherently sinful or shameful. This is a strength because it recognizes the nature of what is, even if it also immediately seeks to bury the knowledge. It is also a strength to the extent that it provides—in *some* instances—a more tolerant view of what humans are capable of doing and how they should be dealt with when they fail to measure up to the standards society has established for them. The weaknesses concern the artificial hierarchies that are constructed in order to save humans from their shame and the resort to an otherworldly author of the ground that prevents the socius from going over the abyss into chaos. In turn, the rites and the secular events that are designed to contain the furies within humans both control and extend the reach of those furies, thereby guaranteeing a perpetual oscillation between relative order and a threatened socius. One might not choose to argue that the secular and social authorities depend on human shame for their perpetuation—otherwise they could solve the problem and dissolve their hierarchies—but it is true that their rites of purgation provide them with a system that ensures their future presence because the rites always cause further shame, and thus the need for further rites.

The liberal vision takes a far more benign view of human nature, one that is predicated on the notion that shame is a *learned* response to situations that aren't inherently abject. It relies upon the Romantic vision of our animal nature that presupposes that self-awareness and shame are two unrelated aspects of human consciousness that can be separated through the implementation of the proper political agenda. The liberals would derive their strongest truth from the fact that the social system does indeed reinforce shame at every level of its hierarchical articulation of life, and their proposals to overcome the artificial hierarchies are the most compelling feature of their program. At the same time, they presuppose that it is possible for humans to live without shame, that a perfectly egalitarian society would provide an openness and candor that would keep people from constructing their lives around the festering ooze of shame and resentment. Again, there is a good bit of truth to this notion, and its conception of the socius derives its power from the vision of an equitable and equal society, a vision that even conservatives now generally at least pay lip service to, even if they then comfortably retreat to the hierarchies that dispense greater favors to them. If all political systems are predicated on a conception of what human nature is, what it is capable of, and where it ought to be channeled in the future, the liberal vision provides the most attractive view of political authority, for it assiduously works to dissolve the artificial barriers that create differences between people that feed on their resentment and shame. If we are to imagine an ideal community, we must begin with what the liberal vision argues for and strives to achieve.

At the same time, the liberals' failure stems from their unwillingness to confront the psychological obstacles to their ideal city. Shame is unquestionably a condition that society shamelessly manipulates for its own ends, and it disseminates the spores of the abject to as many locations as possible to guarantee greater control over the lives of its constituents. Working under the knowledge that shame must be dealt with in order to preserve order yet can never be openly discussed, every society has found ways of employing this contradiction at the center of the human world, and in making use of this knowledge, the systems have like the Thebans of old only guaranteed temporary pockets of peace in a world dominated by the perpetual return of the violence that hides out on the periphery of every community. The oscillation between peace and threatened chaos may not come so readily in generational cycles as it did in the past, but it still exists for all that. And the liberal vision has so far refused to see that even if these factors are brutally manipulated by society for its own ends, the factors themselves preexist the social implementation of their consequences.

One of the problems the liberals would face if they were

to confront the intrinsic nature of human shame is that it is difficult to imagine a political vision that is based on an awareness of it. Again, neither the conservatives nor the liberals really address shame. Both seek to hide it, the one in order to preserve a system that confers benefits upon those who want it hidden, the other because it has never found a way of distinguishing between the shame all humans feel and the manipulation of that shame for political purposes. And in today's world where symbolism at times seems to be nearly everything, it is hard to imagine a political program based on a slogan like "We will give you back your shame" or "Share the shame and save the next victim" or whatever. Because humans do not speak of their shame and are encouraged to repress it even as its effects spread to most social domains, they would not likely find it appealing all at once to have to admit in public to the shameful drives and thoughts they might have.

The abject is taboo, is that about which nothing can be said, and so it is in one sense the chief obstacle to a more equitable world, both because our shame is predicated on difference, and hence on envy, and because we have all collectively decided not to say anything about it. If the liberals refuse to talk about it and build a political vision out of a denial of the abject, they are only doing what political visionaries have been doing for millennia. It is difficult to rouse the people to change without promising in one way or another to eliminate that most elemental of human problems, the revulsion we feel toward ourselves, and so we have yet to find ways of building a political program out of our awareness of the unavoidability of the abject in human existence, and we have yet to find a way of making such a program sound appealing, achievable, and virtuous as well.

The liberal refusal to confront the nature of the abject suffers from another flaw as well, and it is a more serious one, for we can at least begin to imagine a world in which it would be politically appealing to citizens to have a system based on a knowledge of their shame—at least as long as it offered an agenda that would diminish the effects of the abject and the deliberate manipulation of it—and can therefore work toward eliminating the more obvious barriers to an egalitarian society that was truly predicated on the free flow of human energies. But the liberal vision's chief flaw is that it too is based on the same hierarchical intentions as the conservative ones it opposes, however much it might seem otherwise. It has not escaped from the authoritarian world it purports to erase; for the most part it simply imagines another kind of authoritarianism that has the liberals as the authorities. In part this is due to the fact that power is an attractive and enticing commodity, and once one has a taste of it, it is hard to let it go.

But the more important reason inheres in the contradiction that all liberal visions are stuck with: they seek to do things for the benefit of those less privileged than they are at the same time that they must obviously usurp the voice of those very people. The intent is noble, and the plan is to give the people back their voice once their rights have been established, but we have yet to find a system in which that actually happens. The most obvious failure of this kind has taken place within the communist regimes that were once presumed to be heading toward the withering away of the state, an illusion so old and discredited by now that even the communists themselves have for the most part abandoned it. But the liberal/socialist democracies of the West have faced the same problem and done no better with it. Once one is committed to giving everyone a fair chance and a decent life, one moves closer and closer to a world where one's freedoms are limited, one's voice usurped, one's future narrowed by others who know better what that abstract beast called "the people" truly needs and desires. Even if the liberal vision is not a "Trojan Horse" that brings subversion into the city only to rewrite the hierarchies in favor of those who overthrew the old rulers, the results are generally precisely that simply because the process of deauthorization has yet to be imagined. Once authority is established, it is hard for the authorities (and for those who rely upon them) to give it up.

To put the problem still another way, one could say that zeal inevitably tends to shade into zealotry, regardless of the political system that is being advocated, yet the liberal vision is predicated on the elimination of zealotry, that blinding faith in one's own conception of the world that excludes the vision of others. In part this is a difficulty that arises simply out of the need to gain adherents to one's cause. In order to do that, one must work up and through the zeal for one's ideas that people are inclined to have, and the problem then is simply how to control that zeal and keep it from becoming zealotry, both on the part of the people as a whole and for the leaders as well. Politics depends on the careful assessment and manipulation of those forces that reside in the center of shame and that are presumably to be rooted out by the liberal vision, but how is the vision to root out that upon which its effectiveness depends? How can it learn to abandon the care and feeding of zeal within the people once it has prompted them to imagine a world where the egalitarian impulse directs the flows of the socius? And likewise for the leaders: how to escape from the fires that prompted the vision that drove them in the first place?

This can be all the more a problem for a viewpoint that inevitably plays out its egalitarian goals on the basis of envy, even if at times the envy appears in reverse form: the people imagine the lack of fairness in the lives of those individuals they support, and so even if the unfortunate citizens on behalf of whom the leaders fight do not themselves feel particularly resentful of their position within the socius or envious of those above them, the party itself must be committed to precisely that kind of resentment and envy if it is to succeed. And this is again not to argue that the liberal agenda is therefore corrupt and self-serving, for it seems to me to offer the only viable course for a future society. The problem of relying upon resentment and envy at the same time that the vision denies the inevitable human attachment to these shameful feelings is so important precisely because it is a major obstacle to be overcome if the liberal program is to be consonant with its own rhetoric.

If zeal breeds zealotry, which can easily overcome the egalitarian goals at the center of the liberal vision, it also focuses our attention on the final problem the liberal faces: the liberal agenda is based on the shame of its members, yet

denies shame as a ruling force of political life. It asserts that
the arbitrary inequalities that the socius has produced are
inherently shameful and degrading abuses of human potential, something that is more than true enough, and yet it
seeks to shame people into changing the inequities of the
system. Likewise, so-called "liberal guilt" may not be the
only motive in play in the attempts to right the wrongs of
the socius, but it is clearly a part. The leaders of the party
that opposes social injustice are invariably those who have
fared rather well in the system, and I believe that we can
certainly attribute the best of motivations to such people, at
least in the abstract. I do not want to argue that all altruistic
acts are basically selfish or guilt-driven, even if there may be
some truth to that as well. The desire to have a more equitable world can be a genuinely noble one, and there is no
reason to think otherwise.

But there is also shame at work here, most obviously the
shame that comes from feeling degraded by the lowly state
of another, the wretched condition of the poor reflecting in
turn on our own conception of existence. To one who is well
off, the totally abject condition of a "street person" who has
no home, lives out of garbage cans and sleeps on heating
grates, calls into question both one's own well being and
one's definition of the human. Such people shame us precisely because the inequities in their context, particularly relevant to our own, remind us all too vividly how little stands
between us and such a "lower" condition. For us to feel good
about being human, for us to be able to mitigate at least some
of the shame we face when we see the real poor of this
world—both in our own countries and in the even more
horrific conditions that prevail in some of the lesser-
developed nations—we have to imagine a world in which
everyone is capable of living the fortunate lives we find ourselves in the midst of (that is, if our politics is liberal). Again,
I personally find this to be as noble an ideal as one can
imagine, but it also seems to me to be clearly based on a
denial of the human shame that makes us feel badly in the
face of another human whose life seems so pathetic to us. It
degrades *us* to have to see such an individual, shames *us* to

be living so well when this other creature lives in such poverty, and so a good part of our motivation would inevitably be driven by an attempt to create a world in which the abjection of the poor wouldn't undermine our conception of the human, general or particular.

Thus, in the West the liberal vision is predicated on the notion that the shame that degrades those less fortunate members of society will disappear once the inequities of the world are redressed through the efforts of those who see the ideal community as one in which everyone has an equal chance to share the benefits of the socius. But this assumes that the shame at being human will disappear once such a condition is brought about, and only the perpetual presence of the poor in the world keeps the liberal from realizing that he has confused two goals: the noble one of seeking to create an egalitarian society is conflated with the less noble one of attempting to deny his own shame through his efforts on behalf of others less fortunate than himself.

The confusion of these motivations can lead in turn to a third effect being woven into the fabric of the agenda: quite often it is also the case that the shame from which the liberal is fleeing through his attempts to create a better world has nothing to do with what he feels when he confronts the poor. Rather, the sense of abjection he feels in the face of the poor is really the shame he feels toward *his own being*, irrespective of questions of equity and ill treatment. Zeal is invariably predicated on the desire for a certain kind of *purity*, and the *need* for that purity doesn't usually begin when one confronts the poor of the world for the first time. It comes from an inner drive to purify oneself of the abject one finds inside oneself, the futile attempt to purge oneself of all those impurities that make one feel shameful about the nature of one's being, most usually about one's *bodily* being. Once again, I do not want to suggest that such a motivation vitiates the liberal vision, for I do not think it does. And even if this motivation were something that needed to be considered in a political light, it would have to be contrasted with the conservative vision that wants to deny the abject altogether, in oneself and in others, assuming that the best choice within the socius is simply *to act as if that which de-grades humans doesn't exist.* This motivation is even more sus-pect than the one that is based on a desire to rid oneself of the shame of being, for it attempts to deny the force of shame altogether, and in so doing it refuses to deal with any of the inequities of the world.

The liberal may well be partially motivated by a desire to eliminate the shameful aspects of being through the zeal of the drive for equality; I would argue that movements for equality are *always* based on this desire, and I would assert further that this problematic origin of the quest for equality doesn't ultimately undercut the vision itself as long as it leads eventually to the realization that politics is finally inca-pable of eliminating shame. And *this* is what the liberal par-ties have yet to confront, though again it must be said that the only virtue of the conservatives in this respect is that they simply refuse to have anything at all do to with the abject of human existence—they continue to live the bour-geois dream that suggests all of the shameful parts of life go away if one acts as though they don't exist.

But the liberal very much wants to get rid of the shame within himself and very much wants to get rid of the poor who remind him of the shame inside of us all. The need for purity of motivation, undercut from the beginning by the shame one is in flight from, thus often leads to a kind of shrill posturing on the part of liberals, for they are too often unwilling to address the mixed nature of their motivations, firmly believing that only the purest of intentions can justify the somewhat suspect program of action that is based on speaking out for equality and justice for those whose voices too often seem to be quiet and indifferent. If one is going to usurp another's voice, particularly when one is arguing that one is doing so for the benefit of the other, then one is prodded out of conscience to believe that one's motives are singularly pure. It is hard to acknowledge that one will also get something out of the actions on behalf of the poor, hard to concede that all human choices involve a mixed bag of interests, some of which can be "good," others of which can be quite suspect.

If the liberal refuses to admit the degree to which his agenda is based upon his own self-loathing and shame, if he at the same time exploits the sense of shame in others to promote his ideas, and if he also must consequently convince others whose position is less fortunate than his that their position in life is shameful, then there is a problem with the nature of the liberal's discourse. We would recognize this much more clearly if more gains had been made on behalf of those whose lives are demonstrably abject, for then we could see the degree to which our goals were in fact predicated on the impossible illusion of eliminating shame entirely through the eradication of the poor. If the poor are always with us, they are so because shame is always with us, and this fact has yet to be addressed. In some respects this remains the fundamental problem with the liberal vision of life in particular and with political activity in general. To this point, regardless of party or country, politics has refused to address the most basic of human facts: shame. It has tried to will it out of existence, declared it null and void; or it has placed it into the camp of the other and exploited the other—or the *idea* of the other—in order to keep the shame at the edge of the awareness of the people rather than at the center; or it has argued that shame is purely a function of socioeconomic conditions that can be addressed in order to eliminate it altogether. None of these approaches works simply because shame is *not* a sociopolitical phenomenon—even if the sociopolitical world shamelessly exploits its existence—simply because, therefore, it is not to be eliminated by a major jobs or housing program, or even by a totally equitable distribution of income. Such a distribution would only force us to confront for the first time the central cause of all sociopolitical concerns: how to deal with the shame that can never be acknowledged but that drives us all the same.

A purely political response to the abject, then, abjures from the beginning that which it needs to work: an awareness that shame is not originally a political matter, that it only becomes so as a result of its presence. If shame marks the beginning of the social world, the social world needs quite a history to develop all the ways we have found to deny that the socius begins with the shame of being human. In our own day, the problem of shame is made more problematic because the religious structures through which it was to be dealt with no longer function properly. In some respects the very presence of a liberal vision demonstrates the failure of the religious sensibility, for it takes over where the religious failed, albeit in an indirect way. It seeks to address—often with the same apocalyptic and millenarial fervor—the same human situation that the religious world previously dealt with through the consolations of a future world to redress the evils of this one and through the divine arbiter who would mete out the eventual fate of us all in the face of human corruption that prevents all humans from getting that which is appropriate to their lot. Politics at this level is no longer about social stability and order; it is about changing the socius in order to eliminate that within it which is perceived to be evil. And no doubt in our own day we are still too dependent upon the religious framework out of which the liberal sentiments grew to realize how totally the liberal vision fails to address the fundamental situation the religious confronted.

In many respects the history of the liberal movement demonstrates how closely attached it was to the mainline religious groups whose sentiments were directed toward relief of the poor at least as much as toward healing of the soul, and this connection is still strong today even when "secular humanism" is much more the driving force and the religion itself only a backdrop to the main event. This connection to and yet difference from the religious is precisely what the fundamentalist conservatives have perceived so well in their attacks upon liberals, arguing that in the guise of humane and godly ways they advocate the most godless and inhuman of programs, and it is also therefore this connection that allowed a good bit of the conservative movement to cover itself in the clothing of religious sensibility as well. The resurgence of the religious right here and elsewhere reflects in part simple opportunism, but it also suggests two other legitimate, if quietly hidden points: the liberals are indeed finally articulating a structure that is not based on a theological ground, even if its images derive from the religious world; and the liberals have no way of dealing with the godless world they seek to put into place. In both respects the fundamentalists are right. Many liberals are quite convinced of the consonance between their religious fervor and their political zeal and remain unaware of how incompatible liberalism is with a religious system based on the shame of original sin and abjection. Because Christ sought to address the problems of the poor, the liberals believe that their drive for equality is indeed just an extension of God's plan, or at least it can be so argued. But the fundamentalists realize that *any* secular humanism is predicated on a denial of God and on a denial of that which generated Him in the first place: the human shame we find first in Adam and Eve.

If it is true from a philosophical perspective that the logical consequence to be derived from the end of the religious world is a full awareness of the aesthetic domain out of which our religions grew, and if it is also the case that the liberal viewpoint has often been most virulent in its attacks on the aesthetic as a bourgeois subterfuge, then we have to ask ourselves about the reasons for the virulence of these views. Why haven't the liberals tried to *fuse* their politics with a general aesthetics? Why have they instead sought to eliminate the aesthetic altogether? And why have they done so with such hatred of the aesthetic? The most plausible answer would seem to be that they have sought to undercut the aesthetic because they have quietly—and not so quietly— attempted to meld the *religious* and the political, and to be successful in doing that they have no choice but to continue to deny the force of the aesthetic, as the religious has always done. This would seem to be all the more true in a context wherein the liberal viewpoint is indeed a *vision* of the promised land at the same time that it doesn't quite want to go all the way toward declaring the degree to which it is a secular rewriting of the biblical conception of paradise. That would create problems because it is sacrilegious. Again, the liberals want to deny the religious through a secular vision of the promised land as a completely egalitarian society at the same time that this totally human vision is simply a reduced ver-

sion of the promises of eternal life in the Bible. In this sense
the liberal vision comes at times perilously close to a secular
religion, one self-consciously constructed to usurp the place
of the religious and at the same time draw its strength from
that which is denied by the very presence of the egalitarian
fervor underlying the liberal cause.

The liberal viewpoint is predicated on a complex and
contorted series of interconnections that is finally incompatible and inconsistent. It denies the shame that drives it forward, for to accede to the inherent nature of the abject is to
mitigate the furies that can be unleashed in the face of injustice; it asserts a purely secular vision of human communities that is based on total equality; and as a result it relies on
the religious vision of paradise in order to ground in a plausible manner its political goals. It wants to partake of the
religious and to deny it at the same time and refuses to see
the contradiction. And in so doing, it undercuts the only
domain—the aesthetic—that could finally give its perspective the plausibility that it requires while at the same time
allowing it to address the shame that was excluded in the
very beginnings of the liberal movement. In the midst of this
context, the liberals can indeed work for change and achieve
a good many of their goals, and for this we should be grateful, particularly when in many ways we find ourselves in the
midst of a conservative backlash in all too many parts of the
world today. But for them to have a consistent political vision
with a viable articulation of human possibility, they shall
have to confront the tangles in their present views.

When the political returns to discover the necessity of the
basic shame upon which it is based, it will then begin once
again to see how politics is finally dependent on the aesthetic. Put another way, we can say that it will find that shame
and beauty are a necessary couplet, one that must be understood in terms of the difference that is written into their
pairing and the essential union of their origins. If we begin
with the aesthetic nature of the world and the inevitable

connection to that world that all human activities have, the first thing we recognize is that beauty and shame come forth as a result of the orientation we have toward our fundamentally aesthetic natures. If we construe our activity as taking place within the flows of the fields of natural play, we see the beauty in terms of which the patterns make themselves known to us because we situate ourselves within them. If we begin with the aesthetic and focus on ourselves via the real or imagined gaze of the other, then we feel shame in the midst of our *difference* from that world that we can nevertheless not totally escape. The presence of the gaze itself—our awareness of it and its force over us—demonstrates our difference from the aesthetic world of which we are still also inevitably a part, but in doing so the gaze freezes us out of the flows of the fields and thereby makes us seem to be so totally other that we find ourselves to be the freak of nature, the aberration on the periphery that walks without cover through the world, naked before its own awareness of the strangeness of its life.

Once we discern the interlinking of beauty and shame that defines the human context and recognize that their difference is marked by the angle of vision and the degree to which it paralyzes the one who is seeing, we come to understand better the nature of our relation to ourselves and to the world as a whole. The most important factor to be derived from this new understanding is that we can see how our shame is at first a revulsion toward ourselves that is based on our *difference from* the other locations that constitute the flows of the fields rather than on our *connection to* them. We have thought for millennia that the original site of abjection presented us with a self-loathing based on our bodily natures when in fact the first moment of shame had to do with the difference of our bodily natures from those other bodies around us. This is what the story of Adam and Eve covers up, for it moves from their shame at the knowledge of good and evil to the feverish work to cover up their natures before the invisible presence of God. This version of origins has already erased the real situation, that our revulsion stemmed from our difference from the *embodied* world; it hides from the outset the essential knowledge that has driven the human species from the beginning. Once the knowledge of our difference from the other locations within the flows of the world has focused our attention on ourselves, the shame transfers itself from the self-loathing that comes from *difference* to the self-loathing that derives from the *same:* we are shamed by our bodies and their private parts and their excretions, those phenomena we have so obviously in common with the other animals on the planet. We have no difficulty recognizing this kind of abjection simply because it remains present throughout life. The shame of our *difference* from the rest of the world, however, becomes more and more inaccessible as we age; it is that which Kundera argues we find in the idyll, in that conception of paradise whose sole link for us as adults is the animal kingdom. So we transform the shame we felt at our difference from the animal world of which we were a part into a nostalgia for a greater linkage to it even as we are filled with loathing for the sheer animality of our lives.

Because our shame is first of all to be found in the presence of that world we find our difference in, it is also immediately evident that beauty is its corollary, for beauty is to be discerned in those moments when our difference from the aesthetic world is erased, when we realize that the differences are for the most part really superficial ones, that our flows are part of the much larger ones around us. This too is a moment we invariably mistake, and that accounts for the two different versions of beauty we have created, the one based on an awareness of the flows of the world, the other based on the false paradise of a frozen world without flows. Because our lives oscillate between the two poles of shame and beauty, we have come to assume that beauty must be defined in terms of *the momentary absence of shame,* when in fact it makes just as much sense to define shame as *the momentary absence of beauty.* The distinction may seem to be irrelevant, but it is crucial both in the definition of the human and in the definition of beauty, for if one perceives beauty as being that which relieves us momentarily of our shame, one inevitably comes to the conclusion that beauty's distinguishing characteristic is *oblivion*. We desire beauty in order to forget ourselves and our shame, pure and simple. In some senses this is clearly true, but to construe life and beauty in these terms is to create a world in which the primary goal is oblivion rather than beauty, for oblivion can be had in any number of ways, whereas beauty is a specific kind of human event to be distinguished from, say, mere intoxication or a self-induced hallucinarium. Our culture has become incapable of making the distinction precisely because it has reduced beauty to the simple forgetfulness of shame.

When shame is seen rather to be the momentary negation of beauty, the human situation appears to be considerably different. First, we can see how dependent the experience of beauty is on the experience of shame, how they are inextricably connected. The contrary version is continually trying to sever the link between the two—that is precisely the location of the nostalgia inherent in our conceptions of paradise. Second, we realize therefore that the shame that marks our difference from the flows also makes us aware of our place within them, albeit in an ironic way. Third, we recognize that there are two ways of life that are predicated on their different relationship to shame. There is that mode of being committed to oblivion that is forced to practice repression, projection and the like in order to flee from the shame of being human, however much the devices through which one momentarily escapes one's shame inevitably force one all the more insistently to face it yet again; and there is that mode committed to an awareness of how our lives are *naturally* aesthetic, how we don't have to seek out oblivion to hide from our shame but rather can simply learn better how our experiences allow us to slide into the flows of the fields around us without the necessary work of repression. We are in this sense more in than out of the aesthetic, though we think otherwise, and we don't have to work to "get into it" so much as we have to work at avoiding trying to get out of it. Our misunderstanding of the origin of shame, our location of it within the sameness to rather than the difference from the flows of the world, leads us to think that a further immersion into the flows will increase rather than decrease our shame. On the contrary, we come to find that we are always already a part of the flows and don't have to immerse ourselves into anything. We simply have to learn how to turn off the focus of the gaze.

To phrase the matter one more way, we can say that there is an exact parallel between our origins in shame and our everyday lives. We begin as part of the world of flows around and within us, and we spend most of our everyday lives as part of this world of flows. Usually we never think to question our relation to the flows and so remain unaware of how much of our day is in fact spent in this manner. Shame arrives at that moment when we step out of the flows through an ironic awareness of them and our place within them; it is that first split within the human that suggests it is two rather than one. When it comes, we work assiduously to hide from it, to run away from it or cover it over, and the more obsessively we work at hiding from it, the more difficult it is to escape from it. Then, if we are fortunate, we come to see that the easiest way of dealing with the shame that is part of being human is simply to accept it for what it is, and this in turn allows us to move back within the unselfconscious flow of the fields, always to emerge from them again to contemplate our difference and our shame, but not to escape the counterpull back into beauty.

In our daily lives we occasionally choose to focus our gaze upon ourselves, though this is not always marked by feelings of shame, and it is easy for us once we have resolved whatever problem prompted our gaze to shift in the first place to return to the flows with which we began. Only when something within the flows brings us up short do we split ourselves away from them, and we do so then for the most part only to find ways of resolving our conflict with the flows. Day in and day out we thus more or less naturally move between those moments when we are comfortably within the flows of the fields and those where our difference from them becomes more or less acute. The more acute our difference is, the more we focus our gaze upon ourselves and the harder it is for us to get back within the flows. The flow *between* self-awareness and unself-conscious play within the fields becomes disrupted, and at times it is difficult to recover it because we get caught up in the gaze and lose sight of the flows.

But for the most part we have no great trouble moving between the flows and self-conscious feedback loops within them, and this is the same pattern that is found in our movement between shame and beauty. The difference is simply that in our daily lives the experience is not generally as intense as it is at those moments when we are clearly in the midst of beauty or shame, and so we experience the shift without the emotional complement that we associate with the words "beauty" and "shame." After one adjusts more or less well to the fact that one is a self-conscious being, one doesn't always experience shame in the face of the gaze. Indeed, it could be said that maturity is a cultivated *indifference* to what one is, a cultivated indifference that allows one to avoid feeling shameful every time one's self is focused on, either by oneself or by others. Given the repetitions of life and the need to be what one is, over time both the self-conscious moments and those of unself-conscious flows within fields have a more or less neutral tone to them, do not carry with them any particular intensities unless specific circumstances call them forth. We continue to find ourselves in the midst of the moment of beauty as well, and likewise for shame, but the perspective that comes from repetition makes them harder to discern.

If shame emerges from the aesthetic nature of the world rather than the other way around, we are not prompted to envision the aesthetic as a mode of oblivion—"We possess *art* lest we *perish of the truth*"[2] is the statement of a man who acutely desires oblivion, who is desperately tired of thinking about himself and his difference from the flows of the fields. It is an assertion that tells us how often Nietzsche failed to measure up to his own understanding of the aesthetic nature of the world and masterfully encapsulates the bourgeois attitude toward art and beauty that has driven our culture for several hundred years now. But there is an alternative, and it would be something akin to "Art tells us the truth so we don't die of shame." Art is that which prompts us to overcome our obsession with the gaze by allowing us to see the flows that evade the focal point of any look that freezes us in time. Art brings us back to the aesthetic with which we began so that we can see we never left it. And it provides us with the truths to be found within the flows and our experience of them that are the only real wisdom humans ever achieve. And art gives us back the indifference to ourselves that we need in order to be fully human.

What is more important in the present context, though, is for us to see how the two ways we construe the relationship between beauty and shame affect our conception of human existence and thereby give shape to the kinds of political systems we construct. The problem in a way is the same one to be found in the difference between "We possess *art* lest we *perish of the truth*" and "Art tells us the truth so we don't die of shame," for the pragmatic consequences of these different views conjure up radically different political states. We continually forget that our vision of both shame and beauty affects the way we deal with everything in our lives, even if shame and beauty are modes of being we experience relatively rarely. Because they are not insistently in evidence every moment of every day, we tend to assume that they are therefore unrelated to the normal events that carry us through the day. As "exceptional" moments rather than the norm, they seem to be so different from the kinds of experiences that generally face us as to be irrelevant to our consideration of the minutiae of everyday life. But in fact the small things in life are interpreted in terms of these two most intense kinds of human experience, and as a result, our attitude toward these experiences has a major effect on the way we think about the lesser events through which we build our daily lives and construct the bridges between past and future that create the continuities we perceive as our "self."

If our shame is first a response to our difference from rather than our similarity to the flows of the world the gaze has temporarily removed us from, what changes in our conception of pragmatic life and the politics that would seek to address that life? In a sense, nothing at all would change simply because the shame, the desire to eradicate it, and the inability ever to do so would remain. But we can at least begin to see that the self-loathing that comes out of our awareness of being bodily creatures is not in itself the chief reason for our shame, that the origin of it is rather in our awareness of falling out of the flows we desire to be an unself-conscious part of. We have all too easily accustomed ourselves to thinking that it is our bodily natures that we want to negate when in fact just the opposite is true: we want to destroy that which marks our difference from the flows of which we are still a part, self-awareness. And we want to do this not because we don't want to be reminded that we are bodies but rather because we don't want to be reminded that we *know* we are bodies. True, the body is for us a site of fascination and loathing, a mixture of that which entices and that which puts us off. This blend of desire and disgust is precisely what generates our shame in the face of the bodily. But our shame at our self-awareness comes not from a knowledge of the disgust and desire we find ourselves feeling when we see our bodies but rather from our inability simply to *be* a body and nothing more. When our shame surfaces, we assume it has only to do with our rejection of bodily existence, hiding from the deeper truth that we are really running from our self-awareness. The manipulations of the socius can in some respects work as successfully as they do precisely because they can focus our shame on the bodily aspects of life while exploiting our shame at our self-awareness with impunity.

Knowledge of the dual modes of human shame makes us aware of our tendency to focus on one mode in order to hide more fully from the other, but it also makes us see how much our society is consequently pervaded by what Freud called the death instinct, for that is another term for our desire for undifferentiation, and it marks our first modern awareness of the fact that the real problem is not the bodily at all but rather the self-awareness that makes us feel different from the flows around us. In this context it is not an accident, however coincidental it might seem, that the flows of the body are that which we find most loathsome. It is as though these flows, which are among the most significant ways our bodies regulate their relationship to the flows of which they are a part, remind us too much of the ways in which we are removed from the larger flows. The flows disgust us to the extent that they seem our primary—or perhaps our *only*—connection to the world. Their "messiness," their gravity-driven movements, their stinks and textures are seen to be the mark of the other inside of us—how could *we*, after all, make these things that are coming out of our bodies (one is always struck by a child's first amazement at the shit that emerges from it, its captivation by this strange otherness coming out of its body without its bidding)—but in the end our disgust comes from the fact that there is *not enough* of that other within us, that the flows that seem to regulate our relation to the world do so in only a cursory way, only a *bodily* way, when what we desire is the measurement of all our flows in consonance with those around us. We want once again to be undifferentiated from the flows we first perceived our difference from in that moment of self-awareness that declared us to be *human* tissue.

With an awareness of these quite different modes of shame that derive from different aspects of self-loathing, one is better able to understand the forces that drive one's life, and one is consequently better able to imagine a socius that would address real human needs without cultivating fantasies in order to extend power over the lives of its citizens. One would be able to distinguish those modes of power that preyed on one's self-loathing from those that were designed to address the conception of the human that could in fact lead to a truly egalitarian society. For an egalitarian system is not possible within a framework driven by shame any more than it is imaginable within a system that promotes itself through an attempt to deny its shame by passing it on to others. This has been the major armature of most societies with which we are familiar, and it works as a form of control up to a certain extent, but it is also always inevitably attached to modes of sacrifice and torture that are the expedients of a world built on shame that is projected onto others while still needing regular modes of expression in the lives of those who always attribute it to the other. We work out of this mode as much today as we ever did, and it is indeed perhaps more shamelessly exploited by the liberal elements of our society than by those who are quite willing to live within the hierarchies that are designed to lift the wealthy above the degradation of the lower classes.

In the end, we might have to conclude that it is simply impossible to separate politics from shame, or to separate politics from the manipulation of the desire for the repression of shame, but we should first attempt to build a political system from a base that has a genuine chance of succeeding at being egalitarian rather than resting smugly satisfied with the relatively egalitarian societies we have built in the face of much greater exploitation of people in other cultures. At the very least we should begin by recognizing that any system designed to shame others into greater self-loathing is not likely in the long run to succeed in doing much more than achieving power for those who have deliberately manipulated others through the repression of their own shame. From there we might return to our connection to the dual forms of shame in the face of our difference from and our sameness to the world and seek thereby to reassess the ways in which shame and beauty can articulate the basis of a knowledgeable life and an intelligent social system that truly begins to address the needs of its citizens. Such shifts would inevitably prompt us to redefine what it means to be human, and this would force us to deal with some of the unpleasant realities of our psychic displacements that we have generally managed to avoid in the past, but they would also provide us with unknown opportunities that would be built around addressing the flows of the world and our relation to them in ways that might better integrate us into them while also keeping our distinctive place within the patterns that articulate the world.

Chapter Four

In the Beginning There Was Beauty and Shame

The story of Genesis provides us with our chief myth of the beginnings of human consciousness; it gives the reasons we have devised to account for what we have characterized as our fallen state. We know that Adam and Eve ate the fruit they were forbidden to touch, and as a consequence they were driven out of the garden. This meant that they would now have to face pain, childbirth would become difficult, they would have to work hard to make the ground yield up its sustenance, they would feel revulsion toward their bodily natures, and they would die. These results are not listed in quite this way in the Bible, and that is interesting in itself. God never tells Adam and Eve that they will henceforth feel shameful about being human and bodily; that seems to be something they are aware of themselves at the very instant they put on the knowledge of good and evil that comes with self-awareness. Instead, God seems to be listing those things that humans have always found the hardest to take, almost, it would seem, in a catch-all way. Women experience great pain in giving birth, yet humans know that for other species the process is not so difficult. Humans do indeed have to contend with the thorns and thistles of what often seems to be cursed ground. They have to perform arduous exercises on the earth in order to make their food, and this too seems a violation of the natural pattern because one doesn't observe other animals having to work so hard and long to sustain themselves (that they may lead relatively shorter, riskier lives is something we tend not to notice).

The phrases of the King James version emphasize the

degree to which life has become a bitter thing: "In the sweat of thy face shalt thou eat bread, till thou return unto the ground; for out of it was thou taken: for dust thou art, and unto dust shalt thou return." This sentence is made to sound fitting—because humans came from the earth in the first place, there is justice in the fact that they shall be covered with a sweaty dust throughout life and finally decay back to simple dirt themselves when they die—but it also carries with it a mean-spirited tone. It is, after all, bad enough that humans will now have to die, to return to the dust. Why does God have to rub their faces in the dust throughout their lives as well? The knowledge of mortality would seem to be more than enough punishment for the sin of knowledge, and one wouldn't think that things would have to be any worse.

In God's dictum we find a curious blend of explanation, bitterness, and self-loathing, but God himself never says "And thou shalt loathe thyself throughout all thy days because thou urinate and defecate and ooze other bodily fluids." Why is this the first thing Adam and Eve experience after eating the apple yet something that is not mentioned again? And why does God choose to lump together the things He does? Is it simply that those three things that most distinguish humans in their own eyes from other species are the pain of childbirth, the difficulties of working to sustain life, and the awareness of death? Or is the collocation here one in which all the elements are related in an intrinsic way? And why, finally, to go back even further in the basic myth, is self-awareness characterized in terms of a knowledge of good and evil? It would seem in general that these things don't all really belong together in any other sense than that they are the main things that human beings have against life—they constitute the major grudges, if you will. Perhaps they simply reflect the kind of chaos that humans all too often seem to think life is.

The terrible sentence God imposes on humans is curious in its own right, and difficult in the extreme. It is almost more than we can bear. But there is one more curious phenomenon here, and that is that God never mentions any real compensations that might help Adam and Eve find their existence tolerable. This would seem to be a particular need of Adam and Eve, for after all, they had experienced the Paradise in which nothing awful existed and thus must have found the contrasting human world devastating in its effects. Why doesn't God give them some good things here too? Why doesn't He say "To help sustain you in the face of all these nearly insuperable burdens, I will give you *beauty?*" Is it simply because beauty was thought to be present from the beginning in the rightness of the world and the beauty of the garden? Are we to suppose that Adam and Eve experienced the beauty of the world after the fall, or did they simply sweat and suffer and finally die? Why didn't God bother to say that He left them the pleasure of beauty because they needed something to sustain them? And why is there no mention of sexual pleasure or the delights of the senses in general? Were these simply to be assumed, or rather taboo subjects that were as unclean as the pigs that were shortly to be forbidden as food?

The story of Adam and Eve is thus in some senses an elegantly straightforward, yet cryptic account of the human self-pity that is described in terms of a fall from an earlier state of grace, but it is at the same time a curious gathering of the human world that leaves out the connecting links that we may well sense at some level but would nonetheless very much like to find more explicitly detailed in any account of why life is the way it is. From a purely secular context, one can argue that these lapses and connecting links are the result of the relative irrationality of the people who devised the myth in the first place. Even if it does in some respects found Western civilization, it by no means follows that the biblical account needs to have the kind of coherence we expect from our narratives in a rational age. Perhaps the very elegance of the story comes from the elusiveness that in part derives from the conundrums its establishes. At the same time, the power of the story prompts us always to think that there is a deeper logic to its connections and divagations, so we question it one more time in the hope of probing yet a bit deeper into the mysteries of human consciousness.

It certainly makes perfect sense for humans to group together those things about life that they find most difficult and declare them to be the result of a fall. After all, the biblical account is designed to tell us why life is the way it is, and those things we find most mystifying are the aspects of life we most abhor. When we compare our lives to those of the other animals, the pain of childbirth and life in general, the need to toil as much as we do, and the awareness of death do indeed seem to be the major things that distinguish us from them, so they could easily enough be imagined simply as the result of the kind of species we are. One might have to stretch the argument a bit to suggest that the pain of childbirth is due to the increased intelligence of the species that provides the knowledge of good and evil, but beyond that link, the pain and suffering of existence and the awareness of death are closely connected throughout life. That these in turn should have something to do with our need to work the earth in the face of thorns that undercut our efforts and prick us and make us bleed can clearly be linked to the knowledge that allowed humans to stop their hunter-gathering ways and cultivate a particular space year after year. In our culture, this sense of a relatively settled space that we cultivate with effort in order to sustain ourselves does indeed reflect a certain definition of what it means to be human and therefore provides at least a localized assessment of what life involves for us.

These woes that God imposes on future humans thus seem understandable, and we certainly experience them painfully enough in a regular way to believe in their importance. The nastiness of the curse—and the implicit self-pity that writes out the penalties from God—suggests the human attitude toward the life they have been given, its general unacceptability, and they do so chiefly in terms of the pain and death that are the central elements of the decree. What is striking once again is that God does not refer specifically either to the shame and self-loathing that Adam and Eve felt *before* they were thrown out of the garden, or to the good and evil that they learned of when they ate from the tree. We can assume that the evil of which they learned dealt with shame and sin against God, at least as things develop, for they do indeed feel the gaze of God upon them once they have eaten the fruit and thus recognize—or interpret—their act as evil. And we can consequently also assume that the good of which they learned had to do with the ways of God as the Bible proceeds to establish them at great length. But if we confine ourselves specifically to the first books of Genesis, we might wonder why God didn't say more about the evil of which they had learned and the good that must have come with such knowledge. By the time of Moses the rules about good and evil have become consummately important, and yet God doesn't even think to say much about them in Chapter Three. Nor does He stress the shame that Adam and Eve felt when they first knew of themselves as self-conscious creatures.

Indeed, the only real clue we get about the nature of the good and evil of which Adam and Eve must have learned when they ate the fruit comes from God's concern that if they stayed they would also eat of the tree of life—this suggests at the very least that the act of disobedience would eventually prompt them to be disobedient again and thereby take of the fruit of the tree of life and usurp God's privilege there as well. They have *learned* what is good and what is bad, what is desirable and what is not, and would doubtless apply that understanding to create the best circumstances for their lives. They would perhaps have to live in shame, that which they acquired with the first bite of fruit, but at least they wouldn't have to die. On the other hand, if they really only became mortal once they left the Garden of Eden, we could assume that the myth simply has inconsistencies in it that reflect what humans construe as their lot (and their desire) while at the same time suggesting that God had to work to ensure His own pride of place.

Good and evil, then, are not really referred to at any length, and we are left to wonder just what they comprise and how they fit into the shame that wasn't present at their generation. We could very easily say that the first bite demonstrated to Adam and Eve that that which made them feel shame was evil whereas that which they perceived to be beautiful was good, but we have no real basis for establishing this definitively. We could argue that the knowledge of the good was basically derived from the taste of evil—the shame made them realize what could eliminate shame, the aesthetic experience of the world—or we could hypothesize on the contrary that the knowledge of evil came out of that first bite only because they always already had their prior sense of the good life they were leading to contrast it to. There can be no real way of determining these questions precisely, and for the most part there is no reason why we should need to know specific answers to them. But we do need to ask why self-awareness leads immediately to shame, why self-awareness in turn leads to a knowledge of good and evil, and why finally those things in turn lead inevitably to the curse that God metes out to Adam and Eve as they leave the garden.

The most logical genetic explanation for these events would simply be that Adam and Eve achieved self-awareness and therefore a sense of shame, and this in turn allowed them to see their lives in a different light. They could assess the nature of their existence because they could abstract from it and gauge it by the lives of the other species around them. They could also note their otherness in terms of their relative hairlessness and their upright posture and thereby feel the shame of difference from the other species, a difference that would in turn lead to other kinds of shame that would come from imagining others looking at them the way they were now capable of looking at themselves, abstractly and from a depersonalized distance rather than from the inside. At the same time, their self-awareness would not extend to the point where they could make sense out of the kinds of things animal species tend to do, and so their shame would be still further increased. Other animals would both establish their terrain with their excrement and thereby mark off a clean space for living that was "protected" in a way. They dealt with their territorial and hygienic needs in the same gesture and could do so without the least self-awareness. These are simply what would seem to be protective mechanisms written into the nature of living species.

Adam and Eve were not likely to note the territorial and hygienic functions of excrement, though, and so would have to think about just what it was, where it came from, and what should be done about it. And they were not likely to mark off in a self-conscious way their own personal space with it in the knowledge that the smell of their shit would make their territory known to other species. Nor were they likely to be aware of the possibilities for infection that would come about if their excrement contaminated their food supply or water. The animals didn't have to think about what to do with this by-product of life because within their lives it more or less took care of itself. For Adam and Eve, who were truly capable of recognizing the strangeness of these emanations from within, these seeming violations of their own private beings, there must have been a great shock, particularly in contrast to the lives of the other animals. And inasmuch as the gaze of the other translates easily enough into the *smell* of the other, it would almost immediately follow upon the self-awareness of Adam and Eve that they would translate the "bad" smell of the other's excrement as a disgusting odor with the collateral sense of something (and someone) totally and repulsively other and by the final, total otherness of death.   °

Morality comes in this way out of the smell of the other's shit, a smell that is at some level transferred back to oneself—if the other's excrement smells so offensive to *me*, then my excrement must smell as offensive to him. And the circle completes itself by returning to the shame that came from the perception of nakedness. Shame is in some sense nothing more than the awareness that the excrement that comes from one's body and that carries with it an odor that is recognizably one's own and therefore not repulsive must indeed smell repulsive to anyone else and thereby reveal one's total difference from every other living creature. It might in this way be better to argue that the gaze in all its literal and metaphorical manifestations is really a derivative explanation of the first moment of shame. First there is the *smell* of the other that repulses, the smell that makes one recognize how one in turn smells to others; then there is the abstract, visual articulation of the unseen God who can "see" into Adam and Eve and realize that they are now different as a result of the act of disobedience that created the chasm between them and God.

Regardless of whether or not one begins with the shame of vision or of smell, the otherness that is written into it is paramount, the difference from that to which one was originally united. At that point one is both committed to inscribing one's own personal circle through the smell of one's excrement at the same time one can feel the loss involved in having to establish and defend a space that is isolated from the great unity from which one came. And this is the moment of human civilization. Retrospectively the moment is always a *moral* one, even if it isn't precisely that in the first place, for humans and their societies proceed to build themselves on the basis of the sacred smells that differentiate *mine* from *his*, kin from alien, and the edifices thus constructed invariably declare that which is within the sacred circle to be good while asserting that which is beyond the marker of the smell to be evil and dangerous. The shit at the edge, both *of* us and yet irretrievably other, is the sacred border that determines the morality of the individual or the tribe, the mark of our shame and the hem of the garment we weave to protect ourselves from the others beyond.

We have learned over the millennia that it is not always wise to interpret the world in this way, that the xenophobia written into the morality of the smell can be destructive in the extreme and is at the very least a reflection of that first moment when we projected the smell of our shame onto the other, when we declared the evil to inhere in someone else and decided that our own regime could only be good. The essentially conflictual nature of human societies has been defined in terms of this smell of shame and its projection onto the other, and we have come to see how our species needs to overcome this most fundamental of our urges. We have also learned that the best way to do that is to separate the smell from the morality, even if we also have difficulty in doing so. The vulnerability inherent in broadening the range of smells we consider to be "ours" is difficult in its own right, and it goes against ages of learned responses in opposition to that urge. Even more, such broadening breaks down the border that separated one from one's shame—there is no other to attribute it to, no border that keeps it at bay—and so it comes back to one as one's ownmost possession, that with which one's sense of self began.

At the same time, it would be foolish to attempt completely to overcome our fear of and distaste for the smell of the other—if such a thing were even possible—simply because there is indeed a wisdom in that smell. However much we can in our rhetoric argue that we are all members of the great human community, we all also depend on a knowledge of the other for our bodily and psychic survival. Even in the best imaginable of human worlds, it would be necessary to be able to sort through the "smells" that attached to the language of the other in order to discern as much as possible the motivations underlying the rhetoric. It does no good to conceive of a future in which all discourse is "true," devoid of intentional or unintentional shadings that mislead the listener, simply because even the most we could hope for— human acceptance of the shame of their existence—would not keep people from being the forked creatures that they are. The means through which one acted in the world might change, and the attitude one brought to one's life might be different, but the duplicity that came with the first bite in the apple defines us as a species and is simply not eradicable. Given that, one always needs to know both what is other— where the borders of the individual leave off and those of the other begin—and what in a larger sense can be construed as part of the same community. Shame is in one sense simply the ever-fluctuating border between those two relationships, and it articulates our ongoing sense of self and other throughout life. It simply ought not to be construed in moral terms.

When one moves from the moment of shame in the Garden to conceptions of good and evil, one runs into another problem, though, and that is that within the individual and the society as well good and evil can be distributed two ways. It may make the most obvious sense to assert that the good is that which is within my own circle, the evil that which is on the other side of the border, but the gaze of otherness can have the opposite effect as well: the good can be that which the other possesses, the evil that which is our own lot. The need for the border is the same in both cases, but it is used to contrary purposes. In the overall mix of life the borders are defined both ways. The individual finds some of the things in his circle to be good and some evil, and some of the things outside of the circle to be evil and some good. But we have yet fully to understand the mechanism that determines these outcomes, even if we have come to realize how both work on the threshold of the shame that separates them. Yet before we can move on to think through the development of the nature of the good and evil in human life, we have to learn about these oscillations between the two at the threshold between self and other.

Here our problems are defined in part by the all too glib psychologizing about such phenomena that goes on every day. We all recognize when our shame prompts us to desire the "good" of the other, just as we realize when our own good stands up in the face of whatever the other might offer. But how does an individual know which is the case? What internal mechanism allows one to sort through these oscillations in an intelligent (or not so intelligent) way? For the most part there would seem to be no viable way to determine such a thing, for we can never know until after the fact when our choice has been the proper one. In a purely neutral setting, one could argue that an individual chooses the good on the basis of his or her own sense of the situation as long as that sense is quite clear. When it is not, the person may base choices on the assessment of others whose viewpoints are valued. And in part this shift to the viewpoint of the other might come from simple curiosity to see what the other's good is like. If this were the only scenario with which humans had to contend, we could assume that over a lifetime most of them would become adept at discerning when to rely on the good as it was determined from their own sense of the world and when to "borrow" from a valued other.

As the serpent makes clear, though, the good as determined by the other is also—and perhaps primarily—determined by mimetic rivalry. Eve eats of the apple because the serpent convinces her that she will then possess the knowledge of God of which He is unfairly depriving her. The devil preys on what she *doesn't* know and have in order to get her to do something that she is not inclined to do herself. One can assume that Adam eats in turn for the same reason: he is made to feel that Eve has something he must also have, just as she has something that so differentiates her from him that without possessing it too, he will find too great a chasm between them. This desire as lack that drives humans and their sense of the good is indeed the devil's work, the motive for determining what is good that is always suspect even if it is based on what might otherwise be called a healthy curiosity. What distinguishes the serpent's tongue from curiosity is that the serpent convinces Eve that she can *possess* something she doesn't already have, thereby persuading her that her life as it is remains insufficient. One can be both curious and satisfied with one's existence, at least in a general way, but mimetic appropriation works on a different basis.

Self-awareness breeds a knowledge of what one has and what the other has, even if only in a superficial way, and once the individual finds the world shaded by that kind of understanding, an assessment of the good becomes problematic, for one can look at the world through one's own eyes or through the eyes of another, and one cannot always specifically tell when one is doing which of the two. If Adam and Eve ate of the tree of the knowledge of good and evil, both the Bible and the humans who follow after it are far more adept at defining what is evil than in establishing what is good. This may be why even God is rather silent at first about what good they have learned of, why He fails even to mention it. And it may also be that the sense of the good is primarily derived from a negative mode: we discover what is "evil" for us and thereby establish that what is good must be that which avoids the evil we have found.

One could argue from another angle that God in effect sowed confusion by leaving Adam and Eve with the awareness of good and evil they acquired by eating of the tree while also depriving them of the fruit of the tree of life. Only *that* fruit, with its prospect of permanent existence, would allow humans properly to distinguish good from evil without some Other to lay down the rules that establish the two. Once again Milan Kundera understands this problem very well indeed, as we see when he tells us about our confusion via a discussion of Tomas's attempt to decide whether or not to attach himself to Tereza:

> We can never know what to want, because, living only one life, we can neither compare it with our previous lives nor perfect it in our lives to come.
>
> Was it better to be with Tereza or to remain alone?
>
> There is no means of testing which decision is better, because there is no basis for comparison. We live everything as it comes, without warning, like an actor going on cold. And what can life be worth if the first rehearsal for life is life itself? That is why life is always like a sketch. No, "sketch" is not quite the word, because a sketch is an outline of something, the groundwork for a picture, whereas the sketch that is our life is a sketch for nothing, an outline with no picture.
>
> *Einmal ist keinmal*, says Tomas to himself. What happens but once, says the German adage, might as well not have happened at all. If we have only one life to live, we might as well not have lived at all.[1]

Without an Other who determines what is right and what is wrong, Kundera suggests here, we are stuck with the necessarily preliminary nature of all our choices in a world where the effects of the choices are never merely preliminary because once done they cannot be undone. So without a ground for our knowledge of good and evil, we cannot properly decide in any particular case what we should do; we simply have no way of comparing one moment with another to provide a sufficient context for understanding. What happens once might just as well not happen at all because our lives are made too much out of the accidents that come about from not knowing what to choose in any particular situation.

Of course Kundera is exaggerating here, for it is not strictly true that we have no basis for comparison and thus no way of determining what the good is at any particular moment. Our lives do have patterns, and the repetitions—even if they are always different—do allow us in many cases to have a fairly good sense of what the appropriate choice is in an individual situation. The problem comes about when we are contemplating decisions with major consequences. Tereza presents Tomas with a problem because his adult life has been predicated on not attaching himself to one woman and because he knows a continued connection with Tereza will force him to choose otherwise without knowing what the consequences will be. He senses that a major change will come about, but he cannot properly assess what price he will have to pay if he chooses Tereza, nor can he discern what unexpected delights will come from such a choice. It is perhaps strictly true that *all* of our choices are distinctive in this way, and so there is never a proper basis for comparison, but humans learn how to analogize more or less carefully and thus come to act in most cases on the basis of past experience. Only when their experience provides them with no equivalent context do they face the terrors of indecision.

As Kundera implies in his assertion of the adage that *Einmal ist keinmal,* human choice is based on the absurdity of only being able to choose once, of not being able to try one thing out and then another and *then* to make our choice. To have chosen once is to have changed the situation, so even if one in turn decides that the other possibility would have been better, one's life is no longer in the place it was before the initial decision. Kundera contemplates this problem in order to think through Nietzsche's notion of the eternal return, a gauge, in Kundera's mind, for measuring human choice in a radically different way: "Let us therefore agree that the idea of eternal return implies a perspective from which things appear other than as we know them: they appear without the mitigating circumstance of their transitory nature. This mitigating circumstance prevents us from coming to a verdict. For how can we condemn something that is ephemeral, in transit?" (4). On the one hand, the idea of the eternal return creates a framework through which a particular choice is no longer seen as something ephemeral, and therefore something to which mitigating circumstances always attach. This places an impossible burden on each choice, for it must be made in the knowledge that one will have to make it again and again *forever*. On the other hand, this perspective suggests that we are therefore better off with choices that are to be made only once in the midst of the ephemeral circumstances of life. It may be true that what happens once might as well not have happened at all, but that is preferable to a world in which we had to relive the same decision over and over again eternally.

One could argue that the concept of the eternal return and all of its heaviness demonstrates to us the value of the ephemeral at the same time that it provides us with a framework through which to gauge the choices that only come once, and that seems to be a major part of what Kundera himself—like Nietzsche—is interested in. In this sense the eternal return occupies the same space that the tree of life occupied in the Garden of Eden. If God denies Adam and Eve the tree of life, He thereby denies them what they need to have in order to be able to make fitting use of their knowledge of good and evil. Without the fruit of the tree of life, they are condemned to rely on God for an assessment of what is good and evil, for there can be nothing in their ephemeral lives that would allow them to understand the basis for a determination of the good. The idea of the eternal return appears in place of the tree of life precisely because God is dead, because the Other that would give us a fitting gauge for an assessment of good and evil no longer exists, and without that Other we are (at least temporarily) incapable of discerning good from evil.

So Nietzsche proposes an artificial standard through which to measure our actions. If we do not live forever, if we have been deprived of the tree of life, we can at least *imagine* living forever, and can imagine living the same life over and over again forever. However painful this idea might be—and it is so precisely because we should have to live through all those wretched moments of life yet again, knowing full well how awful they were—it is in Nietzsche's eyes the only standard we can make use of that would help us put our choices into the appropriate context without resorting to still another outside determiner of human events. That Nietzsche's standard is "artificial" ought not to be construed in the wrong way; this doesn't mean that it is deceitful or untrue or anything like that. It merely provides us with the vision of the other that we already possess as a result of our self-awareness, a vision that is simply turned once more to be construed as seeing our lives repeat themselves eternally in the same way. Nietzsche has taken the gaze of the other with which Adam and Eve began in that first moment of shame and given it back to each of us in the full knowledge of both the shame and the beauty that it can reveal to us. He has told us that the tree of life is nothing more than this gauge of our choices, the measure through which we can best assess what is right and wrong at any particular moment.

Kundera aptly summarizes what he takes to be the chief effect of this vision of the eternal return: "If every second of our lives recurs an infinite number of times, we are nailed to eternity as Jesus Christ was nailed to the cross. It is a terrifying prospect. In the world of eternal return the weight of unbearable responsibility lies heavy on every move we make. That is why Nietzsche called the idea of eternal return the heaviest of burdens (*das schwerste Gewicht*)" (5). However terrifying the prospect may be, though, both Kundera and Nietzsche are intent on demonstrating to us the value of heaviness. The eternal return may create a weight of unbearable responsibility for us, yet it also provides us with a way of making sense of our choices and establishes a way through which to make them more intelligently. We are then burdened with a kind of responsibility that we have tried to avoid in the past, but this again is simply the final problem all humans must face, the contradictory one of the burden of their choices and the responsibilities that accrue as a result of them in the midst of an ephemeral world that mitigates the effect of any particular choice because, after all, it will only happen once and be gone: *Einmal ist keinmal.*

Nietzsche returns the responsibility for our choices back to us. The devil did not make Eve eat of the fruit of the tree of the knowledge of good and evil in this assessment of human life; Eve herself, constituted out of dust *and* curiosity, living with the sense that the fruit could poison her, took the risk of tasting it and was indeed poisoned in a sense even as she achieved what she desired, knowledge of good and evil. Like a child on the threshold of the realm of experience, Eve couldn't really know what she wanted when she desired knowledge of good and evil, for only after the experience of it could she understand what was involved. But for all that she desired to be a full adult, a mature human being with awareness of what was at stake in her actions. Yet once she achieved such knowledge, she immediately tried to get rid of her responsibility for it. She blamed it on the serpent, as Adam in turn would blame it on Eve. Once a context is created in which the word "responsibility" can really have meaning, Adam and Eve want to run from the responsibility they thought they desired. And if the eternal return presents us with the heaviest of burdens, it does so only because we, like Adam and Eve, are still running from the responsibilities that come with a knowledge of good and evil. We still refuse to accept our own maturity and would prefer an other to come and rescue us from the knowledge we couldn't help but want yet couldn't help but find unbearable at the same time.

When one observes the ready abdication of responsibility that Eve and Adam employ immediately after their awareness of good and evil and connects this abdication to Socrates' argument that knowledge of the gods' savagery ought to be buried in order to inaugurate and preserve the order of the Republic, one is prompted to go back and reread these myths of origins with an eye for what is particularly self-serving about them. If God is portrayed as a harsh and vengeful deity in Genesis, he is also depicted as a selfish ("jealous") God. He very greedily wants to hoard the tree of life for Himself. He refuses to let Adam and Eve become totally like Him, even if He did specifically make them in His image. Certainly these actions make God more forbidding precisely to the extent that they carry with them the all too human resemblances that are to be found in the early Greek gods. They establish His authority by demonstrating that He will not brook very much human resistance. He is clearly determined to preserve His prerogatives even at the expense of the death of the species, as we find when the great flood appears and comes close to achieving precisely that. God's furies seem to be quite similar to those that drive humans, then, which at the very least makes His actions more understandable than they might be.

If we assume that God has projected onto Him the attributes of a great and forbidding Father, we can see the self-justification that humans achieve through Him. It is true that Adam and Eve disobeyed, but a human might well wonder about the nature of the punishment, which seems harsh in the extreme. There is no question that God's sentence engenders the self-pity that afflicts humans today, for it makes life far more burdensome than it should be, more almost than humans can bear. If humans thus constantly whine about their condition, as the Israelites repeatedly do to Moses as they push him to rebel against God, we see that they have set up the justification for their whining in these early chapters of Genesis where their fates are meted out with such vengeance that they are still reeling from all they must suffer. There is a considerable amount of self-pity to be found in the story of Adam and Eve, and another fair degree of self-justification at the rebelliousness of humans in the face of the burdens with which they must deal. And it is not just that the forced labor, the sweat and the pain and the mortality all came from an act of disobedience rather than being consequences of life itself, though that is a good part of it. After all, Genesis states quite clearly that *things could have been different and originally were*. Life didn't have to be the way it turned out. It could have been pure bliss. If humans have a tendency toward nostalgia, it is certainly present early on, for we find its roots in Adam and Eve and their maturation into a painful, mortal existence that they don't complain about as we do but nevertheless provide the justification for our own later cries of sorrow.

If one is looking for the necessary details to account for another aspect of human shame, that tendency toward a denial of life and responsibility through projection and denial, it too is found in good measure in Genesis. The serpent takes the blame and suffers the consequences for his seduction of Eve, an act that preys on her innocence and curiosity, and God's fury, projected out of the shame that comes from the gaze of self-awareness, accounts for the largest share. Beyond presenting their excuses to God for what they have done, Adam and Eve don't really say much about their plight after God sends them from the garden, though their excuses in themselves suggest that they don't feel totally responsible for what they have done. But if we humans choose to measure what they have done and what they paid for it, the scales are overbalanced, the humans overmatched, the battles unfairly joined from the beginning. How could a simple human hope to contend with the forces surrounding him? On what basis did God even think that humans had a reasonable chance? To be sure, we cover this ground with the free will that God has given us, but the free will only deals with the problem of disobedience. Adam and Eve could choose to eat of the fruit of the tree of the knowledge of good and evil even though God told them not to, and in this sense they had free will. But, as with the humans to be found in Kundera's novel, they didn't have a chance to rehearse this choice—they couldn't play it out once and then decide whether to go ahead with it our not. And given this, Adam and Eve's lot is truly human from the beginning. They were forced to live with the intolerable circumstance of having the free will and the curiosity to make different choices yet were forced to live with consequences of which they could have had no true knowledge beforehand.

It would seem that Adam and Eve have written into them the human resentment and self-pity that come from an assessment of the world as a place that is too hard to master and live with, and if Adam and Eve are quite willing to blame the serpent, or Eve in the case of Adam—or God—in some respects that could be construed as a small crime in the face of insuperable odds. Humans have been overmatched from the beginning, even before they faced the pain and mortality they now live with every day. They have been stretched to the limits of their capabilities simply because they *know* what their lot is like and feel shame in the face of it. And if they have therefore like Oedipus sought to put their eyes out because they were repulsed by their situation in the world and the inevitable guilt that is attached to it, Genesis gives them no reason to think that the desire for oblivion is wrong. It may on the surface blame the humans for what has happened to them, but we have a fairly strong sense of fair play that would invariably determine that the human lot is in excess of any crimes they might have committed.

In this sense one could go so far as to project human self-pity and self-justification onto the natural world itself. If we are a species that is constituted out of the flows of the natural world, and if we have at the same time been that species that more than any other threatens the future of those flows, we do so precisely because the heritage we have has made our lives almost unbearable to us, and the result is that we fight against our fate and seek to achieve vengeance on a world that is too difficult for us even as we hope to find the kind of oblivion that will keep us from having to face the difficulties of life. If we are nature's greatest experiment, nature itself would seem to have made a mistake by playing out a species with self-awareness and shame, a species that consequently could find ways of dealing with that self-awareness and shame that increased the destructive potential of the species far beyond what it would need to acquire a sustainable food supply. The more naturalized version of human rebellion comes down to the same thing: a revolt against the paternal figure out of self-pity and resentment, a story that has its origins in Genesis, even if the literal reading of the account would suggest otherwise.

Adam and Eve are first given the ability to make their

own choices without knowing fully the consequences of those choices, and then they are punished so severely as to guarantee eternal resentment. God expresses His disappointment in them and resentment toward them by banning them from their place of privilege, and they in turn will be resentful throughout their lives because of the pain and suffering they will have to endure. The shame and the degradation that comes with their lot will be reinforced by the duplicity in their minds that will attempt regularly to find a reason for their suffering and a victim onto which they can project their disgust over what it means to be human. They may have eaten of the tree of the knowledge of good and evil, and they may consequently know good and evil, but they don't know how to distinguish between them, for the only basis they arrive at is the shame that they feel after a choice has already occurred. They can be *told* what is evil and instructed to avoid it, in which case they don't really know it themselves; or they can find out for themselves, but only by committing the act and determining how the imagined gaze of the other will react to it.

The problem of evil and its connection to the fact that humans have no ready standard for determining it relates in turn to their problems with the good and discerning it. This situation is more clearly established in the second creation story, the one about Cain and Abel. On the basis of the slender evidence available in the biblical narrative of Cain and Abel, it is difficult to account for God's responses to the offerings of the brothers. There seems to be no readily identifiable mark that distinguishes them beyond the food types from which they derive. And this is certainly Cain's difficulty, for he cannot fathom why his offering is less valuable than Abel's:

> And in the process of time it came to pass, that Cain brought of the fruit of the ground an offering unto the Lord.
>
> And Abel, he also brought of the firstlings of his flock and of the fat thereof. And the Lord had respect unto Abel and to his offering:

But unto Cain and to his offering he had not respect. And Cain was very wroth, and his countenance fell.

And the Lord said unto Cain, Why art thou
wroth? and why is thy countenance fallen?

If thou doest well, shalt thou not be accepted? and
if thou doest not well, sin lieth at the door. And unto
thee shall be his desire, and thou shalt rule over him.

And Cain talked with Abel his brother: and it
came to pass, when they were in the field, that Cain
rose up against Abel his brother and slew him.

Cain gets no indication in this account why his offering is
less pleasing than Abel's, and the result is that he gets angry.
God asks him in response "If thou doest well, shalt thou not
be accepted?" without really explaining to him what it is he
should do, or for that matter what he has done wrong. Is his
offering insufficient because it is from the fields rather than a
blood sacrifice like Abel's? Because it doesn't have the sweet
smell of burning fat that God loves so much? If so, Cain
would seem to be in the midst of a change over which he has
no control, the switch from a species that lives by eating
fruits and other vegetable matter to one that lives through
the destruction of other animals. Cain has no idea that vegetable sacrifices are no longer satisfactory and that animal sacrifices are now preferred, and so he is prompted to make
choices and do good without knowing everything he needs
to know to do so. His response, excessive as it is, only reflects in kind the original excess of God when he threw
Cain's parents out of Eden. He kills Abel without really understanding the consequences, for as the first murderer he
really wouldn't know what he was involved in; indeed, as
the first person to witness a human death, he would not be
in a position to anticipate sufficiently the consequences of his
act.

When God sentences him to the life of a vagabond that is
built out of still more difficult tilling than his father had to
face, Cain cries out "My punishment is greater than I can
bear. Behold, thou hast driven me out this day from the face

of the earth; and from thy face shall I be hid; and I shall be a
fugitive and a vagabond in the earth; and it shall come to
pass, that every one that findeth me shall slay me." God is
merciful when He hears Cain's cries and puts a mark upon
him to preserve his life, but the mark itself ignores the fact
that Cain's lot is little different from Adam's, or from what
Adam's should in fact be, for once humans enter into the
realm of animal consumption and sacrifice, they must also be
aware of the fragility of their own life, of the possibility that
everywhere they go they too will have to worry about being
slain. Cain thus suffers the unbearable burden of learning
the full consequences of blood sacrifice, even if he was the
one who tried to satiate God's desires with vegetable offerings. Cain's burden is almost more than a human can bear,
but not quite, so he can live on in the knowledge of his
bloodiness, his awareness of the stain of shame that marks
his face and declares him to be the killer the species had
become. If we needed an account of the transition to a meat-
eating society, and if we also needed a sketch of the first act
of human violence against another human, Cain certainly
supplies both. But he also suggests that he was unfairly sin-
gled out to bear what no human should have to bear, an act
of violence, the knowledge of that act, and the shame there-
from that would bedevil him the rest of his days.

How could Cain know that Abel's sacrifice was good and
his was bad? Did he deliberately try to short God by giving
him less than the best of his crop and thereby incur His
wrath? Should he have known that vegetable sacrifices were
no longer sufficient? Or was he by nature simply a malev-
olent person? Whatever the case, he clearly is the individual
who is allowed to say what Adam and Eve must feel with the
same intensity: that their lot is simply far too much to bear,
that the difficulties of being a human are such that no one
should wish to be one. And if these two stories are designed
to tell us something else, to provide us accounts of human
failings that inaugurate the terrible realm of suffering and
death that we need not have entered into if our first parents
and their children had not made the wrong choices, to demonstrate to us the need for piety and humility and the love of

God; what they really tell us beneath the surface is that humans have been resentful of their lot and its lack of clarity from the beginning and have worked on the politics of self-pity ever since.

In order fully to lay claim to the self-pity that is found at the beginning of the human story we also need briefly to connect it to its twin brother, self-righteousness, for that is the more obvious message in Adam and Eve's story, and in Cain and Abel's. It is the text that is designed to cover up the subtext of self-pity, the fig leaf that hides the human shame with which we all began. God had to be invented to allow us the self-righteousness that *almost* covers up our self-pity and our shame. In the beginning, there was shame, which engendered self-pity, which engendered self-righteousness. Adam and Eve have to learn how to obey God or they will be punished further. They have sinned grievously, and their shame is great. As a result, they are thrown out of the garden, over which they feel self-pity: life is now too hard to bear. But they are told that if they are godly creatures, their lives will be bearable. If they sacrifice properly and do well in their works and uphold the Lord, their lot will be improved. So they work assiduously to hew the line God has established for them, confident that if they can just maintain their adherence to it, they will not fall back into the shame that engendered the self-pity in the first place. They seek to replace the shame and the self-pity with the self-righteousness that comes from doing well in the eyes of the other in order to turn the frozen gaze into a friendly one. Their praises sung to the Lord will make them right with the world and will overcome their difference from that gaze sufficiently to relieve them partially of the burden of shame.

To be sure, in the Bible Adam and Eve are not told to be *self*-righteous. Instead they are to learn how to live in the righteous ways of God. In this sense they will *become* righteous without being self-righteous, though in the end it becomes difficult to distinguish between the two states. And whereas Adam and Eve can presumably keep the two separate, we who follow in their wake are not so fortunate; we have come to see that the two inevitably collapse on one

another. As Socrates demonstrated, the central human difficulty is how to deal with the shame that comes from the
knowledge of our bloody origins and our bloody potential,
and the only way we have devised to escape from that
knowledge is through *sacrifice*. Shame creates an authority
for whom sacrifices can be designed that will remove the
taint of our abjection, that will wash us clean in the blood of
the lamb; but we become all the more bloody as a result of
the sacrifice, and so have still more shame to repress or deal
with in other ways. Our response in turn has been to project
our abjection and self-pity through the sacrificial motif onto
others in another way: through the self-righteousness that
comes from the *difference* of godliness. We can distinguish
ourselves through the rituals we use to pay fealty to the
authority we built up out of the shame of the gaze we felt at
that first moment of self-awareness: Abel's sacrifice is *better*
because he does it right, whereas Cain, whose sacrifice is
noticeably different, obviously is doing something wrong.
Of course the Bible doesn't present Abel to us as a self-
righteous individual who flaunts God's positive response to
his sacrifice, who rubs it in Cain's nose with the sweet smell
of the fat. But certainly the effect upon Cain would be precisely that, even if Abel was purely well intentioned. Abel's
sacrifice is accepted—which would seem to mean that his life
is going well, in contrast to Cain's—and therefore Cain feels
the subordination of Abel's righteous acts, which could also
be *self*-righteous acts, which indeed would *have to be* self-
righteous acts. Cain simply wants what Abel has, a life that
is working well, one of which God has approved. He cannot
account for his failure any more than he can account for
Abel's success, but the lack of fairness he perceives drives
him to the fury that ends in murder.

Sacrifice is an act whereby one seeks to assure oneself a
good life, and if it works, it inevitably leads to self-
righteousness simply because one thinks one has learned
how to overcome the shame and the self-pity that engender
an unhappy existence. This in effect is the knowledge of
good and evil that attends Adam and Eve's first act of disobedience. The result is that humans ever afterward devise

codes of sacrifice to cover their shame with self-righteousness, to overcome their self-pity through an extravagant act of denial. The codes themselves change from society to society, but the conviction they breed with success—and the difference they establish from the codes of others—leads finally to an arrogant self-righteousness that can perhaps *almost* keep shame and self-pity out of play. But always only *almost*. And as with the blood sacrifices themselves upon which our own tradition bases its self-righteousness, the problem is always that the excesses of the self-righteousness lead to a countervailing shame. Just as the mania of the manic-depressive leads inevitably to the depression, just as the fever of the sacrificial crowd leads to acts that are unthinkable without the fury of collective energy, which leads in turn to great shame once one returns to one's normal state and recognizes what one has done, so too do the energetic explosions of self-righteousness finally plunge one even further into the muck of abjection once one's energy has been expended.

In physiological terms there is a very simple explanation for this phenomenon called the rebound effect. If one, for example, chooses deliberately to repress nervous system activity through the consumption of alcohol, one can be assured that when the effects of the alcohol on the nervous system wear off, it will rebound to a higher than normal state instead of simply returning to its previously normal condition. From a lowered level it will spring to a higher level that prompts the jitters, the headaches that come from shrunken blood vessels, and the like. Human physiology is such that all affective states work in this fashion: an extreme movement in one direction, once overcome, tends to lead to an extreme movement in another direction rather than an immediate return to normal conditions. And the oscillation between shame/self-pity and self-righteousness partakes of the same feverish movements and thereby guarantees the perpetuation of the shame it seeks to dispense with through the righteous acts in the first place.

We need once more to restate this relationship among shame, self-pity and self-righteousness simply because it is the armature of social action today as much as it ever was. No political system can make sense without an understanding of the dynamics of shame, self-pity, and self-righteousness. Shame does not always engender self-pity, for if it did the human condition would indeed be intolerable. Instead, self-pity follows only as one possible response to it. Acute repression is also a way of dealing with the abject, and self-flagellation is another direction one can take in responding to the shame of being an embodied creature. In the case of self-flagellation, one's energies are directed only toward oneself, so even if they are intensely articulated, their effects remain localized. When one represses one's shame, it can reappear in any number of guises, but generally it moves in two directions: back to the self-flagellation one is trying to overcome, or toward an attempt to find an origin for the shame. And the origin inevitably engenders self-pity. One feels shame because one is a bodily creature, for example, and then looks for a reason to account for this strong feeling. One can easily conclude in our context that God made us or the world wrong and blame Him for those feelings. If He had properly constituted us in the first place, the accusation might go, we wouldn't have to suffer this debasement in the face of our natural state and would thereby feel much better about who we were. But then we would feel guilty about thinking such things and would perhaps grow worried that God would know what had passed through our minds and would seek vengeance, and this would prompt us to repress the thought.

Inasmuch as the gaze that self-awareness is based upon can be trained and is regularly cultivated by the socius, however, there quickly become any number of alternate sites one can demarcate as the origin of it. One can imagine the gaze as emanating from one's parents, and then come to blame them for the undue shame one feels, or one can turn to one's peer group, or even to some more impersonal force, though such abstractions usually come later in life: one can find the origin of one's shame in one's stature, or physiognomy, or some particular trait, or one's class or gender or race. And when one arrives at this point—particularly when one can locate the shame in terms of a more abstract social feature like class or gender or race—one has then found the means of transforming one's shame into self-righteousness. Instead of flagellating oneself for the shame one feels and blaming it all on the inferiority that seems to be one's lot, one can blame the feelings of abjection on the other who established the differences that guaranteed that shame would attend to one simply because of one's class, gender or race, regardless of the quality of one's being.

The difficulties involved in the assessment of shame come from our tendency to be blind to the ways it drives us, which in turn leads us to look for victims—either ourselves or others—to blame our abject state on. And in all too many cases there are indeed genuine reasons for locating such victims on the basis of those who might discriminate against us as a result of our class, gender, race or some other clear marker. Inasmuch as we know such discrimination exists, it is reasonable to consider its relationship to the shame we might feel in the face of our humanity, just as it is reasonable to try to overcome that discrimination if it turns out to exist. The difficulty comes about when the very real possibility of discrimination is turned into a mode of organizing one's life—and again, for whatever reason; it could, after all, be that one believes one's parents discriminated against one simply because one was the third child and therefore got less love and attention (and it could be that one is right). Instead of creating a scenario for one's existence that takes the inevitable shame of being human into account as only one aspect of one's being, one decides instead to turn the social gaze that would diminish one solely on the basis of class, gender or race back on itself—a more than legitimate action in many contexts—and then build one's life upon reprisals against that site of discrimination. One thereby continues to define oneself almost exclusively in terms of one's shame, only now that shame has been covered over with a veneer of furious self-righteousness: because one does not *deserve* the shame one feels, because it unfairly attaches to one's self-awareness, one is justified in focusing all one's energies on eliminating the source of that unfairness.

As always, one is right in thinking that one does not deserve to feel shame in the face of what one is; it is simply something that is attached to the human lot, not something one has earned. The Bible called this shame original sin and sought thereby to make us responsible for it, and in many respects that makes better sense than blaming someone else for it, for if it is an inevitable part of being who and what we are, we can hardly blame anyone for our being so. Likewise, when one connects shame to a social context like discrimination, there are indeed far too many cases where one is equally right in thinking that one doesn't deserve to have the socius focus only on that which causes one's shame. This is an inherently unfair way of judging individuals, for it fails to take the person's own nature into account. So there is every reason why the shame should lead either to self-pity or to self-righteousness. Except for what the Bible called original sin, that which ought to keep any human away from the zealotry of self-righteousness and the intense redirection of the gaze that it practices in order to hide from its own demons.

Even if the Bible introduces the concept of original sin in order to place the responsibility for our shame on us, it also demonstrates how little that keeps the fires of self-righteousness from blazing away. One only needs to note that the Israelites, that people enslaved by the Pharaoh and completely humiliated through their subjection, turned that greatest of shames into the fury that convinced them of their right to appropriate other people's land. Once freed of the Pharaoh's bonds, the Israelites concluded that in return for the abjection they suffered in their slavery, they deserved their own kingdom. They took their shame and their lack of a homeland and turned them into the singular cause that directed the society for millennia. They *deserved* the homeland their God had promised them; after all the shame they suffered, they adopted a God who promised them that in return for their fealty to Him, He would erase their shame by giving them the lands to which they were entitled. Once again, the issue here is not whether the Israelites deserved to be enslaved by the Pharaoh; of course they did not. This kind of collective enslavement is no better than individual enslavement, and the abjection it leads to is even worse because it is both individual and tribal. It also goes without saying that the continued form of this abjection, known today as anti-Semitism, is as abhorrent as it always was, particularly from cultures that ought by now to know full well what the consequences inevitably are when an entire group of people is unfairly discriminated against in this way simply so that the discriminators can escape from their own abjection by placing it on the Jews or someone else.

What is striking in the biblical context, though, is that it asserts through original sin that we are all condemned by dint of being human to feeling shame, to being stuck in the muck of abjection, and we must not assume that the shame we feel comes from an outside source—like God in particular, but like any other other as well. At the same time, the chosen people of the Bible survive and prosper (to the extent that they do) precisely on the basis of a self-righteousness that comes from the projection of their shame onto other people. They are compelled to see their lot as determined by original sin even as they deny that this is so via their conviction that God has given them a promised land in return for the troubles they didn't deserve. The only thing that is required of them in return is a social structure that is completely determined by the nature of their shame and the way to overcome it, that is, by giving total fealty to the divine Other.

God in this sense is that Other who in His authoritarian way gives us what we want: He authorizes our self-pity and the self-righteousness that will allow us to fight to overcome our shame through His insistence that everything in our lives ought to be interpreted on the dual grid of original sin/redemptive Other. God takes no responsibility for our state of abjection, yet He promises a means of escape from it through total devotion to Him, a devotion that allows us in turn to project our shame onto those others who are un-

believers, who do not have the authorization of God to overcome their shame. If we are polluted by original sin and have
no way of ever escaping from it, God—the only pure site in
the world—can help us deal with our abject lot by providing
rituals of cleanliness that mark off our difference from others
and thereby demonstrate how our purity places us above the
unclean other. As Nietzsche argued, this scenario does not
so much provide a means for dealing with life as it offers us a
way of *denying* life: God gives us the cleanliness we need in
order to overcome our feelings of shame by demanding that
we give up the world of the body to which our shame is first
attached. And in turn He corrupts us by making us feel that
we are superior to those who have not so denied the body
and thereby remain unclean. He fans the self-righteousness
that forces the shame of the world onto the other through
the collective gaze of the religious sensibility and then tells
us to pride ourselves on our courage. That we have made use
of our self-righteousness to escape from our shame and have
thereby denied, if only for a moment, the abject state of
original sin, is something that doesn't seem to matter.

All authoritarian regimes are based on the manipulation
of human feelings of shame, and those regimes begin with
God and the paternalistic world of which He is a part.
God/the Father takes the shame that exists within any human and trains it to be shame in the face of God/the Father;
having done so, God/the Father then promises the abject
child to eliminate the shame through the simple expedient of
obedience: one feels shame because one is not right with the
Lord, or is not consonant with the wishes of the Father, and
so one only needs to subscribe to the regime of the Lord or
the Father in order to escape from the shame that projects
His fierce gaze so unrelentingly upon us. The promise of
God/the Father is always the same: the end to our shame
through total self-denial. If we want to be rid of our abjection, the only way to accomplish that is to deny who we are,
to become like our accuser, to occupy the space of the omnipotent gazer who forces us into the corner of shame with
His intense vision.

But unfortunately, even if we are all at times attracted to

the notion that we can overcome our shame by becoming the Other who gives us our shame in the first place, we can never achieve the goal that is outlined by God/the Father because we are always only who we are: ourselves. We can *never* be the other who God/the Father is precisely because He is other and always will be; only the schizophrenic can be both himself and the other at the same time. For the rest of us, there can only be those moments when we think we have become the other that will keep us from being the shameful creatures that we are, and those moments of still greater abjection when we come to realize that, no, we have failed miserably once again to become someone else and thus have not dispensed with our shame. This is why self-righteousness is *never* the solution to the shame of our abject condition, regardless of the mode of self-righteousness, regardless of whether it originates in the zealotry of a religion or in a more secular form that is based on something like class, gender, or race. Self-righteousness provides a temporary antidote to the abject but leads to greater shame after the inevitable fall back into the self from which one was in flight to begin with, prompting yet another round of violent denial and even greater shame when one falls again.

The Bible had the proper response to self-righteousness when it invented original sin, but it then took the wrong course by training that original sin to work against the humanity it was found in. To be sure, the self-righteous fury of the Israelites accomplished great things, just as the divine violence upon which Western civilization has depended has created great monuments and technologies that demonstrate our self-importance. No one doubts that the furious attempt to deny the shameful origins of one's being through the projection of a self-righteous itinerary can lead to wonderful achievements. What is in question is whether or not we as a species can afford such a method of development anymore and whether we should employ such methods at a time when we have finally become aware of the mechanisms through which they operate. Our zealotry has led to fearsome consequences of its own, even if it also continues to promise us a means through which we shall be able to escape from the shame of the human world, and only our continued attempts to bury our shame have kept us from dealing as we should with the consequences of the world that we have built out of the denial God/the Father has offered to us as an antidote to the poisons within.

Within the sociopolitical world in general we face the same situation in terms of different questions: whether we choose to continue to drive the machine of the socius through the projection of our shame onto others—the projection that generates discriminations on the basis of class, gender, race, creed, and the like, *and* the projection that prompts some of those so discriminated against to direct their own furies of self-righteousness onto the original sites of discrimination—or whether we find a means through which we can begin to assess what our humanity entails without immediately finding a scapegoat to account for those aspects of our lives that engender abjection.

One of the ways we can reconsider our sense of the human is to question what is written into the notion of original sin upon which so much of the Western edifice is based, even if unintentionally so. If we assume that the Bible confers original sin upon all human beings as an inevitable part of their lot, is this a useful way of depicting our lives or something that leads only to the kinds of self-righteousness we have already discussed? One can think of original sin in any number of ways, beginning with the rather literal notion that it simply means we are born with the guilt that Adam and Eve introduced by their act of disobedience. This is certainly one of the standard ways of construing our lot, and it makes its own kind of sense. At another level, we could say that original sin is precisely that context that is characterized by self-awareness/shame/desire. Our original sin is the desire that makes us self-aware, that prompts us away from our shame into a state that would deny our origins. And in many ways this definition of original sin covers the most terrain precisely to the extent that it reveals our "flaw" to be our self-loathing, our denial of life as we find it, our revulsion against the world as it is constituted, and our shame in the face of it and all its bodily squalor.

If original sin is indeed the shame of self-awareness and the denial that comes from it, then it is not really something Christianity developed; rather it is something that the religion did a marvelous job of encapsulating with the concept. For original sin makes it clear that there is no escaping the embodied lot of existence, no way we can avoid the full consequences of being human, including the denial of the human that comes out of our shame, including the force of desire that the Bible finds sinful in itself. We may or may not agree that desire is sinful, but there is no doubt that it derives in part from our shame and hence carries with it the emotional constituents that would be covered (and extended) by the word "sin."[2] Shame itself provides the feelings of revulsion that would make one feel opposed to oneself, willing to deny the being who has those emotions, and thus sin is a logical, if particular, extension of an affect that antedates its existence. As Nietzsche repeatedly argued, the sense of good and evil that derives from the notion of sin leads to a vision of humanity that is in many respects life denying, and hence destructive in its own way, but there is a logic to that vision nevertheless, and it is predicated on the affective constituents of shame, the feelings that attend our awareness of the gaze we invented.

The concept of original sin thus accomplished several things. First, it established the fact that to be human is to feel shame, to be born with an "original sin" that "taints" one's being. There is no escaping from this phenomenon, regardless of what terms one uses to describe it. Second, original sin leads to a structure of good and evil that reinforces the shame humans always already feel about themselves, chiefly because the good and evil are derived from the feelings that shame is: good attends to the absence of those feelings, evil that which we find in the presence of shame. To be sure, like any other structure, Christianity had to work to broaden the regions where humans would feel shame, even if without quite knowing this. But more importantly, it established a grid for evaluating human existence that assumed shame was a far-reaching and powerful motivator of action, and in this it developed an essential insight. We in the modern age who have worked so hard to deny our connection to shame have forgotten how much it is a part of our lives. We haven't gotten rid of it so much as we have trained ourselves to ignore its signals. Just as a child who feels shame over its acts of excretion can literally refuse to let them emerge (and thereby pollute itself even more), so too we have increasingly refused to let our shame show its face. Original sin has the virtue of asserting that even when it doesn't show its face, it is still within us, not to be denied even if it can be hidden.

Perhaps the most obvious reflection of the degree to which we have practiced a thorough-going repression of shame came in the 1970s when we tried to believe that sexual activity was capable of being unconstrained and uncontaminated by the sense of sinfulness Christianity gave to it. We thought that there was no reason it had to be covered by feelings of shame, that it was in itself a "pure" activity reflective simply of our bodily natures. So the sexual revolution allowed much greater freedom in this domain, and doubtless convinced some that sexual activity is not necessarily connected to shame in any way, that Adam and Eve's initial act of weaving fig leaf garments for themselves was an accident of our history rather than an intrinsic aspect of self-awareness. That "Love ha[d] pitched his mansion in / the place of excrement,"[3] as Yeats put it, seemed irrelevant to the ideology of the time; that the smells of sex were both intoxicating and offensive seemed to be merely a matter of training.

In rather quick succession, however, we discovered several things. One, it seemed that sex in and of itself, practiced purely for the sake of the activity, had a higher boredom quotient to it than we expected. That is, the act in and of itself, even through a variety of postures, lost some of its enticement when it became routine. It seemed to be more intoxicating when it was somewhat shrouded over with a sense of the shameful, of the forbidden. When it was declared open and free, it seemed that over a short period of time its excitement depended on more and more bizarre forms of sexual activity. In relatively short order orgies and sadomasochism and the like were appearing in mainstream contexts like advertisements in fashion magazines and even news magazines. And far from being an expression of the freedom of the sexual urge, these manifestations—leading up, one supposes, to that subgenre of pornography called the snuff film—suggested that in order to maintain a certain level of excitement in the face of readily available sexual activity, one had to invent ever-new thresholds of shame to violate: the excitement came from crossing borders that presumably were purely fictive, even if they did provide the momentum for those who were arguing that sexual activity need not be constrained by feelings of shame.

Even at its "freest," the sexual revolution depended on shame for its pleasures, devoted itself indeed in many respects to an exploration of the modes of shame and their connection to the various forms of bodily expression. And then suddenly some time near the end of the 1970s, as if by magic, the sexual revolution pulled back—and this was, it should be remembered, well before any AIDS scare raised its horrific visage—retreated from the ever-expanding borders of expression to a more constrained view of sexual activity. Our mores did not return to the ones that had been in play in the 1950s, but there can be no doubt that for some reason we as a culture did pull back, did come to feel an individual and a collective shame in the face of the direction the sexual revolution was leading us. As always, there are those who still maintain that there is no intrinsic connection between sexual activity and shame, but for the most part we as a society came to the conclusion that even if our religious views had made sex far more guilt ridden than it ought to be, it seemed to have a certain amount of shame attached to it regardless of religious perspective.

What was so striking about this conclusion was that it was in its own way "reasoned out" more or less collectively and more or less in a short period of time. Even granting that American society has traditionally been more "puritanical" than its European cousins', the fact is that within a six-month period one could trace the recession of the wave of sexual freedom. All of a sudden the broader-based soft-porn magazines started pulling back from their increasingly perverse displays of sexual activity, and in doing so they were only reflecting the barometric pressure of the socius itself. If there were individuals who continued to fight on in the belief that a shame-free sexuality was indeed possible, the collective will of the majority retreated without ever publicly sounding the bugle. It was sufficiently shamed by what it saw, and by what it was doing, to turn around without speaking of the change and return to more "conservative" forms of social expression. Indeed, the revulsion that was a part of this turn contributed to the broader-based revulsion that American society began to feel by the end of the seventies that led to the exploitation of shame by conservative and fundamentalist exponents who continue to force their narrow vision of human behavior onto the socius at large even today. If the conservative tendencies of the last decade have succeeded as well as they have, it is because they were able to exploit the shame the socius felt at its own collective degradation through the excesses of the sixties and the sexual revolution of the seventies.

This is *not* to say that either the exponents of the sexual revolution or the fundamentalist preachers of hell and damnation today have any real idea of the shame they are putting to their own uses, any more than they have an intelligent notion of what "natural" sexual expression is. Both camps exploited shame in different ways—the one using it to increase the intensity of sexual pleasures, the other sublimating it into the theopolitical furies that ride the same crest of bodily energy through mob action—and both exploited it without knowing fully their own complicity in that which they sought to deny or constrain. Likewise, neither one has helped in any way—other than through the expression of excess that prompts the majority back to some kind of ill-defined "happy medium"—to establish the limits or even the nature of the sex/shame couplet that is always so much of an issue in human communities. The fundamentalists seek to return to the eternal verities as they see them (except for their leading preachers, who are capable of transcending the narrow borders the rest of us must adhere to), whereas the exponents of sexual freedom have forgotten that the revolution came to an end before AIDS and thus reflect wistfully on the rich possibilities they had before this awful scourge ruined their fun.

Likewise, even with all of the surveying that has gone on for more than thirty years, the "scientific" community has no more to say about sex and shame that is useful than the extreme positions do. Once we get past the fact that sex is coupled to shame, we are lost. We have found no way of describing the limits of the relationship; indeed, we have never seriously attempted to do so. The result is that both sex and shame continue to be exploited by people who have little understanding of the volatile mixture they are dealing with. The virtue of a conception of original sin in the midst of this situation is that it at least prompts us to concede that sexual attraction *and* repulsion are both predicated on the shame Adam and Eve first felt when they recognized themselves as sexual, bodily creatures. The more we move away from that kind of awareness, the more our motives become hidden, our impulses driven increasingly by repressed forces and displaced desires. The more we retreat into the comfortable notion that our sexual behavior and the shame that attaches to it are definitively laid out for us in the Bible, the more we are likely to repress urges that only find other ways of expressing themselves.

"Original sin," then, works well as a constant marker of human shame. It works less well as an origin for the establishment of a full-blown axiology, for there is no way that good and evil can be distributed along a continuum that is determined chiefly by the abject. The root of the problem here gets to the fundamental difficulty inherent in the concept of original sin: the word "sin." In declaring shame to be a mark of *sin,* Christianity asserts that therefore every shameful feeling is derived from a sinful state. If one feels shame, one must have sinned, in mind if not in body. Given this viewpoint, one can simply delineate good and evil on the basis of that in the midst of which one feels shame: if shame is present, it is evil; if shame is absent, it is good. This works well enough for a society that has no other means of regulating human behavior, and it certainly has the virtue of depending on affective states that most humans do indeed feel, but it is based on an erroneous assumption—that shame is invariably a marker of "sin" or wrongful behavior— and leads to an idiosyncratic and generally repressive system of values. Good and evil, right and wrong, simply cannot be determined on the basis of the original sin of shame. That which repulses us is not necessarily evil any more than that which takes us away from our shame is necessarily good. Yet this is precisely the system of values that is built on the notion of original sin.

If we assume that at least initially most of those areas of human life that engender feelings of shame are *bodily* states, then we can see how the final problem with any conception of original sin is that it stains the entire bodily domain with sinfulness and prompts us to turn away from our natural condition with revulsion. We may well feel abject in the face of our excretions or our sexual desires and forms of expression; we may well be revulsed by the very act of eating, to say nothing for the disgust that can attend any of the fluids that drip and ooze from various orifices. And we may well finally feel self-loathing as a result of the image of our body in contrast to the ideal image of bodies that our society presents us with. But it does not follow from these feelings that shame is the mark of evil.

Indeed, the feelings of shame that derive from one's bodily image are an important reminder of something that our own culture tends to forget: *all* societies depend on images of the body that engender shame in their constituents. Because our own society is presently obsessed by certain forms of mesomorphic or ectomorphic structure that accentuate interest in sexual organs, we assume that the shame that comes from having a less-than-perfect body is a result almost exclusively of the artificial definition of the "right" bodily make-up and the exploitation of our feelings about our own bodies by the advertising media. All this may be true, but at the same time we need to remember that all social systems are built in part on ideal body images, even if those images are always dependent on the needs of the culture. It may be true that some cultures don't seek to exploit the shame one feels in the face of one's bodily image, but inasmuch as there is no "perfect" body even in terms of any of the artificial ideals that various societies establish, virtually everyone within a society finds his or her body to be "flawed" in terms of the ideal. We know within our own, for example, that often those whose bodies are said to be the most beautiful—models and movie stars—find their own bodily equipment to be seriously flawed and are thus full of self-loathing toward the body, all the more so because others lavish so much attention on it. No society escapes from these kinds of measurement, though a society *can* contribute to great self-loathing by encouraging more and more investment in certain kinds of bodily self-absorption, as our own does.

If we feel shame at our bodies, it does not follow that our bodies are *sinful*. If that were indeed the case, we would have no choice but to spend our lives in opposition to our own needs and desires, as all too many do even today. Likewise, shame itself is not an index of "sinfulness." It is a reflection only of a certain disposition toward ourselves that we cannot avoid having; it is indeed "original" in this sense, for it defines an essential aspect of what a human is. When Nietzsche sought to strip away the good and evil that had connected themselves to the physical world of which we are always inevitably a part, he was simply trying to demonstrate the ways in which we have taken the feelings of shame that come from being human and turned them into a system of values that takes us away from our strengths and moves us toward a world in which denial is the only constant: denial of the human world of shame to which we are connected every day in every bodily way. What Nietzsche failed to do was to establish the ways in which shame manifests itself even outside of a system of good and evil that is predicated on them. Like the existentialists who followed him, he was a bit too taken with the notion that human attitudes are created solely out of linguistic forms and hence capable of permutations *beyond* shame: we can make ourselves over in such a way as to eliminate shame, to eradicate the nausea that comes from our self-awareness. Nietzsche himself was not foolish enough to believe that we could eliminate our abjection, and he realized how difficult it would be for us simply to face up to it. But he did contribute to a notion of human malleability that had all too much of an effect on the existential philosophers who came after him and on the social engineers who had so much of a part in the destructiveness of our century.

If we carry original sin back to Adam and Eve and the things that derived from their first act of disobedience, we can see how the turn that was taken there depended on the sinfulness of all those modes of human experience that were connected in any way to shame. At the same time, we confront yet again the problem that Adam and Eve faced: they had indeed eaten of the tree of the knowledge of good and evil, and so they knew there was such a thing as good and such a thing as evil, but beyond the link between shame and evil, they had no way of determining either good or evil. They needed the fruit of the tree of life in order to be able to distinguish between the two, and when God deprived them of the fruit of that tree, He thereby also committed them to the endless confusions that come from any attempt to consider good and evil without a proper ground. In saying this, I don't mean to suggest that Adam and Eve would have had to have been immortal to be able to discern good and evil; on the contrary, "good" and "evil" would become irrelevant terms in a world where no humans ever died. I would suggest on the contrary that what God really deprived them of was not eternal life but a full commitment to the value of *this* life, the bodily existence of sweat and pain and great toil and death. *That* was the fruit that God kept them from eating, and with that fruit they would have been able both to affirm life and to develop a system of values that went beyond the simple yoking of shame/body/evil. "God" was able to do this only because He convinced them that their shame was paramount, that their act of disobedience and the evils that came from it were to create a world that was almost unendurable in its difficulties. Our "sentence" was mitigated in part by the New Testament, but the initial sentence to original sin and shame deprived us of the tree of life in *this* world, and the New Testament did nothing to alter this fact.

We return then to one of our original questions: when God was dispensing His judgment of Adam and Eve and throwing them out of the garden, why did He make no mention of *beauty?* Why didn't He explain to Adam and Eve that they would now have to suffer greatly as a result of their sin, but that they would still have the beauty that they found in the Garden of Eden, even if it was now to be located in the midst of nettles and thorns? God had declared every element of the creation to be good, and its beauty was evident throughout, yet He never asserts during the judgment that Adam and Eve will know of His presence in the world through its beauty, nor does He suggest that the beauty of the world has any value in general. And yet surely the most striking facet of the planet in some respects is how beautiful it can be, just as the most powerful of human states is the aesthetic one that manifests the flows and patterns of the life around and within us. In terms of the narrative structure of Genesis itself we can see that there was beauty *before* there was shame, and this in itself seems an essential insight into the nature of the world. It may be true that strictly speaking humans could only perceive beauty once they had self-awareness and hence shame, and that shame therefore is that which makes us perceive the world as a beautiful place, but that sense of the idyllic to which Kundera refers also tells us that there was beauty before there was shame. We may recognize its priority only after we feel shame toward our own being, but at that point we can indeed perceive that we were always in the midst of an aesthetic world of great consolation and axiological value.

One can explain the absence of any godly remarks about beauty during the judgment of Adam and Eve by saying that it was not God's intention to offer them consolations but rather to convince them how horribly they would pay for their disobedience. He would leave the virtues of beauty to other eras, as when He declares the rainbow to be a reflection of His promise never to flood the entire earth again in a moment of anger. At that point one could suggest that the connection of the promise of a good and stable world to the rare beauty of a rainbow marks an axiological intersection that can be found in other aesthetically pleasing contexts as well and hence provides a vision of the usefulness of beauty. In this way there would be no need for God to mention to Adam and Eve that the beauty of the world would be a special consolation to them when their struggles became too much to bear.

More pertinently, though, it would seem that God would want Adam and Eve to ignore the beauty of the world. Even though He has not specifically promised them eternal life and thus had not yet become part of a religious system that focuses human attention on the prospect of another life at the expense of this one, we can surmise that the beauty of the world and its potential intoxications are such that God doesn't want Adam and Eve to think that there are any special consolations in it. They have, after all, already succumbed to the temptation of eating what must have been an especially luscious fruit even though they were told not to, and so God could surmise that with their free will and their fallen state they would be more than likely to discern and make use of the beautiful things of the world without His comments about them, so much so that the things of the world might take them away from Him.

At this early stage of the Bible, there is as yet no serious mention of elaborate codes of values to live up to any more than there is a real promise of eternal life—after all, God deliberately removed Adam and Eve from the garden in order to keep them from eating of the tree of life. But in failing to mention that beauty was one of the sources of pleasure and comfort in the world that would help Adam and Eve to bear their difficult lot, and by not suggesting that it would provide some kind of ground for their consideration of good and evil, God seems deliberately to be withholding knowledge of that which could be a potential threat to Him. It is certainly true that the the Bible does not progress very much farther before there are regular accounts of people who have been swayed from their faith in God by the pleasures of the world and any number of graphic accounts of what happens to such people. It is as though God did not yet quite properly know the potential threat of the beauty of the world to His regime in the early chapters of Genesis in spite of the fact that He made it well enough to be beautiful in the first place, and it was still well enough constructed to be beautiful even after life became a series of endless trials for every human who lived. Either God Himself did not know how powerful the beauty of the world was—and how much of an inducement it was to move away from his commands—or else He did indeed know this and didn't mention its consolations to Adam and Eve in the hope that they would not discover them.

The one thing that does seem certain is that there should be some restatement of the beauty, the value of the world, and the connection between the two as God places Adam and Eve on the course of the future generations of human beings. If Adam and Eve now possess the knowledge of good and evil and yet have been deprived of the fruit of the tree of life, they need some way of establishing more clearly what is good and what is not if they are going to be able to make their way in the world. Without the fruit of the tree of life, there are only two possibilities for a ground to their knowledge of good and evil: God's commandments and rules, or the beauty of the world. Clearly our tradition moved in the direction of God's commandments and away from an axiological system based on the aesthetic mode of being that is the one we are most comfortable with and the most pleased to experience. Over time we re-established the connection between beauty and axiology when our sacrificial ways were translated more and more into symbolism: when people were weaned of their need to worship particular images, false images that had appeal because of their beauty and tangibility, then there could be a church that would meld the laws of beauty into the worship of God through the production of art devoted to His glory, from the construction of the church edifice itself to the mosaics and paintings and the like that adorned the church and other areas of life that centered around religious life. But first the beauty of the tangible world and the production of tangible images of beauty had to be separated from the religious in order to keep humans from returning to their worship of graven images of false gods.

When one argues as I have that we in the late twentieth century must come to see that any system of values we hope to make use of in the future must be derived from our aesthetic understanding of the world, one could see this from the traditional religious viewpoint in two ways: as a return to the worship of graven images that deny the intangible world of beauty that God declared to be our potential lot if we refused to succumb to the lure of the tangible beauty of the planet we presently reside on; or as a return to the beauty of the creation with which God began, a return that seeks to demonstrate the necessity of building our axiology out of the beauty of the world that is inevitably attached to the shame that makes us want to run from both the tangible and the bodily. In the second possibility there is certainly no necessary commitment to graven images of any sort, nor is there a belief in artificial gods that have been made out of human desire. If there is a belief that the beauty of the world and the aesthetic mode of being through which we perceive it are capable of providing us with a sense of the good that will sustain us throughout our lives, there is no argument for the worship of beauty, or "nature," or golden images of eternity.

On the contrary, while there may be celebration of the wonders and delights of the world, there is no attempt to build an edifice that would defy the laws of time. The creation itself is good enough and beautiful enough on its own and has no need of a remoter charm; the tree of life in this return to the beginning is not a tree of eternal life for individuals, except in the most metaphorical of senses—having lived, we all inevitably play a part in the unfolding future of the planet and the species even after we are dead—but it is a tree that lives through the frangibility of its individual constituents and their ephemeral natures. The tree of life itself becomes a reflection of the possible directions one can go once one perceives both the beauty of the world and the knowledge of good and evil that comes from the self-awareness and shame that attends it: it can be a manifestation of our desire for the eternal in the face of the excruciatingly brief lives we recognize more and more as we age to be slender and short threads, a displaced and graven image of an eternal world of beauty that puts the earth itself to shame. Or it can be a measure of our feelings about our present lives, a tree that mitigates the shame we feel at being human by its indifference to our abject state—it has no need continually to remind us of our "shameful natures" even if it does nothing to eliminate them either—and by the awareness of the flows and forms of the world with which it provides us that allow us to work through our own individual sense of what is good and proper for us within those flows. This tree of life is always a tree that reflects the moment and the potential of the next moment as well rather than putting the present into a negative context by suggesting the possibility of a better future.

What we choose to make of the tree has always been up to us, for it is one of the founding images of human societies and has been determined in any number of ways. One interprets the tree of life in terms of the desires that flow through the community, and if those desires never change, they are always shaped by the local contexts that give them utterance, determining that the tree shall be the last forbidden fruit or the one we eat from every day. And if our culture has chosen for millennia to see its fruit as the one we never managed to eat of, it has increasingly suggested just the opposite over the last century or so. It has prompted us to look at the world and the tree of life at its center in a new way, one that would rewrite our relationship to the flows of the world through our deliberate reintegration within them.

What more than anything has held us back from this new interpretation of the world has been our lack of conviction about our own natures and what they want and can live with. We have been able to avoid a full confrontation with this problem for so long only because we could always find a way to reconcile that feature of our special mode of being that we so pride ourselves on—our desire for *knowledge,* our interest in finding out what the world was all about—with the consequences of that knowledge. Now we have had to face the fact that our knowledge has brought us to a point where we must either concede with T. S. Eliot that humankind cannot in fact bear very much reality and thereby confess that we sought knowledge only as long as it fulfilled our desires for a world beyond the ephemeral state we find ourselves in, or we must do what we can to elaborate out of the flows in and around us a sense of the right and fitting that is wholly consonant with our position in the midst of a world that may not be the Garden of Eden but that has its own endless beauties and charms and wonders. The fruit of this tree has always been within our grasp, yet so far we have been unwilling to stretch our hand in its direction. If there were a "natural" step for us to take at this point in the development of our civilization, I would argue that it is precisely the time for us to take the fruit of the tree of life and eat it in spite of our shame.

Epilogue

At the End

Our century has provided us with momentous change and deep uncertainty about the future course of the world, and there are as a result good reasons why we should be as confused and troubled about our prospects as we have ever been. One could attribute our difficulties to the pace of change, to the technology that seems to increase the velocity of our lives more every year, to the residues of the industrial age that are only now beginning to show us how flawed our understanding of the world was, or to something more traditional like a lack of commitment to the kind of values that would allow us to project a future for ourselves with confidence. I have argued that more than anything we are in the midst of a fundamental reappraisal of the circumstances of our civilization, one that takes us back in many ways to the kinds of originary problems to be found in Genesis, in *Oedipus Rex*, or in *The Republic*. In an important way the West has always been driven by a schizophrenic posture: on the one hand, it prided itself on its desire for knowledge, and on the other its central myths declared that we would find the truth unbearable. Oedipus had to poke out his eyes to keep from seeing his shame, Socrates sought to bury the shame of the gods—and hence of the humans—so that it could no longer be found within the Republic, and Adam and Eve were banished from the most delightful of habitations as a result of their desire for—and shame in the midst of— knowledge of good and evil.

In spite of these founding myths, we have chosen to think of knowledge as that which would finally redeem us, particularly in the past few hundred years since we have developed greater and greater confidence in the human ability to shape the world according to our own designs. Even today there are many who would argue that our only chance for survival on the planet is to proceed on the basis of our longstanding commitment to reason and to the structures we have built on the basis of it. These people will have nothing to do with ideas about human shame and fallibility, for they believe that such thinking defeats our enterprises before we start out. Only by extending, or attempting to extend, our Faustian reach will we be able to resolve the problems we have created by our earlier attempts to wrest control of the life of the planet for ourselves. Or so one school of thought today would have it. Regardless of how much evidence there might be that the desires driving this vision of human accomplishment are deeply flawed—and perhaps fatally so—there is no way to argue with people who are convinced that even if our great achievements have leached all sorts of deadly poisons into the world as well, to change course would mean renouncing the value of everything we have done up to this point, and that would be a denial of our own centrality to the world.

That such sentiments do not necessarily follow from the argument that our knowledge has taken us to a point where we need to change our conception of things is beside the point from the perspective of those who see any critique of the Western mode of development as a brutal attack on the part of those who would love self-destructively to see it collapse under its own weight. Again, the unfortunate thing in this respect is that the positions toward our future seem to be so mutually exclusive. Each of us tends to have a viewpoint that connects itself to a particular attitude toward our history, and we defend that viewpoint. One of the great benefits of our commitment to reason was that it allowed us to think that people were truly convinced by reasons, that one could indeed reason a problem through and change one's mind—and others' as well—as a result of an ironclad line of argument. We have come to see, however, that human conviction is predicated less on reason than we thought, and so we no longer have that easy out when it comes to the defense of our positions. We have declared all arguments to be what they are—different forms of persuasion—and therefore also have to admit that there is no way to change people's minds through the rational exposition of ideas alone. One seeks to persuade, but the differences in viewpoints seem particularly extreme at this juncture in our system, so the possibilities for persuasion are not what one might hope, regardless of one's perspective. There is simply nothing to be done about this, and so it must be taken as a given from which we begin.

However much we might like to think that our culture has been based upon a kind of grand commitment to the quest for knowledge, though, and however much we might want to celebrate the ways in which we have put this feverish desire for the truth to work in the developments that have sprung from the quest, there have always been others who would argue that our pursuit of the truth was in fact at the very least based upon an initial—if not a *continual*—denial of truths we knew all too well, the kind that Socrates tried to bury when he banished the poets. In this version of our history, our quest for knowledge was in fact rather an attempt to deny what we all secretly knew about ourselves through a rational superstructure that would lift us above the muck of human abjection and place us on the same plane as the gods. The motivations for this denial of what is have varied from place to place, and the variety of reasons for a rejection of the given is in itself a striking phenomenon. Some, like Socrates, argued for the burial of our deepest knowledge of the human out of regard for the ideal polity. His argument implied that the average human was simply not capable of bearing the weight of fundamental human shame and was all too likely to make use of the violence of the gods/humans if he saw any kind of representation of it. The benevolent dictator derives from Socrates' views, the leader who convinces himself that he shall keep to himself the knowledge of human horrors so that the polity itself can live in the belief of its cleanliness. This pact is predicated on the deliberate obfuscation of human truths and the expulsion of anyone who would be inclined to offer up the knowledge that is declared sacred, and it assumes that one can actually keep the abject sufficiently repressed so that people will come to believe they have denied nothing.

We still have examples of Socrates' approach to human existence today, most obviously in totalitarian countries, but it would seem that there is a limit to how well and how long the leaders can keep the truth from the people even after the truth-tellers are banished and art is filtered through a grid of sociability. More and more we have created a world in which it is almost impossible to keep humans from knowing what it means to be human. One can attribute this change to the global dissemination of information through television and other media, through increased contacts between peoples thanks to air travel and the like, or to the fact that many cultures have shaped themselves through a long enough history to keep the awareness of bloody human possibilities always in mind even if the leaders try to bury this knowledge. In a world that encourages forgetfulness in order to flee from the truths we know too well, however, it is most likely the nearly omnipotent gaze of the others who are always viewing other societies that has put the most pressure on cultures to face up to their origins. For the most part even the obscurest corners of the planet face continual observation by other nations, and even those who declare their indifference to the gaze they find obtruding on their actions are doubtless affected by it in some respects. The pressure of that gaze simply bears too much resemblance to the initial gaze that emanates from the shame of self-awareness for us to be able to block it out, regardless of our cultural or social make-up. In this respect it would seem that the "media" that contribute so much to the gaze have indeed prompted considerable change in the world simply by their presence.

The most striking—and most lamentable—form of Socrates' desire to bury the knowledge of the actions of Kronos and Ouranos comes less from totalitarian countries, though, and more from the democratic ones like our own, and especially the United States, where it would seem that the entire social world is based on a continual denial of the abject. In the last ten years in particular there has been a kind of mania of denial that has been predicated upon all kinds of minor trouble signs that would suggest the need for a serious reappraisal of direction on the part of the socius. Instead of undertaking that reappraisal, however, the country seems to have chosen deliberate ignorance in the face of the future, and if the large and small corruptions that have emanated from this chosen ignorance have not been any worse than those to be found in some of the earlier periods of our history, they are more shameful simply because they have been so intentionally indulged.

If earlier eras had their forms of corruption and denial, it was generally the leaders and the wealthy who practiced them, whereas today it could be said that most of the people in the country are at least embracing a form of deliberate and self-conscious denial, fully suspecting that they are only postponing some terrible crisis to come. If not everyone has cynically taken up the forms of corruption that have appeared in most sectors of the society, that is less important than the indulgence that has appeared in the face of such crimes. We have chosen to be ignorant of our own shame and of that of our leaders as well; we have preferred to assume that their behavior has been *normal* and *appropriate* at the same time, for if we were to recognize properly the degree to which their corruption was based on both greed and a denial of the abject, we would have to recognize how much we had in common with them. If our leaders have shamelessly proclaimed their actions virtuous and have for the most part carried the day on the basis of such declarations, they could have done so only to the extent that we ourselves didn't want to admit that they were in fact producing a scurrilous society whose motivations for action were totally suspect, if all too understandable.

We have collectively practiced denial because there is much we want to deny, yet most of what we have chosen to ignore would seem to embrace the minor forms of shame. The most inexcusable lies we have told ourselves have to do with the millions of people whose lives have virtually been sacrificed to our well being and denied at the same time. It is not an accident that the average foreign visitor from whatever country is first and foremost struck by the great riches and great poverty that exist next to each other in this country, a nation presumably devoted to the ideal that all members of the socius have a right to share in its benefits. If a democratic system is designed to distribute the power to all in order to ensure an equal hearing for all, our country has certainly demonstrated that the one doesn't follow from the other. More people have the right to vote and exercise various forms of power in the United States today than ever before, and yet we find ourselves in the midst of a society that has almost completely written off anywhere from 10 to 20 percent of its people. And it has done so *shamelessly*, fully aware of what it was doing and yet quietly denying it every day when the evidence was faced, whether it was shown on the drive to work through the worst areas of the city one inhabits or on the nightly news when the accounts of drug-induced murder and destruction in the ghetto appeared in graphic images.

It could be argued that a society is inevitably measured by that which other societies see in it that it itself most denies, or by the degree to which its own gauge of the socius differs from the assessment of other societies. Naipaul, again, was most shocked by the defecation habits of the Indians, even though his ancestry was Indian, because he couldn't account for such shameful ways of dealing with human waste. He simply refused to believe that humans were capable of treating such acts as though they were of a piece with normal conversation among friends in the open air. Finally Naipaul realized with even greater shock that the Indians were able to defecate so openly precisely because they refused to admit that they were doing so. A visitor from almost any other culture—developed *or* undeveloped— would have been greatly shocked by the habits of the Indians, yet the Indians themselves were totally oblivious of their practices. The degree to which they repressed their knowledge of this shameful habit was so strong that they didn't even recognize what they were doing. They continued to converse with friends fully as though they were not also defecating at the same time. Such behavior is invariably among the most shameful in Western countries, yet in India it was simply normal behavior.

A similar form of shock attends the great spread between wealth and poverty in our country today, and what is most astonishing finally is less the scandalous degree to which we have allowed our "egalitarian" culture to be so driven to extremes than it is the fact that *we no longer recognize that this is so.* We have chosen simply to *deny* that poverty exists, that vast segments of the population have been written off, and we have succeeded so well in denying the poverty all around us that for all practical purposes it no longer exists for us. It is as though we have pulled down our pants or lifted our skirts and started defecating in the middle of a conversation with an acquaintance without any real knowledge of what we were doing. It is as though we have denied that which is most obvious about our everyday world *out of shame and horror,* but also out of *fear.*

And our shame ought far more to surround our deliberate repression of our knowledge of the poor and their plight than to concern our willingness to let the wealthy and the powerful grab everything that isn't nailed down. The two, of course, are related, for we have chosen to ignore, with a few exceptions, the vast power and money grab that has been going on for a decade and more for the same reasons we have chosen to deny the increasing poverty that is an inextricable part of it: to admit that the horrors of corruption and poverty are as profound and as deep as they presently are in our society would force us to confront certain facts about our own motivations that don't bear looking into. If we have let the rich and powerful do what they have done, that is only because we ourselves should hope to be able to do likewise; if we have let the poor continue to rot in their ghettos, that is because we have assumed there is an equation between their suffering and our potential for a better life. If, in other words, there is such a great disparity between *our* view of the United States and the views of visitors, it is chiefly because we have realized at one level what we refuse to accept at another: that the relatively smaller share of the world's wealth that we shall be acquiring in future decades will inevitably mean either the diminution of our individual shares or else the kinds of increased poverty we see at the lowest level in order to perpetuate as much as possible the shares we already believe ourselves entitled to. Rather than face this redistribution of national wealth, we have chosen to exclude an ever-larger number of citizens from any kind of economic well being in order to guarantee our own portion. This may not be an act as heinous as Kronos', but it comes close.

It may well be that Socrates' desire to bury the knowledge of human shame was based on his assessment of the human capacity to lie to oneself that derives from an awareness of the abject. He surely must have known how easy it was to convince oneself that one had no part in shame, and his general contempt for the ability of the average individual to confront the full context of human life may well have been based on a belief that humans weren't capable of dealing with all their motivations. But I think even he would be shocked by the degree to which entire societies can so wilfully lie to themselves, can so deliberately deny what is most evident about their make-up and character. He had no real experience with the larger forms of democracy that are practiced today and thus would have great difficulty imagining the lengths to which the people within them have gone to practice his more localized form of denial. Socrates was fully aware of the modes of collective hysteria and self-delusion that are to be found in *The Bacchae* and the like, so he understood that large groups could be taken over by manias that kept them from knowing what they were doing, but this is a different form of collective delusion, for it is based upon extreme behavioral conditions. Mobs do not recognize what they are doing precisely because they have put off their self-awareness, have been taken over by the upsurge of nervous system activity that creates oblivion in its wake; and mobs do not finally take their members away from the abject but force them to see it all the more graphically once they return to their "normal" state.

It could be argued that the United States—and some other countries as well, though perhaps to a lesser extent—are practicing similar forms of collective hysteria, but the constituent elements of hysteria are not sufficiently in evidence for us to draw that conclusion. A true mania does indeed put out of the mind any knowledge of one's actions and their abject nature, whereas we today have not done so. We are still self-aware enough to recognize—and to *rationalize*—the problems we see around us. If we have in some senses totally denied the poverty upon which our well being depends, we can still see it and pay lip service to dealing with it, albeit in increasingly half-hearted ways. Our shame thus derives from the fact that we are *not* mad, are *not* taking part in a collective rite that has momentarily purged from us an awareness of what we are doing. Our behavior on the contrary is like that of the Indians defecating on the public road—they do so not because they are swept up by the intense energy of a crowd but simply as a regular matter of course, as part of their normal lives. We too practice the denial of our shame as a normal part of everyday life and as such demonstrate too well the degree to which we are caught between our knowledge of what we have done and our desire to hide from it.

Whether the form of denial that Socrates argued for is assumed by the leaders of a culture or is a collective act of an ongoing or temporary nature is in some senses irrelevant, but in another sense it is most important, for the collective, non-hysterical denial of shame in the midst of which we find ourselves is far more degrading than an attempt by one's leaders paternalistically to keep the truth from the citizens. The paternalistic regime is based on the assumption that the citizens themselves couldn't bear the truths the philosopher kings keep to themselves, and it is based also on the history of human societies that suggests that collective manias can overrun and destroy a culture at any moment and therefore need to be contained by keeping the people in deliberate ignorance. But it never has really put its members to the test, for the true measure of humans is not whether they are capable under certain forms of duress of destroying their own cities through collective violence but whether they can do so as a part of the ordinary course of their daily lives. Totalitarian regimes do not test humans in this way; only democratic systems do. And democracies have thus placed within the sociopolitical context the largest of questions to be addressed to humans: whether they are capable of building a society on the basis of what we know about human nature or whether social systems can only grow from collective delusions of one sort or another. Ten years is too short a time to be able to answer this question, but there can be no doubt that those who have taken Socrates' view of how to deal with human shame have sorely tested the alternative vision as well.

In some respects one could say that the implications of the story of the Garden of Eden are similar to those to be found within Socrates' argument for silence. From the Christian perspective, after all, one assumes as a matter of course that people were born into sin and will continue to sin, however much they may try not to. This would be reason enough for Socrates to banish the poets, for their horrible truths might well prompt people to sin more than they would if they weren't reminded that the gods too performed bloody acts. But Socrates sought to bury the knowledge of what Christianity calls original sin, whereas it is the cornerstone of the Judeo-Christian tradition, that declaration which grounds and centers human life: we are born in the image of God, perhaps, but our first act was one of disobedience, the result of which was original sin, the result of which is that our lives take place in the midst of the abject that Socrates thinks he can bury. There is no burying the abject in the Bible, even if any number of Christian denominations over the millennia believed that it could be buried through one device or another, from indulgences to the acquisition of power and wealth to simply being born again. The Bible itself seems rather to be committed to the notion that we are born in sin and remain sinful throughout life, even if we are redeemed in the Christian account of life. The abject is not something to be escaped from within Christianity but rather something to be written into the body like the mark of Cain: our humiliation in the face of it ought to be part of our daily awareness of who we are.

Needless to say, the Christian vision of human existence

moves in different directions from the one predicated on the grandeur of Western accomplishments or on the need to bury our shame as far away from consciousness as possible. At the same time, the variety of responses to the human situation from within the Christian context is so great that it would be difficult to establish a standard perspective in any kind of definitive way. Although the basis of the religious viewpoint ought to be found in the notion of original sin and the redemptive grace of Christ, original sin is not taken as seriously in some segments of the Christian population as it is in others. The shame that attaches to it is at times mentioned, at times exploited, at times put to sociopolitical uses by both left- and right-wing denominations, but it can also be more or less ignored as an overly harsh judgment on humans and their potential. If we were to focus on the notion of original sin in general, we could suggest that it would offer humans a different perspective to the extent that it would keep them from burying the origin of human shame and force them to be fully aware of it. Original sin is that of which we should always be mindful, and attached to its open acknowledgment of human frailty is in turn a conception of humility that also alters our viewpoint on life. There are no arrogant leaders who seek to hide from their constituents the truths about the world they find themselves in but rather priests and ministers who share with their parishioners the same sin and the same humility before God.

The humility that springs forth from the general concession of original sin has its advantages over the burial of human abjection simply because it does keep our awareness focused on one of our major limits, the revulsion we inevitably feel toward that which we conceive to be shameful in our existence. The religious denomination can choose to emphasize our abjection and degradation and thereby shamelessly exploit the feelings it is supposed to address, but it can also simply acknowledge the human condition as it is without ruthlessly putting it to any kind of totalitarian uses. Nor are the humility and shame that are put forward in Christianity necessarily constricting when it comes to action in this world: again, denominations of both the left and the right seem quite content to address the ills of the sociopolitical in accord with their own views. And if there is a serious residue of denial of the bodily in Christianity and a rejection of this world, for the most part that vision of religion seems to be in decline.

On the other hand, Christianity does argue for a vision of human life that promises an ultimate elimination of shame, just as it predicates both the beginning and the end of that shame on the omnipotent gaze of God. In so doing, it has developed from a plausible sense of what shame *feels* like to the one who first experiences self-awareness and the sense of the vision of the other that comes with it, but it also in turn promises solutions to that shame that depend upon an other that removes the problem from our hands even as it makes us most responsible for it. At the same time, it has transmuted shame into *guilt* and thereby created an insuperable burden for humans to bear that exacerbates rather than relieves them of the shame they face. There are variations of response, but in general Christianity is indeed based on the development of guilt and the transference of the solution to the Other in the face of whom we are to feel guilty and ashamed.

The pliability of the Christian vision is demonstrated by the variety of sociopolitical responses that emanate from it in our time, for in many respects a good number of what may be characterized as positivists come from the ranks of the church, those people committed to the notion that human evil is, if not eradicable, at least capable of being seriously diminished either through the "containment" of human evils Christianity provides (the right-wing response) or through a greater and greater push for egalitarian treatment of everything and everyone on the planet (the left-wing response). Usually there is no attempt on the part of the right to do anything more than control human instincts through the structures and strictures elaborated by the Bible, but the left-wing viewpoints are often at least tacitly committed to the notion that hard work and good will can indeed bring about heaven on earth: we *can* all live together in peace if only we put our minds to it.

And whereas this sentiment is one that we ought seriously to consider, all too often it springs from a series of pieties that denies the abject that is always inevitably a part of life. The fervor of commitment to a better world keeps from view the fact that there are always certain phenomena to do with human nature that, inexplicable and ineradicable, do not disappear merely as a result of good intentions. This doesn't mean that the need to work for the general conceptions embodied in the liberal viewpoint isn't essential to our future well being on the planet. It only suggests that the strengths of the commitment to change the lot of humans so that the world becomes more equitable and egalitarian tend to be undercut when those espousing the viewpoint refuse to see any limits on human potential and at the same time may well also believe that change depends on God's will or God's plan for us. Such a viewpoint undercuts paternalism even as it defends it, and works out of the humility of original sin even as it denies it as an inevitable part of life.

The positivists in general—including both those who are attached to the church and those whose religion is purely social change—are committed to noble ideas about the future of the species, but the implementation of their commitment can be as condescendingly hierarchical and oppressive as the paternalistic perspective they seek to overcome. The superciliousness and zeal that emanates from these positivists is predicated not only on the fearsome force of their own desire but also on a serious miscalculation of what the species itself is capable of. Their push for change often ends up causing reactions that work against the very transformations that are necessary, and even if some of these reactions are inevitable simply because of the variety of possible responses to our world, there is no inherent reason why one must undercut the force of one's viewpoint by asserting it with the same sense of omniscience and omnipotence that is being attacked within the system that depends on the gaze of the Father to regulate our shame. This contradictory position, difficult though it may be to overcome after millennia of use, is precisely part of the problem rather than its solution, and while we may effect some useful change through the imposition of yet another paternalistic viewpoint (this time named something else in order to hide its origins, something like "maternalistic" or even "egalitarian"), in the end we shall find ourselves with different names flowing through the same hierarchical grid that arbitrarily seeks to limit the flow of human and other kinds of energy on the planet.

Another irony inherent in the positivist viewpoint is that it bases itself on a commitment to human potential that is predicated on a denial of the past of the species, or, to put it another way, it assumes change is possible only as long as we ignore all the markers from our past that suggest change is only possible *in some respects.* What guarantees the repetition of the past is that the positivists refuse to understand a very simple point that develops out of the paternalistic system they seek to overcome, a point best expressed, perhaps, by Wallace Stevens in "Esthétique du Mal" when he is considering the question of the origin of human suffering:

> It may be that one life is a punishment
> For another, as the son's life for the father's.
> But that concerns the secondary characters.
> It is a fragmentary tragedy
> Within the universal whole. The son
> And the father alike and equally are spent,
> Each one, by the necessity of being
> Himself, the unalterable necessity
> Of being this unalterable animal.[1]

Stevens' words here begin by reflecting the traditional religious and social attitude toward that which we despair over in our lives. He agrees that it "may be that one life is a punishment / For another," as that is clearly the main argument of our own civilization, demonstrated in the idea that the son's life is punishment for the sins of the father's, a viewpoint that traces our origins in the Oedipal story, in the Christian vision of God and His fearsome might that metes out punishments to His children from one generation to the next, and in the paternalistic social structures that have been built up over the millennia as well. In some respects it is precisely this notion of guilt and punishment that must be eliminated if we are ever going to establish a socius that is truly egalitarian, and the positivists—particularly those who focus their attacks on the paternalism of our current system, be they feminists, Marxists or simply individuals who believe in equal rights for all—are intent on eliminating the structures upon which this guilt and punishment are based. That is all to the good and a necessary part of the struggle against the inequities that dominate the society.

The problem comes from either knowingly or unknowingly employing the same form of guilt and punishment, the same threats and condemnations that the previous system made use of, and the main reason for this flaw in the liberal viewpoint is that it fails to attend to the other half of Stevens' point. It *may be* that one life is a punishment for another, Stevens tells us, but even if that is so, it is a minor point, "a fragmentary tragedy / Within the universal whole." Lives may truly in some senses work out at times according to a guilt-and-punishment structure that passes the blows down from one generation to the next, but we have focused on this minor structure so much that we have missed the "major / Tragedy," the "force of nature in action" that we see in the fact that "The son / and the father alike and equally are spent, / Each one, by the necessity of being / Himself." To be within the natural world, according to Stevens, means that one is inevitably going to "spend" oneself on being always and only who one is. The notion of being "spent" in this way may seem unimportant, or perhaps even peculiar, yet for Stevens it is indeed the major tragedy to be found in our natural lives. We are simply forced through the way things are to spend ourselves by the necessity of being *only* ourselves, which to Stevens also means that we are stuck with "the unalterable necessity / Of being this unalterable animal." Some things can be changed, but in general we are quite simply an "unalterable animal," our natures determined more by the natural world of which we are a part than any of us has ever wanted to admit. And given this fact, we have no choice but to spend our lives being who we are.

Now in some respects there is no reason why any of this should trouble us. After all, if we like who we are, we should be quite pleased to spend our lives being just that. Yet Stevens' remarks suggest that we have a problem with being who we are, that in the end we really want to be something or someone else, and thus spend our lives futilely trying to be someone else and ending up always only being who we always already were. Put in the sociopolitical context, one could say that in some respects, given the inertias in the system, one should be grateful for *any* impetus toward change, regardless of the camp from which it comes or the direction it seems to be taking. If one doesn't like the direction, one can hope to alter it after the useful changes are effected.

From another angle, however, it would be necessary to distinguish between the desire for change that is predicated on self-loathing and the desire for change that is predicated on self-confidence. If one's impetus for change, that is, comes from a desire to be other than who one is, if one hopes to overcome the necessity of spending one's life being only who one always already is, then it would seem that there may be surface changes brought about by one's actions, but in the end the *structure* that one opposes will remain, for the structure that is opposed in the paternalistic system is predicated on a denial of the human condition, on a refusal to believe that we must spend ourselves on being who we are. More pertinently, positivist to the end, it is really predicated on the origin of our necessity, that we are forced to be this "unalterable *animal.*" It is our animal natures that we continually try to deny through the implementation of this or that social program that is designed to guarantee greater this or better that. We are simply trying all too often to eliminate the constraints that our animal nature places upon us because they force us to concede the presence of a shame that will never go away. One can thus choose to work out of a circle that attempts to deny the shame that is part of who one is and end up with ever-increasing self-loathing, or one can begin by acceding to the unalterable animal nature one has and the shame that comes with it and work from there.

What is most striking about our sociopolitical system is that it has yet to think through precisely the possibility that

Stevens articulates so masterfully in his description of the way our lives are spent. After all, a conservative within our system would be one who bases his viewpoint on the unalterability of human nature and the belief that only social structures keep him from becoming *nothing but* the animal that he always in part is. And a liberal is almost invariably one who believes that everything can be changed, that there is no animal nature that constricts our behavior, no limit to human potential *if only we set our minds to it*. This is indeed a secular kind of religion that is devoted finally to denying essential aspects of who we are, and there is a good reason why this fundamentally religious viewpoint must deny that we have no choice but to spend our lives being the unalterable animals we were destined to be: because, as Stevens tells us, this is the major *tragedy* of human existence, and our religion is designed to find a way around the tragic nature of life. To concede that life is indeed tragic is to accept the fact that there are certain unalterable, natural, *bodily* facts about our being that will *never* be changed, that must be accepted from the beginning. This, of course, is tragic because it means that there is no way around the most horrible of human necessities, the requirements of aging and death that come along with life.

It may be that the positivist liberals want to deny the essentially tragic nature of existence because they themselves cannot accept this inevitability, or because, like Socrates, they believe that nothing good can come from telling the field troops of the movement that the changes that will be implemented will not find ways of dealing with the tragic nature of life. Whether the motivation is the purely cynical and manipulative latter possibility or the deliberately self-deceiving one of the former, the result is always the same: a perpetuation of the vicious circles that are presumably going to be eliminated through the pragmatic action of the movement. Even if we assume the most beneficent of intentions and the most noble of motivations, it is hard to imagine how individuals whose practice is so devoted to denying the limitations of human life can distance themselves from the kinds of hypocrisy they so legitimately decry in the current political regimes that shamelessly exploit the populace's desire for a utopian future in the guise of a nostalgic past. The liberal movement is perpetuating precisely the same fallacy for precisely the same reason: it is hard to mobilize people for change when one admits to them at the outset that the things they most want to have changed—the essentially tragic nature of life and the inevitability of being the unalterable animals they are—cannot be changed by *any* movement because they are not products of a sociopolitical system but rather simply a part of human existence. Politics in the late twentieth century is too often built upon precisely this kind of deliberate deception, regardless of viewpoint, regardless of intentions. And it is because of this that the system itself is bound only to repeat different forms of the same kinds of denial, the same kinds of paternalism, and the same kinds of arbitrary hierarchy as the ones we have seen for millennia.

If conservatives *resist* change because they believe it will indeed always only repeat the same forms of human brutality that already exist, and if liberals *promote* change in the belief that we can escape from being who we are, why isn't there also a third possibility: that we promote change on the basis of a general assessment of that which *cannot* be changed? Why can't we begin by assuming that our (more or less animal) natures are constituted by certain unalterable factors and then seek to change that which is truly capable of alteration? The liberal positivists are increasingly intent on telling us that "human nature" is a *fiction*, so in their standard incarnation they shall surely not be interested in any viewpoint that begins by assuming that certain things are inevitably part of the world. Because the givens of human nature have been extended and exploited, because shame has been turned into guilt and manipulated by a whole range of political regimes from the largest levels on down, liberals tend to be committed to the notion that the very idea of an unalterable nature is an elaborate ruse that is contrived to keep people in their places.

Human nature, so this theory goes, is whatever the social structure says it is. It is a totally pliable medium that is made to take the shame of whatever commandments dominate it.

And given the fact that there are any number of sociological studies that would back this perspective up, they are invariably grasped and thrust in our view as demonstrations of our foolishness at believing in anything so retrograde and essentialist as a human nature. The liberals of our day are indeed often positivists precisely to the extent that they base their fragile illusions on the social sciences that are clearly grounded in and predicated on the notion that human nature is pliable. If it were not, there would be little for these disciplines to do. Given this, and given the fearsome desires to hide from the self-loathing that generates so much of the steam of any number of liberal movements, one is not likely to see a ready kind of acceptance for the notion that one must begin by accepting what cannot be altered before one can usefully work toward modifications of what can be changed.

Nevertheless, one must ask again why it isn't possible at this juncture of history to imagine a sociopolitical framework that is both committed to the notion of change *and* based on an assessment of those unalterable features of being human? Why can't we imagine a politics that seeks to rectify the gross injustices of our present system at the same time that it accedes to the limitations of the species that seeks to alter its destiny? In a straightforward way this would seem to be the question that our civilization poses to us at the end of a rather long series of developments, even if it is also the question that was posed to us at the beginning and throughout the course of our history. It is the question that places us in the midst of the abject from which we have been in flight for millennia, and as such it has been the shaping force that articulated the contours of our response to the world. As Nietzsche demonstrated, all too many of those contours are negative in nature, imploded shapes that reflect a revulsion over and rejection of the body and the shame to which it is necessarily attached, and that remains as true today as it did a hundred or a thousand years ago, if not more so.

As a culture, we have not moved very far from our beginnings when it comes to our relationship to the abject, and perhaps Julia Kristeva best encapsulates what that relationship is and what we must do to live through it: "The border between abjection and the sacred, between desire and knowledge, between death and society, can be faced squarely, uttered without sham innocence or modest self-effacement, provided one sees in it an incidence of man's particularity as *mortal and speaking*. 'There is an abject' is henceforth stated as, 'I am abject, that is, mortal and speaking.'"[2] The very junction of our humanity comes at the intersection of our sense of mortality and our linguistic nature, and that is the location of the abject. Kristeva here urges upon us the need to face squarely that which can no longer afford to be hidden, and she argues that we can indeed face our shame "without sham innocence or modest self-effacement" as long as we are willing to begin our assessment of who we are with the simple statement "I am abject, that is, mortal and speaking." In a way, nothing more is required of us when it comes to facing the shame out of which our nature has grown and through which it continues to develop, though such a simple assertion requires its own kind of courage, quiet though it be.

More to the point, even if we as individuals can imagine a context where it is possible for us to begin in the midst of our shame, it remains an open question as to whether or not a social system can be based upon such knowledge, particularly when the foundation of society would appear to correspond more to Socrates' act of burial of the abject than to a close confrontation with it. As Kristeva points out, "Defilement is what is jettisoned from the *'symbolic system.'* It is what escapes that social rationality, that logical order on which a social aggregate is based, which then becomes differentiated from a temporary agglomeration of individuals and, in short, constitutes a *classification system* or a *structure*" (65). Defilement, and its inevitable connection to shame and the abject, is precisely that out of which the social structure constitutes itself through the act of denial. The sacred circle of the classification system that a society is develops from the abject that is placed outside the circle in the context of the *other*. We begin with our own revulsion, project it into another space and thereby create the periphery in terms of which the social circle will be constructed. And if this is so, then we are really confronting the question of whether or not a society can be constituted on the basis of its own defilement and abjection when in the past it has always drawn its rationality from a denial of them.

In a way it simply *does not make sense* to argue for a society based upon its own shame because the definition of a social structure is in effect "an aggregation of individuals that is constituted through its collective rejection of its own defilement and shame and the projection of that sense of abjection onto the other that inaugurates the particular symbolic system out of which the socius develops and through which its identity is established." This is the crux that we are called upon at this point in our history to address, and it may well be the ultimate test of our capacity as a species. At the very least it requires a response that differs greatly from the ones espoused by Socrates, by the celebrators of Western genius, by those committed to the biblical vision of original sin, and by the positivists of many stripes who boldly assert the coming of a new age that demonstrates only the repetition of the same old world by its refusal to begin with the abject from which the symbolic system originates.

In the end we are left with the coupling of shame and beauty, with that first moment that is always upon us when out of our shame we come to recognize the beauty that we missed before our self-awareness brought us a knowledge of good and evil. It would seem at this juncture in our history that we may never know why we begin with such a peculiar thing as shame, or why the abject remains a part of our lives regardless of our attitude toward it. It may well be that the strangest of all human phenomena is that we feel shame in the face of our naked bodies, the unaccountable beginning from which everything else seems so implausibly to come. This is a mystery about which we know no more today than we ever did, in spite of the inquiries made by psychoanalysis, cultural anthropology, and the like; it is the surd which, making no sense whatsoever, is nevertheless the beginning of sense, the beginning of the reason through which we assess our position in the world. We carry that surd around with us today as much as we ever did, and our behavior and our societies are as dependent on it as they ever were, even if we still manage almost always to forget the degree to which our entire sense of the world depends upon it.

That we may never properly understand the nature of our shame, however, is no reason for us to continue to seek to deny it, any more than it is a reason for us to fail to see how the beauty of the world—and the aesthetic flows on which it is based—is the twin of the abject, the other side of our nature that gives us the only sense we shall ever have of how we fit within the patterns that we can see as we trace our development out of the shame from which we have fled yet never left behind, out of the abject that provides us with the wonder of the world as the antidote to our sense of degradation and revulsion. We may have lost the tree of life when we tasted of the tree of the knowledge of good and evil, but we gained a perception of the aesthetic through which we can construe the good of our lives in the face of the shame that defines us as a species and yet always prompts us to question what our future as a species can be. We continue to be a question that is posed to the world, a query that so far in our history has always had the same answer. But we are also a question that can have more than one rejoinder, and the world awaits our new response.

Notes

Introduction: In the Beginning There Was. . .

1. *The Dialogues of Plato,* trans. B. Jowett, Volume II (Oxford: Clarendon Press, 1953), p. 222. Subsequent quotations are from this translation and will be noted parenthetically with page numbers in the text.

2. My understanding of the imitative violence embodied in these myths of origin—and my reading of *Oedipus Rex* in particular—is indebted to the work of René Girard, and especially to his important book *Violence and the Sacred,* trans. Patrick Gregory (Baltimore: Johns Hopkins University Press, 1977). For a fuller account of my agreement with and difference from Girard's work, see especially the following: *The Play of the World* (Amherst: University of Massachusetts Press, 1981), pp. 63–84; *Imitation and the Image of Man* (Philadelphia: John Benjamins, 1987), pp. 74–77; and *The Fate of Desire* (Albany: State University of New York Press, 1990), pp. 195–202.

3. Sophocles, *Oedipus the King,* trans. Stephen Berg and Diskin Clay (New York: Oxford University Press, 1978), p. 63. Subsequent quotations from the play are from this translation and will be noted parenthetically with page numbers in the text.

4. Hesiod, *Theogony/Works and Days,* trans. M.L. West (Oxford: Oxford University Press, 1988), p. 9. Subsequent quotations are from this translation and will be noted parenthetically with page numbers in the text.

Chapter One: In the Beginning There Was Beauty

1. See my *The Values of Literature* (Albany: State University of New York Press, 1990).

2. Wallace Stevens, "Esthétique du Mal," *Collected Poems of Wallace Stevens* (New York: Knopf, 1954), pp. 313–325.

3. Nathaniel Hawthorne, "My Kinsman, Major Molineux," in *The Celestial Railroad and Other Stories* (New York: NAL, 1963), p. 32. Subsequent quotations are from this edition of the story and will be noted parenthetically with page numbers in the text.

4. I am assuming here that the open society's system of laws has more or less satisfactorily addressed the basic inequities that are found in any social structure, not because this is true but rather because it would seem that the general tendency still continues in that direction, even in spite of the current trend in the United States and elsewhere to roll back the attempts to redress previous inequities.

5. See Daniel Bell, *The Cultural Contradictions of Capitalism* (New York: Basic Books, 1976), pp. 146–171.

Chapter Two: In the Beginning There Was Shame

1. See Friedrich Nietzsche, *On the Genealogy of Morals*, trans. Walter Kaufmann (New York: Vintage Books, 1967), p. 89.

2. John Berger, "Muck and Its Entanglements," *Harper's*, Vol. 278, Number 1668, May, 1989, p. 60. Subsequent quotations from the essay will be noted parenthetically with page numbers in the text.

3. Milan Kundera, *The Unbearable Lightness of Being*, trans. Michael Henry Heim (New York: Harper, 1984), p. 245. Subsequent quotations will be noted parenthetically in the text with page numbers.

4. V. S. Naipaul, *An Area of Darkness* (New York: MacMillan, 1964), p. 73. Subsequent quotations from this text will be noted parenthetically in the text with page numbers. I thank Julia Kristeva and her *Powers of Horror*, trans. Leon S. Roudiez (New York: Columbia University Press, 1982) for reminding me of Naipaul's book.

Chapter Three: In the Beginning There Was Shame and Beauty

1. See V. S. Naipaul, *An Area of Darkness* (New York: MacMillan, 1964), pp. 11–26.

2. Friedrich Nietzsche, *The Will to Power*, trans. Walter Kaufmann and R. J. Hollingdale (New York: Random House, 1967), p. 435.

Chapter Four: In the Beginning there Was Beauty and Shame

1. Milan Kundera, *The Unbearable Lightness of Being*, trans. Michael Henry Heim (New York: Harper, 1985), p. 8. Subsequent quotations from the novel will be noted parenthetically in the text with page numbers.

2. I would argue that desire is also manifested in the curiosity that prompts Eve to eat the apple, and that is what I would characterize as desire as *fullness* rather than lack. For an elaboration of the distinction between the two forms of desire, see my *The Fate of Desire* (Albany: State University of New York Press, 1990).

3. W. B. Yeats, *The Collected Poems of W. B. Yeats* (New York: Macmillan, 1956), p. 255.

Epilogue: At the End

1. Wallace Stevens, *The Collected Poems of Wallace Stevens* (New York: Knopf, 1954), pp. 323, 24.

2. Julia Kristeva, *Powers of Horror: An Essay on Abjection*, trans. Leon S. Roudiez (New York: Columbia University Press, 1982), p. 88. Subsequent quotations are from this translation and will be noted parenthetically with page numbers in the text.